DATE DUE

THE STRATEGIC PRESIDENT

THE STRATEGIC PRESIDENT

Persuasion and Opportunity in Presidential Leadership

GEORGE C. EDWARDS III

PRINCETON UNIVERSITY PRESS · PRINCETON AND OXFORD

Library of Congress Cataloging-in-Publication Data

Edwards, George C.
The strategic president : persuasion and opportunity in
presidential leadership / George C. Edwards III.
p.   cm.
Includes bibliographical references and index.
ISBN 978-0-691-13947-0 (cloth : alk. paper)
1. Presidents—United States. 2. Political leadership—United States.
3. Communication in politics—United States. I. Title.
JK516.E324   2009
352.23'60973—dc22   2008039432

British Library Cataloging-in-Publication Data is available

This book has been composed in Utopia

Printed on acid-free paper. ∞

press.princeton.edu

Printed in the United States of America

10   9   8   7   6   5   4   3   2   1

to Carmella

whose power to persuade is not in doubt

Contents

Preface

IN THE FALL of 2005, I began a memorable year as Olin Professor of American Government at Oxford. New senior faculty at Oxford deliver an Inaugural Lecture to an intelligent and worldly university-wide audience. Selecting a topic for such a lecture is not an easy task. For more than three decades, I had studied presidential leadership, trying to understand why others, especially those in Congress and the public, respond to the chief executive as they do. More often than not, I found that the White House was frustrated in its attempts to obtain the support of others. It occurred to me that it was time to reexamine some of our basic premises about the nature of presidential leadership.

The great presidential scholar, and my dear friend, Richard Neustadt, revolutionized the study of the presidency with the publication of *Presidential Power* in 1960. The essence of his argument was that "presidential power is the power to persuade." For half a century, scholars and students—and many presidents—have viewed the presidency through the lens of Neustadt's core contention.

In this book, I take a fresh look at the nature of political leadership, with a particular focus on the American presidency. We typically view leadership as a key, often *the* key, to explaining major changes in public policy. If we are to understand such changes, we must first understand the nature of leadership. The probability of analytical error and even political disaster is high if scholars, the public, and especially presidents misunderstand the true potential of leadership.

I am particularly interested in determining whether presidential power actually is the power to persuade, or whether presidents help to engender change by other means. The question is not whether presidents matter, but *how* they matter— how do they bring about change? In the end, I conclude that presidential power is *not* the power to persuade, and I show that even the most skilled and effective presidents did not create new opportunities for change by persuading others to follow their lead.

Chapter 1 discusses the nature of leadership and the widespread understanding that persuasion is central to the success of leaders, and reveals the lack of evidence of the persuasive power of the presidency. It then raises the question of whether the most effective presidents employ persuasion to reshape the political landscape to pave the way for change, or whether they are facilitators who recognize and skillfully exploit opportunities in their environments to achieve significant changes in public policy. If recognizing and exploiting opportunities are critical leadership skills, scholars and presidents alike need to understand both the limits of persuasion and the possibilities of facilitative leadership.

In chapter 2, I focus on perhaps our three greatest presidential communicators: Abraham Lincoln, Franklin D. Roosevelt, and Ronald Reagan. I examine their level of success in moving the public to support their policies and find that typically the public was unresponsive to their appeals. It usually takes events, not presidential persuasion, to change public opinion.

The next chapter investigates how presidents, rather than shaping public opinion, may sometimes exploit existing opinion to move their agendas. By focusing the public's attention on the issues it wishes to promote and encouraging the public to see its proposals for dealing with those issues in a positive light, presidents may increase their chances of success. At the same time, a wide range of factors constrain their ability to focus the public's attention and structure its thinking.

Chapter 4 looks at Congress and examines the famous "Hundred Days" of Franklin D. Roosevelt, Lyndon Johnson's Great Society Congress, and Ronald Reagan's significant policy changes in 1981 to determine whether the success of these presidents was the result of persuasion. I find that rather than creating opportunities for change, all three presidents recognized that they were governing in periods of especially favorable conditions for passing their agendas and effectively exploited these circumstances while they lasted.

Chapter 5 investigates presidents governing in more typical circumstances. I first examine the presidency of George H. W. Bush, who took office with perhaps the worst strategic position of any president in the twentieth century. Then I focus on his son, George W. Bush, who began his tenure with a tenuous majority in Congress and a loss in the popular vote for president. Like their predecessors who governed in more auspicious circumstances, the degree of success these presidents enjoyed resulted from the interplay of circumstances and their skills at understanding and exploiting them.

Chapter 6 reassesses our understanding of leadership and offers an appreciation for facilitative leadership. It also suggests lessons for scholars, questions that bear exploration in light of a better understanding of the potential of presidential leadership. Finally, I suggest that we need to consider the broad implications of the limitations of presidential persuasion for basic strategies of governing.

I am especially grateful to several people and institutions for their support and advice. The University of Oxford provided the initial impetus for this book, and the Department of Political Science and especially Nuffield College supported its early stages. The Department of Political Science at Texas A&M University continues to be an extraordinary place to work, and the support I received sustained the project.

I have also benefited from the advice of colleagues. Stephen Skowronek was a careful reader who helped me clarify and develop central ideas. Paul Quirk provided thoughtful feedback, as did Stephen Wayne, Bert Rockman, Barbara Kellerman, Bruce Miroff, Gary Jacobson, and Sam Kernell. Chuck Myers was an engaged and insightful editor. I am grateful to all of them.

As always, my greatest debt is to my wife, Carmella, who makes my life worthwhile.

George C. Edwards III
Paris

THE STRATEGIC PRESIDENT

1

Power as Persuasion

LEADERSHIP is perhaps the most commonly employed concept in politics. Politicians, pundits, journalists, and scholars critique and analyze public officials, attributing both success and failure to the quality of their leadership. When times are bad, as people often perceive them to be, the reflexive call is for new—and better—leadership.

The president is the most prominent focus of political leadership in the United States, and the notion of the dominant president who moves the country and the government by means of strong, effective leadership has deep roots in American political culture. Those chief executives whom Americans revere—from Washington to Franklin D. Roosevelt—have taken on mythic proportions as leaders. Anecdotes about the remarkable persuasive powers of presidents abound. Often these tales originate with presidential aides or admiring biographers, fed by the hagiography that envelops presidents and distorts both our memories and our critical faculties.

For example, Garry Wills entitled a book *Lincoln at Gettysburg: The Words that Remade America.*[1] But did they? The evidence suggests a different conclusion, at least when it came the idea of equality.[2] Recent scholarship has shown that few listeners, including soldiers, commented about his speech, and when the press mentioned Lincoln's words at all, they accorded it second billing to Edward Everett's two-hour official oration. Otherwise, the press typically reduced the address to a sound bite—or worse, as in the memorable words of *The Steubenville*

Weekly Herald: "President Lincoln was there, too." Similarly, the press met the president's words with "virtual editorial silence," although some opposition papers greeted the speech with criticism. In a final, although unintended insult, a number of news reports badly misquoted the president. The *Centralia Sentinel* in Illinois substituted "Ninety years ago" for "Four score and seven" and heard "conceived in liberty" as "consecrated to freedom."[3]

What about a generational impact? We know that it took a century to realize Lincoln's call for equality,[4] so it seems rather generous to Lincoln to argue that his few sentences at the cemetery dedication *remade* America. We also know that Lincoln's decency and eloquence did not preclude him from being in danger of losing the election of 1864 until Sherman marched through Georgia. Similarly, the president's own party largely ignored his call in his eloquent second inaugural address for toleration and moderation toward the defeated South. Lincoln was undeniably an extraordinary human being. However, we cannot infer from that fact that public officials and members of the public responded positively to him.

When Ronald Reagan's pollster found that the public overwhelmingly disapproved of the administration's reductions in aid to education, Michael Deaver—the president's longtime public relations guru—arranged for Reagan to make a series of speeches emphasizing quality education. Deaver later gloated to the *Wall Street Journal* that public approval of the president regarding education "flip-flopped" without any change in policy at all.[5] If public opinion did change as Deaver described, it would indeed have been an impressive performance of presidential persuasion. However, opinion did *not* change. Deaver was referring to the addresses, including national radio addresses, Reagan delivered in the spring and summer of 1983. Yet in Gallup's August poll, only 31 percent of the public approved how Reagan was handling education.[6]

Similarly, in his memoir of the Reagan years, Deaver reports that the president was distressed about the lack of public support for defense spending. According to Deaver,

Reagan pulled me aside one day; "Mike," he said, "these numbers show you're not doing your job. This is your fault; you gotta get me out of Washington more so I can talk to people about how important this policy is." I did, and he would systematically add his rationale for more military spending to nearly every speech, and eventually his message would get through to the American people.[7]

In fact, however, public opinion on defense spending did not move in the president's direction, as we will see in the next chapter. One does not have to challenge the sincerity of the author's memory to conclude that such commentary contributes to the misunderstanding of the potential of presidential leadership.

Even though both the public and commentators are frequently disillusioned with the performance of individual presidents and recognize that stalemate is common in the political system, Americans eagerly accept what appears to be effective presidential leadership as evidence on which to renew their faith in the potential presidential persuasion to engender change. After all, if presidential leadership works some of the time, why not all of the time?

Leadership as Persuasion

Despite all the attention to leadership, it remains an elusive concept, and there is little consensus even on what leadership is. According to James MacGregor Burns, "Leadership is one of the most observed and least understood phenomena on earth."[8] Barbara Kellerman lists ten different definitions of political leadership,[9] as does Gary Yukl.[10]

Writers and commentators employ the term "leadership" to mean just about everything a person who occupies what we often refer to as a position of leadership does—or should do. When we define a term so broadly, however, it loses its utility. Making tough decisions, establishing an administration's priorities, and appointing good people to implement policy are core functions of the presidency. Yet these activities are quite different from, say, obtaining the support of the public, the Congress, or other nations for the president's policies.

George W. Bush liked to say his job was to make tough decisions. He often referred to himself as a "strong leader" in this context, and he made strong leadership the underlying theme of his reelection campaign. The president promoted this perception of his leadership with a tough-guy image, as in his use of provocative language declaring that he wanted Osama bin Laden "dead or alive" and his taunting Iraqi insurgents to "bring 'em on."

There is no question that the Constitution and federal laws invest significant discretionary authority in the president. Making decisions and issuing commands are important, and doing them well requires courage, wisdom, and skill. At times, the exercise of unilateral authority may lead to historic changes in the politics and policy of the country. In the extreme case, the president can choose to launch a nuclear attack at his discretion. The consequences would be vast. Most people, however, would not view such an act as one of leadership. In exercising discretionary authority, the president, in effect, acts alone. He does not have to *lead*. At its core, decision making represents a different dimension of the job of the chief executive than obtaining the support of others.

Persuasion refers to causing others to do something by reasoning, urging, or inducement. Influencing others is central to the conception of leadership of most political scientists. Scholars of the presidency want to know whether the chief executive can affect the output of government by influencing the actions and attitudes of others. In a democracy, we are particularly attuned to efforts to persuade, especially when most potentially significant policy changes require the assent of multiple power holders.

An important element of a chief executive's job may be creating the organizational and personal conditions that promote innovative thinking, the frank and open presentation and analysis of alternatives, and effective implementation of decisions by advisers and members of the bureaucracy. We may reasonably view such actions as leadership, and there is no doubt that the processes of decision making and policy implementation are critical to governing. For purposes of this book, however, I focus on leadership of those who are not directly on the president's team and who are thus less obligated to support his initiatives.

RICHARD NEUSTADT AND THE POWER TO PERSUADE

Perhaps the best-known dictum regarding the American presidency is that "presidential power is the power to persuade."[11] It is the wonderfully felicitous phrase that captures the essence Richard Neustadt's argument in *Presidential Power*. For half a century, scholars and students—and many presidents—have viewed the presidency through the lens of Neustadt's core premise.

Neustadt provided scholars with a new orientation to the study of the presidency. Published in 1960, his framework was strikingly different from those of Edward S. Corwin[12] and Clinton Rossiter[13] that had dominated presidential scholarship. These differences were to have important consequences for the way many scholars would examine the presidency over the ensuing decades, as the emphasis on persuasion encouraged moving beyond Corwin's focus on the formal powers of the presidency and Rossiter's stress on roles. In Neustadt's words, "'powers' are no guarantee of power"[14] *and "[t]he probabilities of power do not derive from the literary theory of the Constitution."*[15] Power, then, is a function of personal politics rather than of formal authority or position. Neustadt placed people and politics in the center of research, and the core activity on which he focused was leadership. Indeed, the subtitle of *Presidential Power* is *The Politics of Leadership.* In essence, presidential leadership was the power to persuade.

Following Neustadt's lead, scholars began to study the people within institutions and their relationships with each other rather than to focus primarily on the institutions themselves and their formalities. It was not the roles of the president but the performance of those roles that mattered. It was not the boundaries of behavior but the actions within those boundaries that warranted the attention of scholars. In other words, scholars began to study presidents attempting to lead by persuading others to follow them. The president's need to exercise influence in several arenas led those who follow Neustadt's power perspective to adopt an expansive view of presidential politics that includes both governmental institutions and actors, such as the Congress, bureaucracy, and White House staff, and those outside of government, such as the public, the press, and interest groups.[16]

Two critical premises follow from Neustadt's argument that presidential power is the power to persuade. Both have had a powerful impact on studying the presidency. The first stems from the fact that power is a concept that involves relationships between people. By focusing on relationships and suggesting why people respond to the president as they do, Neustadt shifted us into a more analytical mode. To understand relationships, we must *explain* behavior.

Equally important, Neustadt was concerned with the strategic level of power:

> There are two ways to study "presidential power." One way is to focus on the tactics . . . of influencing certain men in given situations. . . . The other way is to step back from tactics on those "givens" and to deal with influence in more strategic terms: what is its nature and what are its sources? . . . Strategically, [for example] the question is not how he masters Congress in a peculiar instance, but what he does to boost his chance for mastery in any instance.[17]

Neustadt, then, was less interested in what causes something to happen in one instance than in what affects the probabilities of something happening in every instance. To think strategically about power, we must search for generalizations and calculate probabilities. Although he employed neither the language nor the methods of modern social science, Neustadt was clearly a forerunner. His emphasis on reaching generalizations about presidential power discouraged ad hoc explanations and may have been his greatest contribution of all.

The emphasis on explaining relationships has had a positive impact on studying the presidency. Less benign has been the impact of a second implicit proposition. There is an important a prescriptive element in *Presidential Power*. Neustadt's central motivation for writing the book was to offer advice to presidents to help them help themselves with their strategic problem of power, and he remained interested in the challenges of governing. Indeed, tying scholarship to governing is important, because—entertainment value aside—governing is the primary reason we study politics. Underlying his effort to aid presidents in leading was Neustadt's premise that they *could succeed* in persuading others if they were skilled enough at recognizing and protecting their interests and exploiting critical resources.

The view that presidents not only need to persuade but that they can do so has led scholars, commentators, and other observers of the presidency to focus on the question of *how* presidents persuade rather than the more fundamental question of *whether they can do so*. In addition, Neustadt's emphasis on the personal in politics—and the potential success of persuasion—has led some scholars to overlook the importance of the context in which the president operates as well as his institutional setting. Ironically, this focus has also discouraged reaching generalizations about the strategic level of power.

It would be unfair to argue that Neustadt had erected an impediment to understanding the broader patterns of presidential influence. His emphasis on the person in the office certainly discouraged it, however, especially among the less discerning of his readers. Similarly, many scholars and other commentators on the presidency have fallen prey to the personalization of politics and have uncritically accepted, for example, an exaggerated concept of the potential for using the "bully pulpit" to go public.

Presidential Power has remained the most influential, and most admired, book on the American presidency—and for good reason. Its focus on the influence relationships of presidents was a critical intellectual breakthrough that forced us to broaden and clarify our thinking and encouraged us to emphasize explanation and generalization in our research. Yet we must not *assume* the power to persuade. Instead, we need to explore the basic premises of presidential leadership.

"Transformational" Leaders

Although Neustadt encouraged the belief that presidential persuasion was possible, he began with the premise that presidents would have to struggle to get their way. As he put it, "The power to persuade is the power to bargain."[18] Indeed, it was the inherent weakness of the presidency that made it necessary for presidents to understand how to use their resources most effectively. Not everyone has such restrained views of leaders, however.

A common premise underlying the widespread emphasis on political leadership as the wellspring of change is that some leaders have the capability to *transform* policy by reshaping the influences on it. Such "transformational" leadership is the holy grail of leadership studies. An Internet search of the phrase "transformational leadership" will quickly produce more than a million hits. Web sites, institutes, and research studies focus on understanding—and teaching—the principles of transformational leadership.

With so much attention on transformational leadership, there is no consensus definition of the concept. The most prominent advocate of transformational leadership is James MacGregor Burns.[19] The essence of Burns's concept of transformation is elevating moral leadership, transforming both the leaders and the led. This change, in turn, leads to fundamental and comprehensive change in society, values, and political structures.[20] In his work on leadership, Burns focuses more on the goals of leadership than on democratic political leaders actually leading.

Others have adopted the term "transformational" and infused it with broader meaning than Burns originally intended.

Writing on the private sector views transformational leaders as visionaries and catalysts for change who sell their ideas and reshape their organizations. Common to most applications of the concept in the public sector is a belief in the potential of transformational leadership to change the opinions and behavior of followers in the public and actors in institutions and thus effect major change. (The address in one of the first hits in an Internet search for "transformational leadership" is aptly named Changing*Minds*.org.) Burns himself asserts at various points that transformational leaders have an "extraordinary potential influence over followers" and "immense" potential for influence over them. They are event-making individuals who define the forks in history.[21]

It would be easy to become enmeshed in debates about whether a particular president was "transformational." The issue is *not* whether major policy changes that presidents desire occur. They do. Neither is the issue determining when change is large enough that we may consider it to be transformational. That is a matter I leave to others. I am interested in significant changes, whether or not they are "transformational." The fundamental question is whether presidents have the potential to persuade others to follow them. If significant changes in public policy occur, what is the explanation? Can presidents transform politics through persuasion? On the other hand, must presidents persuade in order to change policy?

EXPLAINING CHANGE

The tenacity with which many commentators embrace the persuasive potential of political leadership is striking. They routinely explain historic shifts in public policy such as those in the 1930s, 1960s, and 1980s in terms of the extraordinary persuasiveness of Franklin D. Roosevelt, Lyndon Johnson, and Ronald Reagan.

Equally striking is the lack of evidence of the persuasive power of the presidency. Observers in both the press and the academy base their claims about the impact of such leadership on little or no systematic evidence and seemingly little reflection. There is not a single systematic study that demonstrates that presidents can reliably move others to support them.

Perhaps faith in the potential of persuasive leadership persists because such a view simplifies political analysis. Because broader forces that may influence changes in policy are complex, and perhaps even intractable, focusing primarily on the individual as leader eases the burden of explaining policy change. Faith in the persuasive presidency also simplifies the evaluation of the problems of governing. If it is reasonable to expect the White House to create opportunities for change, then failures of leadership must be personal deficiencies. If problems arise because the leader lacks the proper will, skills, or understanding, then the solution to our need for leadership is straightforward and simple: Elect presidents who are willing and able to lead. Because the system is responsive to appropriate leadership, it will function smoothly with the right leader in the Oval Office. The blame for unsuccessful leadership lies with the leader rather than with the opportunities for change in the leader's environment.

Leadership as Facilitation

The American political system is not a fertile field for the exercise of presidential leadership. Most political actors are free to choose whether to follow the chief executive's lead; the president cannot force them to act. At the same time, the sharing of powers established by the Constitution prevents the president from acting unilaterally on most important matters and gives other power holders different perspectives on issues and policy proposals. Thus, the political system compels the president to attempt to lead while inhibiting his ability to do so.

These imperatives present the primary challenge to his political leadership. Harry Truman, writing to his sister, reflected on the job of president:

Aside from the impossible administrative burden, he has to take all sorts of abuse from liars and demagogues. . . . The people can never understand why the President does not use his supposedly great power to make 'em behave. Well, all the President is, is a glorified public relations man who spends his time flattering, kissing and kicking people to get them to do what they are supposed to do anyway.[22]

Despite Truman's frustration, presidents often succeed in achieving changes in public policy, some of which are of historic significance. Coupling this fact with the lack of systematic evidence that presidents succeed in persuasion and plenty of evidence that they frequently fail to achieve the policy changes they desire presents a conundrum. What explains their success when they have it? If persuasion is not the key, then what is?

If persuasion plays a minor part in presidential leadership, it does not follow that leadership is unimportant. Successful leadership may have another explanation. In some cases, presidents may not need to rely on persuasion because there is already sufficient support for their policy stances. In other instances, there may be latent support that requires activation by the president and his supporters. In all cases, presidents who are successful in obtaining support for their agendas have to evaluate the opportunities for change in their environments carefully and orchestrate existing and potential support skillfully. Although it is not common for students of politics to articulate leadership as recognizing and exploiting opportunities for change, these—rather than persuasion—may be the essential presidential leadership skills.

To sharpen our thinking about leadership, it is useful to contrast two broad perspectives on the presidency. In the first, the president is the *director* of change. Through his leadership, he creates opportunities to move in new directions, leading others where they otherwise would not go. The director establishes an agenda and persuades the public, organized interests, Congress, and others to support administration policies. Accordingly, the president is the moving force of the system. Some may term such leadership as "transformational," and all view it as based on successful persuasion.

A second perspective is less heroic. Here the president is primarily a *facilitator* of change. Facilitators understand the opportunities for change in their environments and fashion strategies and tactics to exploit them. Rather than create a constituency, they reflect and sometimes clarify, intensify, or channel their constituencies' aspirations, values, and policy views. Instead of persuading others to support them, they skillfully work at the margins of coalition building, perhaps influencing a few critical actors, to obtain support for their initiatives.

It is important not to underrate this role. The facilitator is *not* simply one who seizes opportunities as they present themselves and invites people to do what they already want to do. Change is not inevitable, and facilitators make things happen that otherwise would not. Effective facilitators are skilled leaders who must recognize the opportunities that exist in their environments, choose which opportunities to pursue, when and in what order, and exploit them with skill, energy, perseverance, and will.

The director reshapes the contours of the political landscape to pave the way for change, whereas the facilitator exploits opportunities presented by a favorable configuration of political forces. The director creates a constituency to follow his lead, whereas the facilitator endows his constituency's views with shape and purpose. The range and scope of the director's influence are broad, whereas those of the facilitator are narrower.

The question of the relative influence of context and personal skills has also occupied some scholars of leadership within Congress. In their innovative examination of leadership in the House of Representatives, Joseph Cooper and David Brady concluded that institutional context is more important than personal skills or traits in determining the influence of leaders. They found no relationship between leadership style and effectiveness and argue that the institutional context, especially party strength, in which leaders find themselves, determines their leadership style more than do their own personal traits.[23]

The distinction between director and facilitator does not create exclusive categories: my goal is neither to classify presidents nor to resolve an academic dispute. Instead, I employ these types to aid our understanding of leadership by exploring its possibilities. Once we understand the possibilities of leadership, we are in a better position to assess both the performance of presidents and the opportunities for change. Equally important, we will be better positioned to *explain* the success or failure of presidential leadership.

The two categories of leader do not represent a straw man. Instead, they represent leadership types common in the literature on leadership. Sidney Hook contrasted the "eventful man," who influences developments noticeably, and the "event-making man," an eventful man whose actions are the consequences of outstanding capacities rather than accidents of position and who not only appears at but also helps define the forks in the road of history. (Hook expected few event-making leaders in democracies. His principal example of an event-maker in the twentieth century was Lenin.[24])

Burns, arguing that leaders can change contextual forces under certain conditions, criticized Franklin D. Roosevelt for being only an "eventful man."[25] He goes on to argue:

> There is an important difference between the politician who is simply an able tactician, and the politician who is a creative political leader. The former accepts political conditions as given and fashions a campaign and a set of policies best suited to the existing conditions. The latter tries consciously to change the matrix of political forces amid which he operates, in order that he may better lead the people in the direction he wants to go. The former operates within slender margins; the latter, through sheer will and conviction as well as political skill, tries to widen the margins with which he operates. He seeks not merely to win votes but consciously to alter basic political forces such as public opinion, party power, interest group pressure, the governmental system.[26]

This description is a close match to my distinction between facilitators and directors of change.

There is of course a third possibility: a president who is disposed not to lead. Although some occupants of the Oval Office may have fit this description, it is not useful for our purposes. We may learn a great deal about leadership from those who do not succeed in their efforts, but we can learn little from those who do not endeavor to lead.

GREAT MEN VERSUS HISTORICAL INEVITABILITY

It is useful to distinguish the leadership types I employ from the polar positions that characterize the debate over the "great man" interpretation of history. The two sides of this issue assumed their best-known forms in the nineteenth century. In *Heroes and Hero-Worship and the Heroic in History,* published in 1841, Thomas Carlyle argued that great men alone were responsible for the direction of history. To Carlyle, the environment of the hero was generally malleable and thus receptive to leadership.

George W. Bush shares this view of leadership. As conservative columnist David Brooks put it, "When Bush is asked about military strategy, he talks about the leadership qualities of his top generals. . . . When Bush talks about world affairs more generally, he talks about national leaders." Bush "is confident that in reading the individual character of leaders, he is reading the tablet that really matters. History is driven by the club of those in power. When far-sighted leaders change laws and institutions, they have the power to transform people."[27]

Viewing history from quite a different perspective, various schools of social determinists, including the Spencerians, Hegelians, and Marxists, saw history as an inexorable march in one direction, with change occurring only when the culture was ripe for it. They concluded that great men could not have acted differently from the way they did. Tolstoy's portrayal of Napoleon in *War and Peace* is perhaps the most memorable depiction of this view.

Most will agree that these perspectives are inadequate, and we have no need to become mired in this ancient debate. My contrasting leadership types are much less extreme, and the issue is not whether leadership matters, but rather how much and in what ways. It is not sufficient to conclude, however, that sometimes the environment is receptive to change and at other times, it is not. This view simply begs the question of whether leaders are able to influence the environment so as to create the opportunity for change. It also discourages inquiring about the roles that recognizing and exploiting opportunities play in presidential success.

How Presidents Matter

It is common to argue that it makes a difference who the president is.[28] For example, commentators often offer the example of the attempted assassination of President-elect Franklin D. Roosevelt on February 15, 1933, to make the point. If anarchist Giuseppe Zangara had succeeded in assassinating Roosevelt instead of Chicago Mayor Anton Cermak, they argue, the history of the United States would have been different. No doubt. It does not follow, however, that the difference Roosevelt made lay in his ability to build supportive coalitions through persuasive leadership.

Thus, I am *not* suggesting that presidents do not have transformative effects or that they are not independent agents in producing them. Stephen Skowronek maintains that the presidency's capacity to transform American government and politics results from its blunt and disruptive effects. Andrew Jackson forced the submission of the nullifiers and undermined the Bank of the United States, Franklin Pierce deployed the resources of his office on behalf of the Kansas Nebraska Act, and Lincoln bludgeoned the South into submission. All were transformative acts that changed the landscape of American government and politics. I agree. And Skowronek agrees that persuasion was not central to any of these actions.[29]

In addition, Skowronek argues that presidential failures can be as transformative as their successes, with retribution for failure driving political change, jarring loose governing coalitions, opening unforeseen alternatives, shifting the balance of power, and passing to successors an entirely new set of opportunities and constraints.[30] Again, I agree. My focus, however, is on presidents attempting to obtain support for policies that *they* want.

The question, then, is not whether presidents matter. Of course they do. The question is *how* they matter—how do they bring about change? If we are going to understand the nature of presidential leadership and the potential of *persuasion*, we must not conflate persuasion with other dimensions of the presidency such as discretionary decision making. In addition, we must move beyond anecdotes and investigate presidential persuasion more rigorously. Finally, we need to investigate whether facilitative skills are another, and important, dimension of presidential leadership. Thus, it is reasonable to ask whether the most effective presidents reshape the political landscape to pave the way for change, or whether they recognize and skillfully exploit opportunities in their environments to achieve significant changes in public policy. If recognizing and exploiting opportunities are critical leadership skills, we need to understand how presidents exercise them.

The Importance of Understanding Leadership

Debunking exaggerated claims of presidential persuasiveness is not an end in itself. Rejecting simplistic and inaccurate explanations for political change is the first step to understanding the nature of presidential leadership, however. And it is important that we do so.

Understanding presidential leadership provides lessons for scholars and presidents alike. I defer discussion of these matters until chapter 6, after we explore the explanations for successful presidential leadership. It is clear, however, that the stakes of understanding the potential of persuasiveness are especially high for the White House. If the conventional wisdom is wrong and presidents are not able to persuade, much less mobilize, the public or Congress, then presidents may be wasting their time and adopting governing styles that are prone to failure. Presidents—and the country—often endure self-inflicted wounds when they fail to appreciate the limits of their influence.

Avoiding mistakes is not enough, of course. It is important for all of us to understand how successful presidents actually do lead. What are the essential presidential leadership skills? Under what conditions are they most effective? What contributions can these skills make to engendering change? The answers to these questions should influence presidents' efforts to govern, the focus of scholarly research and journalistic coverage, and the expectations and evaluations of citizens. Thus, we must seek a better understanding of presidential leadership in order to think sensibly about the role of the chief executive in the nation's political system.

-◦- -◦- -◦-

Having posed the question of how presidents bring about changes in public policy, it is time to answer it. The most constructive approach is to examine rigorously the actual circumstances and success of presidents, especially of those presidents to whom we most often attribute transformational leadership. In the next four chapters, I explore presidential success in moving the objects of most of their persuasive efforts: the public and Congress.

At the core of my analysis is examining the strongest cases for persuasive leadership. Using best test cases here focuses attention on the most difficult hurdles for a challenge to the conventional wisdom that persuasion is the key to successful presidential leadership. In the best test case approach, the burden of proof is on the challenger. However, if an argument holds for the most difficult cases, the logic of the analysis is that it will hold for others as well.

Thus, in chapters 2 and 4, I focus on best test cases, including the political giants Abraham Lincoln, Franklin D. Roosevelt, Lyndon B. Johnson, and Ronald Reagan, searching for persuasiveness where we are most likely to find it. We want to discover

whether the presidents who led the fights for the most significant changes in public policy succeeded through persuading
others to support their policies or whether their success rested
on recognizing and exploiting existing opportunities for change.

I take a different tack in chapters 3 and 5. There I examine
presidents governing in more typical circumstances. My goal is
to determine whether whatever success such presidents
achieved was the result of the same type of leadership as that
employed by presidents governing in more auspicious conditions. In addition, I explore a variety of forms of facilitative
leadership to enrich our understanding of both its possibilities
and its limitations.

2 Leading the Public
Best Test Cases

THE PRESIDENT's relationship with the public is crucial. Gaining and maintaining office, obtaining support from an independently elected legislature, and increasing the party's representation in Congress depend on public opinion. Can some presidents *change* public opinion and move it to support their transformational policies? Or are they likely to be frustrated in their efforts, as John F. Kennedy insinuated with his suggestion of an exchange from Shakespeare's *King Henry IV, Part I* as an epigraph for Clinton Rossiter's classic work, *The American Presidency*:

> GLENDOWER: I can call spirits from the vasty deep.
> HOTSPUR: Why, so can I, or so can any man.
>   But will they come when you do call them?[1]

Commentators on the presidency in both the press and the academy often assume that the White House can move public opinion if the president has the skill and will to effectively exploit the "bully pulpit." In Sidney Blumenthal's words, in the permanent campaign, "the citizenry is viewed as a mass of fluid voters who can be appeased by appearances, occasional drama, and clever rhetoric."[2] Books that purport to tell politicians just the right words to use in order to persuade the public receive substantial attention.[3] Even those who lament the "plebiscitary presidency" may base their analyses on the premise of the president having established a direct and persuasive relationship with the public.[4]

Equally important, those in the White House share the premise of the potential of presidential leadership of the public. David Gergen, an experienced White House communications adviser, favorably cites Churchill's assertion that "Of all the talents bestowed upon men, none is so precious as the gift of oratory. He who enjoys it wields a power more durable than that of a great king. He is an independent force in the world."[5] He goes on to add that Ronald Reagan turned television "into a powerful weapon to achieve his legislative goals."[6] Blumenthal agreed, declaring that Reagan had "stunning success in shaping public opinion," which in turn was central to transforming his ideas into law.[7]

Similarly, in interviews in the 1990s, Jacobs and Shapiro found among both White House and congressional staff widespread confidence in the president's ability to lead the public. Evidently President Clinton shared this view, as people close to him reported that he exhibited an "unbelievable arrogance" regarding his ability to change public opinion and felt he could "create new political capital all the time" through going public—a hubris echoed by his aides.[8]

The assurance with which presidents, scholars, and journalists accept the assumption of the potential of presidential public leadership belies our lack of understanding of that leadership. Until recently, we knew very little about the impact of the president's persuasive efforts because we had focused on the stimulus rather than the response in examining presidential public leadership.

For example, there is a substantial and rapidly increasing literature focusing on presidential rhetoric.[9] Underlying most of this research is the premise that the president can employ rhetoric to move the public. An individual president may be ineffective and fail to move opinion, but the potential is there. The authors of these fine works concentrate on analyzing *what* the president said. In the process, they make numerous inferences regarding the impact of the president's rhetoric on public opinion. However, scholars of presidential rhetoric virtually never provide evidence for their inferences about the president's impact.[10]

Yet one of the crowning ironies of the contemporary presidency is that at the same time that presidents increasingly attempt to govern by campaigning—"going public"—public support is elusive. In the century since Theodore Roosevelt saw the White House as a "bully pulpit," presidents have often found the public unresponsive to issues at the top of the White House's agenda and unreceptive to requests to think about, much less act on, political matters. When asked about his "biggest disappointment as president," George H. W. Bush replied, "I just wasn't a good enough communicator."[11]

In his memoirs, Ronald Reagan—the "Great Communicator"—reflected on his efforts to ignite concern among the American people regarding the threat of communism in Central America and mobilize them behind his program of support for the Contras. "For eight years the press called me the 'Great Communicator.' Well, one of my greatest frustrations during those eight years was my inability to communicate to the American people and to Congress the seriousness of the threat we faced in Central America."[12]

In the following sections, I examine the opinion leadership of three extraordinary presidents. I begin with the case of our most eloquent president, Abraham Lincoln, whose presidency certainly helped transform the nation. Then I review data on two best test cases for more modern presidential leadership of the public: Franklin D. Roosevelt and Ronald Reagan. A Democrat and a Republican, each president displayed formidable rhetorical skills, and both supporters and detractors frequently commented on their unusual rapport with the public. Roosevelt revolutionized political communications with his famous fireside chats, and Reagan earned the sobriquet of the "Great Communicator." If these political giants could not move the public, it is unlikely that any presidents can. We have much more data on Reagan than on FDR, of course, but even a limited examination of Roosevelt's tenure is instructive.

Abraham Lincoln

No president has exceeded Abraham Lincoln's eloquence in public discourse, and only George Washington can make a similar claim on the hearts of the American people. Lincoln was a brilliant politician who rose to power by expressing ideas on the great questions of his time. Many writers have commented on his talent for establishing a rapport with the public, and there is no doubt that he was skilled at speaking candidly without giving offense.[13] Once in office, did he position himself ahead of public opinion and employ his rhetorical skills to sway the public to support the Civil War and, later, the emancipation of the slaves?

Certainly, many authors have claimed that Lincoln shaped public opinion.[14] The *Wall Street Journal* asked a prominent expert in public relations to name the five best books in his field. His list included a work on Lincoln, and he argued, "Abraham Lincoln's words moved public opinion as no other U.S. politician's have before or since." For example, "However great the public dismay over the Civil War's length and costs, Lincoln succeeded in uniting the country behind him—in large part . . . because of the moral clarity and the eloquence of his appeal."[15] Yet there is nothing in the book—or any other book—that shows the impact of Lincoln's eloquence.

Rather than swaying opinion with the intellectual and aesthetic force of his rhetoric, Lincoln acted in a strategic manner that would be familiar to politicians in the twenty-first century. He invested heavily in reading public opinion, relying on election returns, politicians, newspapers, mail, and visitors (including many ordinary citizens). One of his primary goals in this effort was to avoid moving too far ahead of public opinion. He well understood that any individual politician would fail if he tried to swim against or resist the larger tide.[16] As one contemporary supporter put it, "Lincoln . . . always moves in conjunction with propitious circumstances, not waiting to be dragged by the force of events or wasting strength in premature

struggles with them."[17] Lincoln's task was to identify and promote the means by which he could help advance the larger
forces at work.[18]

To do so, he tapped into the Union's deep well of religious-
patriotic sentiment and effectively channeled the forces of
mainstream Protestant orthodoxy, the most potent agents of
American nationalism. Lincoln's deep familiarity with Americans and his political and social context gave him an extraordinary sensitivity to the direction of events. Although not religious in the sense of formal membership in a church, Lincoln
was "alert to the power of religious opinion and fused appeals
to Protestant millennialism and Enlightenment rationalism."
According to biographer Richard Carwardine, it is "no over-
statement" that "the combined religious engines of the
Union—and the motor of evangelical Protestantism in particular—did more than any other single force to mobilize support
for the war."[19]

Similarly, Lincoln's election in 1860 "depended far less on
his individual appeal than on the skill with which Republican
organizers projected him as the embodiment of the party's philosophy and platform." Moreover, the demonstrations of fidel-
ity to the Union following the hostilities at Fort Sumter and his
call to arms did not require inspiration from the White House.[20]

The president was also a master of timing. "Lincoln's great—
possibly greatest—achievement was to take a stethoscope to
Union opinion and read it with such skill that he timed to per-
fection his redefinition of the national purpose." "Lincoln
openly acknowledged that the steps by which he redefined the
war for the Union as a war against slavery were guided by his
reading of public opinion and that he feared too early an embrace of emancipation would shatter the Union consensus."
This redefinition was successful because he took the initiative
and persisted in his goals, but also because he was acutely sensitive to public opinion and had a gift for knowing when the
public would support his policies. He articulated the rationale
for the war and its sacrifices in terms that he knew from his
reading of public opinion would resonate with mainstream

Unionists and cement the war coalition. When he was confident that the public mood had shifted and border state opposition to military emancipation could be contained, he prepared to act.[21] Thus, he waited for the Union "victory" at Antietam before issuing the preliminary Emancipation Proclamation.[22]

Of course, Lincoln was constantly trying to obtain public support,[23] albeit it less directly than contemporary presidents. After his nomination for president on the Republican ticket in 1860, he never again took the stump. Although as president he spoke to the public nearly one hundred times, most of these instances involved modest, unscripted remarks—to troops passing through Washington, impromptu responses to visiting well-wishers, and statements to visiting delegations of clergymen, free blacks, state representatives, and others. His two inaugural addresses and his speech at Gettysburg were rare exceptions. To disseminate his views, Lincoln wrote carefully crafted public letters on issues crucial to the conduct and outcome of the war to individuals or mass meetings. He designed them to rally opinion and prepare the way for changes in policy. Many of these appeared in newspapers and pamphlets. A core of Republican Party loyalists proved invaluable as interpreters of the administration's purpose to the people, and Republican editors trumpeted the cause of the Union. The administration also imaginatively exploited a formidable network of governmental, religious, and philanthropic organizations, including the Union army, to spread the word, and Lincoln's image was visible in mass-produced woodcuts, lithographs, photographs.[24]

Despite his caution in not getting too far ahead of public opinion, his mastery of timing, and his administration's extensive efforts to influence the public, Lincoln experienced many setbacks. On the core issue of emancipation, "[d]espite his skillful avoidance of partisanship, moral reproach or an argumentative tone, and his emphasis on opportunity for securing change that would come 'gently as the dews of heaven, nor rending or wrecking anything,' his appeal went unanswered."

Poor white laborers and border state slaveowners were unresponsive (encouraging the Republicans to soft-pedal the emancipation theme in the 1864 elections). On the other hand, the president could not convince black leaders of the advantages of freed slaves colonizing another country.[25] In addition, the Republicans suffered substantial losses in the 1862 midterm elections, and Congress did not heed Lincoln's plea for "malice toward none, with charity for all" when it established its Reconstruction policy.

It does not detract from Lincoln's uplifting and highly principled eloquence to conclude that his words were something less than "swords." Although he did have deep popular support, which his personal qualities encouraged and sustained, there is no evidence that he swayed many Americans with his rhetoric. Instead, he was a brilliant politician who mobilized his supporters and carefully read public opinion so as not to be too far ahead of it. His understanding of the public also helped him seize opportunities to move when opinion was disposed to support his changes in policy.

Abraham Lincoln knew full well that he could not direct events, and he was not inclined to doing so. David Herbert Donald remarks in the preface to his biography of the sixteenth president that his volume "highlights a basic trait of character evident throughout Lincoln's life: the essential passivity of his nature."[26] In 1864, Lincoln famously confessed to Albert G. Hodges, the editor of the Frankfort, Kentucky, *Commonwealth*, "I claim not to have controlled events, but confess plainly that events have controlled me. Now, at the end of three years of struggle the nation's condition is not what either party, or any man devised, or expected. God alone can claim it."[27] His equally famous declaration that his policy was "to have no policy"[28] allowed him to bend to the demands of the situation.

In addition, Lincoln did not make a case to either the public or Congress for transforming change. His power came not from challenging or subverting the routine political system or the state itself but from defending the status quo, as Unionists de-

fined it. It was the secessionists who were attempting to transform the system. In contrast, he emphasized and represented
continuity, not radical disjunction.[29] Thus, Lincoln was a highly
skilled facilitator. By brilliantly playing the hand history had
dealt him, Lincoln's facilitative leadership transformed the nation forever.

Franklin D. Roosevelt

Commentators frequently attribute Franklin D.
Roosevelt's early successes in obtaining public support, and
thus congressional action, to his ability to sway public opinion,
especially in his radio speeches. Historian Doris Kearns Goodwin makes a representative argument when she contends that
Roosevelt successfully used his famous fireside chats "to shape,
educate and move public opinion at critical moments":

> After his first address on the banking crisis . . . large deposits began
> flowing back into the banking system. When he asked everyone to
> get a world map and spread it before them as they listened to his
> description of far-flung battles in the Pacific, map stores sold more
> maps in several days than they had sold the entire year. When he
> announced a scrap drive to collect old rubber for reuse, the White
> House was inundated with old rubber tires, rubber balls, rubber
> bands and rubber girdles.[30]

None of these examples, however, represents the president
asking the people to change their minds. People were not opposed to looking at maps or participating in aiding the war effort. Indeed, they were eager to do so. Nor did they offer much
resistance to banking. After all, they had their money in the
banks in the first place. What they sought was reassurance for
their normal inclinations, and Roosevelt provided that brilliantly by assuring the public that only banks that had passed
government inspection and were thus in good condition could
reopen.[31] We should not forget, then, that FDR was moving people in the direction they already wanted to go.

THE PUBLIC'S RESPONSE

Roosevelt faced extraordinary trials as president, from battling the Depression to fighting World War II. No challenge was greater than leading public opinion, however. Some of FDR's efforts, such as his failed attempt to "pack" the Supreme Court in 1937 and his unsuccessful barnstorming the country to purge the Democratic Party of recalcitrant conservatives in the 1938 primaries,[32] have become part of American political folklore. However, these dramatic examples of failed opinion leadership are symptomatic of the frustration he faced in longer-term efforts such as preparing the nation for war or continuing New Deal reforms.

The president frequently found the public unresponsive to his leadership. Occasionally, as in the case of Lend-Lease, we have evidence that the public moved, albeit only slightly, in his direction.[33] More often, however, FDR had to rely on events to educate the public, first for creating a climate supporting domestic reform and then for fighting the war.

Matthew Baum and Samuel Kernell found that "the Roosevelt presidency was unique more in its context than in the president himself." The authors conclude that FDR "was by no means immune to the normal political winds that nip and tug on every president's political support. On a number of occasions, Roosevelt's exceptional political skills failed to insulate him from the negative political consequences of pursuing unpopular policies."[34] When both the left and right attacked him in 1936, his approval declined. As the economy worsened in the 1938 recession, the president's approval again turned down.[35]

Roosevelt did, of course, win four presidential elections, certainly an impressive achievement. Yet, election campaigns normally focus on reinforcing voters' predispositions to support a party and to attract the uncommitted. They generally do not focus on convincing people to change their minds about parties and candidates. We should not be surprised, then, that FDR built his winning coalitions on attracting new cohorts of voters—such as the young, women, the urban working class, immigrants, and the children of immigrants—to the New Deal coalition rather than converting loyal Republicans to support him.[36]

To win an election, a candidate need only convince voters that he or she is a better choice than the few available alternatives. In addition, someone always wins, whether or not voters support the victor's policy positions. Governing is different. The president's policy is just one of a wide range of alternatives. Moreover, delay is a common objective, and a common outcome, in matters of public policy. Neither the public nor elected officials have to choose. Although stalemate may be the president's goal, it was rarely Roosevelt's. Usually, the president wished to convince people to support a positive action. In sum, we cannot infer success in changing minds from success in winning elections.

Roosevelt recognized the limits of his ability to move the public, even if his many admirers did not (he won his first race as governor of New York by a hairbreadth in 1928). As historian Richard Hofstadter put it, "he was content in large measure to follow public opinion."[37] Thus, FDR reminded Upton Sinclair that he could not "go any faster than the people will let me."[38]

To determine how far he could go, FDR adopted a decision-making style in which he let situations develop, crystallize, and clarify, allowing competing forces to battle it out and letting public opinion express itself. Similarly, he made substantial efforts to understand the public's views. He read several newspapers and magazines and had a clipping service catalog many others; he was attentive to the mail, which arrived at the White House in record amounts; he engaged in an extensive correspondence; he sent his wife around the country to serve as his eyes and ears; he heard from state and local party leaders and regional and state administrators; he held hundreds of press conferences, using journalists' questions and his own trial balloons to gauge the public's thinking; and he used his highly developed skills to read the crowds before which he appeared. Equally important, Roosevelt commissioned polls and had access to the results of others. By 1941, Hadley Cantril had established a secret organization, Research Council, Inc., to conduct surveys for the president, and FDR even specified some of the questions he wished Cantril to ask the public.[39]

Roosevelt was typically cautious in his attempts to lead the public. He gave only two or three of his legendary fireside chats a year (only eight in his entire first term) and generally did not focus them on legislation under consideration in Congress. Instead, he devoted attention to several issues in each speech and sought to build broad support and instill confidence in him and his administration—and to decry his political opponents.[40] One study concluded that FDR only used a fireside chat to discuss legislative proposals on four occasions, the clearest example being the broadcast on March 9, 1937, on the ill-fated "Court-packing" bill,[41] a bill for which the president never obtained majority support.[42] His typical radio address increased his public approval by only about 1 percentage point—and then only during peacetime.[43] Even the president's staunchest supporters, relief recipients, had diverse reactions to his peacetime radio addresses, particularly if they dealt with controversial matters.[44]

Interestingly, and contrary to legend, many people—sometimes most of the public—did not listen to his addresses.[45] A poll in April 1939 found that 37 percent of the public responded that they *never* listened to FDR's fireside chats, and another 39 percent answered that they only sometimes listened. Only 24 percent said they usually listened.[46]

PREPARING FOR WAR

The most important issue of the era, world war, provides perhaps the best example of Roosevelt's approach to the public and its response to him. The president responded to changing circumstances like the advent of World War II by seeking popular support from those constituencies most inclined to deliver it rather than by persuading reluctant citizens to support him. According to Burns, "As a foreign policy maker, Roosevelt during his first term was more pussyfooting politician than political leader. He seemed to float almost helplessly on the flood tide of isolationism rather than to seek to change both the popular attitude and the apathy that buttressed the isolationists' strength."[47]

Early in 1935, he urged entry into the World Court, but the Senate refused to ratify the treaty. That same year, the Neutrality Act prohibited him from embargoing arms to belligerents, and he could not remove these constraints in 1936. Similarly, he could not recommend embargoing oil to Italy or lifting the embargo on arms in the Spanish Civil War for fear of losing the Catholic vote.[48] Indeed, for most of the prewar period, Roosevelt lacked public support for even modest forms of engagement in emerging conflicts in Europe and Asia. During 1935–1939, the public supported a national referendum in order for Congress to declare war, restrictions on Americans traveling on the ships of warring countries, prohibitions on American ships sailing in war zones, prohibitions on the manufacture and sale of war munitions for private profit, bans on arms shipments and bank loans to China, and requirements that Britain and France pay for arms from the United States in cash (even though they were at war) and that they carry the goods away in their own ships.[49]

In the years before the U.S. entry into World War II, FDR wanted to move the country from its isolationist tendencies, aid Britain, and rebuild U.S. military strength. Yet he feared a backlash if he moved too rapidly and, as Steven Casey has shown, sought to lead public opinion with prudent caution.[50] He knew he was severely constrained by public opinion and that "he was unable to move except in the direction, and largely at the pace, they [the public] wanted to go."[51]

When he proposed to "quarantine" aggressors in October 1937, the president immediately backed away from any commitment to a system of collective security. As his aide, Samuel Rosenman, put it, "the reaction to the speech was quick and violent—and nearly unanimous. Critics condemned it as warmongering and saber rattling. The president was attacked by a vast majority of the press." FDR had made the mistake of trying to move the public too quickly. Reflecting on the episode, he told Rosenman, "It's a terrible thing to look over your shoulder when you are trying to lead—and to find no one there."[52] For a time thereafter, he hesitated telling the nation about the gravity of the situation, saying the public would not believe him.[53]

There is a range of opinion about the extent of public support for Roosevelt's speech (although not the president's retreat). Some scholars have found that there was substantial favorable response.[54] We will never know the public's thinking for sure. What we do know is that the president ran into opposition from within his own administration and among isolationists in Congress—and that his own aides saw plenty of opposition in the country. They were not impressed by whatever public support existed for FDR's policy. The president felt hemmed in by public opinion, so he temporized.

As war neared, the president still could not mobilize the public and thus felt manacled by isolationists. He could not commit to Britain and France when war broke out or take action against the Axis powers or even aid the victims of the Nazis. Despite personal appeals to senators, Congress would not free him from the shackles of the Neutrality Act in the spring of 1939. He called a special session of Congress after Hitler invaded Poland on August 31, and asked the legislature to repeal the arms embargo. Yet he had to stay in the background because of the widespread fear that he desired dictatorial power. Although he secured repeal of the arms embargo, the isolationists won a number of concessions—even in the face of a world war. The Allies had to pay cash and carry the munitions themselves, Americans could not sail on belligerent vessels, and American ships could not sail to belligerent ports.[55]

It was not until 1940 that Congress, fearing an invasion, began appropriating generously for defense. Nevertheless, Roosevelt felt he needed to resort to the subterfuge of the destroyer-for-bases deal to circumvent potential isolationist opposition and the Walsh Act, passed that year, which stipulated that the U.S. Navy could release equipment for sale only if it certified the equipment was useless for defense. Similarly, he used secrecy to smooth the way for the French and English to purchase ammunition and hid the fact that the United States was patrolling security zones and alerting the British as to the location of German ships and planes.[56]

Roosevelt knew what he was up against. Despite the outbreak of war in Europe, in November 1939, a clear majority of the public still thought Congress had been correct earlier in the year to deny the president the power to decide to whom we would sell war materials.[57] In February 1940, isolationist sentiment was so strong that 63 percent of the public even opposed FDR involving himself in attempting to stop the war in Europe.[58] The next year, the House passed an extension of the draft by just a single vote, and in late July, 45 percent of the public supported releasing draftees after only one year of service.[59] As late as November 25, 1941, 51 percent of the public opposed sending draftees outside the Western Hemisphere to fight.[60]

Even when the nation's attention was focused on foreign policy in 1941, Harry Hopkins, the president's closest aide, remarked, "The President would rather follow public opinion than lead it."[61] In May, Roosevelt moved cautiously toward convoying shipping across the Atlantic to Great Britain to provide protection against German submarines. In preparation, he carefully watched the polls, noting a slight majority in favor. He was looking for a buildup of interventionist sentiment that would "push" him into a policy of convoying British ships. On May 27, he delivered a radio address in favor of convoys, and the telegrams to the White House in response to the speech were overwhelmingly favorable. Nevertheless, he disavowed any convoy plans the next day,[62] apparently in response to indications of opposition.

Indeed, the public was so unwilling to face up fully to the international dangers confronting the nation that even days before the attack on Pearl Harbor, the country was divided and unenthusiastic about war with Japan. When FDR asked Congress for a declaration of war against Japan on December 8, he did not include Germany and Italy in his request, because he felt he had yet to convince the public to fight Germany.[63]

On the greatest issue of his time, then, Roosevelt had little success in persuading the public to follow his lead. Indeed, he found the task so difficult that he typically relied on events to change opinion about the nature of the threat posed by the Nazis and the Japanese and the appropriate national response to it rather than positioning himself ahead of the public and trying to move it in his direction. For example, he did not feel he could persuade the public regarding protecting shipping to Britain in 1940, and the use of his name made only a marginal difference in public support for stronger war policies. Thus, he exploited the fighting between a German submarine and a U.S. destroyer, the *Greer*, to announce a policy of naval escorts of shipping and "shoot on sight" in the Atlantic.[64] He believed that the constraints of public opinion made the timing of initiatives crucial. "Governments . . . can only move in keeping with the thought and will of the great majority of our people," he declared. Thus, when public support for aiding the Allies rose sharply in June 1940, FDR took advantage of the change in mood and announced selling them outmoded planes and arms. Similarly, when he was convinced he had a consensus for expanded American aid, the president asked Congress for the Lend-Lease bill.[65] In this and other instances, consensus occurred only when other elites, especially Republicans, shifted their rhetoric to support the president's policies.[66]

Mindful of the lesson of Woodrow Wilson, who he felt got too far ahead of his followers, FDR tagged along with public opinion and sometimes even lagged behind it.[67] As a precaution, Roosevelt had Hadley Cantril poll the public throughout the war on whether he had gone too far in aiding Britain. Even at the end of the war, he feared a return to isolationism (his pollster wrote him a memo shortly before FDR left for the Yalta conference in 1945 that "internationalism rests on a rather unstable foundation"),[68] and believed that public opinion would force him to bring home American troops in the near term.[69]

Ole Holsti has it right when he summarizes FDR's efforts to mold public opinion in foreign policy as being "calculatedly cautious" and having a "modest impact."[70] There was no alternative. As historian Robert Dallek put it, even the Atlantic Charter did not change public opinion on involvement in war. Had Roosevelt "directly presented his view to the public of what it must do in response to the world crisis, it would have won him few converts and undermined his popularity and ability to lead by confronting ambivalent Americans with a choice they did not care to make."[71]

Ronald Reagan

In contrast to his immediate predecessors, the public viewed Ronald Reagan as a strong leader, and his staff was unsurpassed in its skill at portraying the president and his views in the most positive light. This seeming love affair with the public generated commentary in both academia and the media about the persuasiveness of the "Great Communicator." James Baker, the president's White House chief of staff in his first term, said of Reagan's repeated televised appeals, "Every time he spoke, he moved the needle on public and congressional opinion."[72] Reagan's views were notable for their clarity, and there is little doubt that the public knew where the president stood on matters of public policy. The question for us is the degree to which the public moved in Reagan's direction.[73]

COMING TO POWER

Did Reagan prepare the way for change by leading the public to support his policy stances? The evidence suggests that Ronald Reagan, like presidents before him, was a facilitator rather than a director. The basic themes Reagan espoused in 1980 were ones he had been articulating for many years: government was too big; the nation's defenses were too weak, leaving it vulnerable to intimidation by the Soviet Union; pride in country was an end in itself; and public morals had slipped too far. In 1976, conditions were not yet ripe for his message. It took the late 1970s, which brought long lines for gas, raging inflation, high interest rates, Soviet aggression in Afghanistan, and hostages in Iran, to create the opportunity for victory. By 1980, the country was ready to listen.

Martin Anderson, Reagan's first chief domestic policy adviser, agrees: "What has been called the Reagan revolution is not completely, or even mostly, due to Ronald Reagan. He was an extremely important contributor to the intellectual and political movement that swept him to the presidency in 1980. He gave that movement focus and leadership. But Reagan did not give it life."[74] Anderson goes on to argue that "neither Goldwater nor Nixon nor Reagan caused or created the revolutionary movement that often carries their name, especially Reagan's. It was the other way around. They were part of the movement, they contributed mightily to the movement, but the movement gave them political life, not the reverse."[75]

As journalist Haynes Johnson put it, Reagan "was the vehicle around which conservative forces could and did rally, the magnet that attracted a coterie of conservative journalists and writers and ambitious young economic theorists who proclaimed sacred dogma and argued theoretically pure positions."[76]

William Niskanen, one of the members of Reagan's Council of Economic Advisers, agrees with Anderson, writing that several developments in the generation before Reagan's election set the stage for substantial change in economic policy. As he saw it:

> Lower economic growth, rising inflation, and increasing tax rates led to a popular demand for some change in economic policy. . . . reduced popular confidence in the government increased the appeal of policy changes that would reduce the role of government in the American economy. Several complementary changes in the perspectives of economists and an increasing number of empirical

studies shaped the choice of policies to meet these concerns. . . . [Thus,] there was broad bipartisan agreement in Congress by the late 1970s for the direction of change in each of the major dimensions of federal economic policy.

All that was missing was a president who could shape a coherent economic program and articulate the rationale for this program to Congress, the press, and the American public. For most voters Ronald Reagan was the logical candidate and the logical president for the time. For over fifteen years he had articulated a quite consistent set of views that appealed to an increasing share of the electorate. . . . There are few periods in American history for which a president so closely matched the current demands on this role. Few presidents have had a greater opportunity to guide and shape federal economic policy.[77]

More systematic data support the view that Reagan had a receptive audience. James Stimson concluded, "movements uniformly precede the popular eras." The conservative winds of the 1980s were "fully in place before the election of Ronald Reagan" (just as the liberal winds of the 1960s were blowing in the late 1950s).[78] He was the beneficiary of a conservative mood, but he did not create it. Similarly, Benjamin Page and Robert Shapiro found that the right turn on social welfare policy occurred before Reagan took office and ended shortly thereafter.[79] James Davis also found that pro-defense and anti-welfare conservative trends had occurred by the late 1970s—before Reagan's nomination.[80] William Mayer produced similar findings,[81] while Tom Smith found that liberalism had plateaued by the mid-1970s.[82]

There is another aspect of Reagan's coming to power that is of direct interest to us. Although he was the preferred candidate of the American people in 1980 and 1984, Reagan was also the least popular candidate to win the presidency in the period from 1952 to 1988. His supporters displayed an unusual degree of doubt about him, and those who opposed him disliked him with unprecedented intensity.[83] Votes for him in 1984 were not necessarily votes for his policies.[84]

REAGAN'S REVOLUTION

What happened once Reagan took office? The first six months of Ronald Reagan's tenure have become part of the folklore of American politics. The conventional wisdom is that Reagan went on television and, using the bully pulpit, mobilized the public to support his tax and spending cuts. The image of Reagan leading the public so successfully is a strong one and requires that we examine it more closely.

Budgetary politics, 1981. On February 5, 1981, Reagan made a nationally televised address assessing the nation's economic problems and presenting the broad contours of an economic program. On February 18, he delivered another nationally televised address before a joint session of Congress in which he unveiled his proposals for tax cuts and spending reductions. There is no question that the public was anxious about the state of the economy, which featured high inflation, high interest rates, and rising unemployment. According to Samuel Kernell, the public's response "was muted,"[85] but we can see in table 2.1 that public support for the president's taxing and spending proposals immediately after his speech was quite high. A tax cut during hard times is an attractive option to most people.

On March 30, John Hinckley shot the president in an assassination attempt. Reagan's approval ratings increased by 7 percentage points after the attempt on his life. Within a week of the shooting, White House Deputy Chief of Staff Michael Deaver convened a meeting of other high-ranking aides to determine how best to take advantage of the new political capital the assassination attempt had created. Ultimately, the plan was for Reagan to make a dramatic nationally televised appearance before Congress, which occurred on April 28. The president showed himself to be recovering from his injuries and vigorously threatened legislators with the wrath of the people if they did not support the Gramm-Latta budget reconciliation resolution, which included the president's proposals.

TABLE 2.1
Support for 30 Percent Tax Cut over Three Years, 1981

Date	Favor	Oppose	Unsure/ No Opinion
19–20 February 1981	76	20	4
25–29 March 1981	65	29	6
20–22 April 1981	68	25	7

SOURCE: ABC News/ *Washington Post* poll.

Date	Favor	Oppose	Unsure/ No Opinion
23–24 February 1981*	68	15	17
13–14 April 1981*	67	15	18
18–19 May 1981*	61	20	19
13–14 July 1981*+	56	18	27

SOURCE: NBC News/Associated Press poll.

* Among those who had heard or read about Reagan's economic proposals

+ Question asked about favoring a *25* percent tax cut over three years

We lack systematic evidence of the public's response to Reagan's speech. Kernell describes the president's reception in Congress as a "love feast,"[86] and perhaps it was. We do know that there was no upsurge in the president's approval ratings in the Gallup Poll. Indeed, the polls nearest in time before and after the speech produced virtually identical results.[87] Moreover, it is obviously illogical to employ Congress's reception *during* the speech as evidence of public reaction *following* the speech. We know that in preparation for the president's speech the Republican National Committee stimulated grassroots pressure on Southern Democrats whose districts had voted heavily for Reagan in 1980.[88] The whole point of this effort was to develop support before the speech, and the Republicans seem to have been quite successful in achieving this goal. On the other hand, the figures in table 2.1 show that support for the president's tax-cut proposal among the great majority of the public that had heard or read about his economic proposals *declined* between mid-April (before the president's speech) and mid-May (after his speech) and declined even further by mid-July.

Other evidence undercuts the argument that the public followed the president's lead. In June, Reagan's pollster, Richard Wirthlin, asked the public whether they supported a 10 percent across-the-board tax cut over each of the next three years without attributing the proposal to the president. Seventy-five percent of the public responded that they favored such a proposal. What is most significant for our purposes, however, is that only 51 percent thought that Reagan supported such a policy and 45 percent thought he opposed it! To add to the confusion, 48 percent of the public said they favored no tax cuts in 1981 and that the United States should strive to balance the budget before considering tax cuts for 1983 and 1984. Only 29 percent agreed with Reagan's view opposing such an approach. And 64 percent opposed Reagan's policy of across-the-board tax cuts, favoring a larger percentage cut for those in the lower income brackets.[89]

The next stage in the budgetary process was for Congress to decide on specific budget cuts. By mid-June, however, the White House concluded that the president could not successfully go public on behalf of his spending proposals.[90] The public did not seem receptive to the president's message. For example, in May, 60 percent of the public said they would support increased spending for social programs even if it would require an increase in taxes,[91] and 62 percent favored balancing the budget while only 30 percent preferred to cut taxes.[92] Nevertheless, the administration won by a narrow margin a crucial procedural vote to vote on all the cuts together on one vote, and then the House passed the president's budget.

The most notable example of a president mobilizing public opinion to pressure Congress in the age of television is Ronald Reagan's effort to obtain passage of his bill to cut taxes in 1981. On July 27, two days before the crucial vote in the House, the president made a televised plea for support of his tax-cut proposals and asked the public to let their representatives in Congress know how they felt. Evidently, this worked, for thousands of telephone calls, letters, and telegrams poured into congressional offices. We will probably never know how much of this represented the efforts of the White House and its corporate allies rather than individual expressions of opinion. Nevertheless, on the morning of the vote, Speaker Tip O'Neill declared, "We are experiencing a telephone blitz like this nation has never seen. It's had a devastating effect."[93] With this kind of response, the president easily carried the day.

We must be cautious about inferring the president's success in leading the public from his victory in Congress. The White House was not content to rely solely on a presidential appeal for a show of support. It took additional steps to orchestrate public pressure on Congress. Kernell describes the auxiliary efforts at mobilization of Reagan's White House in 1981:

> Each major television appeal by President Reagan on the eve of a critical budget vote in Congress was preceded by weeks of preparatory work. Polls were taken; speeches incorporating the resulting insights were drafted; the press was briefed, either directly or via leaks. Meanwhile in the field, the ultimate recipients of the president's message, members of Congress, were softened up by presidential travel into their states and districts and by grass-root lobbying campaigns, initiated and orchestrated by the White House but including RNC and sympathetic business organizations.[94]

Reagan's White House tapped a broad network of constituency groups. Operating through party channels, its Political Affairs Office, and its Office of Public Liaison, the administration generated pressure from the constituents of members of Congress, campaign contributors, political activists, business leaders, state officials, interest groups, and party officials. Television advertisements, letters, and attention from the local news media helped focus attention on swing votes. Although these pressures were directed toward Republicans, Southern Democrats received considerable attention as well, which reinforced their sense of electoral vulnerability. The president also promised not to campaign against Southern Democrats who supported him.[95]

In addition, the administration engaged in old-fashioned bargaining on a wholesale scale. Reagan's budget director David Stockman was quite candid about the concessions that members of Congress demanded in return for their support for the tax cut of 1981, including special breaks for holders of oil leases, real estate tax shelters, and generous loopholes that virtually eliminated the corporate income tax. "The hogs were really feeding," he said. "The greed level, the level of opportunism, just got out of control."[96] Stockman recalled, "The last 10 or 20 percent of the votes needed for a majority of both houses had to be bought, period." Similarly, he termed the trading that went into passing the final budget as "an open vote auction."[97] For example, Reagan agreed to raise sugar price supports to induce representatives from Louisiana to vote for his budget cuts in 1981.[98]

After a careful study, Marc Bodnick concluded that the 1981 tax and budget cuts relied heavily on traditional bargaining and that Reagan's going public strategy was not as dominant as the conventional wisdom suggests. Conservative Democrats supported spending and tax cuts because they agreed with them, not because they were afraid of Reagan's public support. For example, twenty-four of the twenty-nine Democrats who supported the president on specific spending cuts were long-time fiscal conservatives. The other five Democrats had conservative leanings, and each made a deal with the White House. The president's public appeals reinforced deals that were already made. Indeed, Bodnick concludes that bargaining had produced a viable tax-cut compromise *before* Reagan's public address.[99]

Beyond the tax cut in 1981. The administration's mobilization of the public on behalf of the tax cut of 1981 appears to be a deviant case—even for Ronald Reagan. His next major legislative battle was over the sale of AWACS (Advanced Warning and Control System) planes to Saudi Arabia. The White House decided it could not mobilize the public on this issue, however, and adopted an "inside" strategy, working directly with members of Congress to prevent a legislative veto.[100]

Reagan went public one more time regarding the budget in 1981. On September 24, he made a national address arguing for further budget cuts. In a Gallup poll of October 2–5, 1981, respondents were asked, "In general, are you in favor of budget cuts in addition to those approved earlier this year or are you opposed to more cuts?" Only 42 percent of the public favored such cuts, while 46 percent opposed them (12 percent expressed no opinion). Gallup asked the same people, "To reduce the size of the 1982 budget deficiency, President Reagan has proposed cutting $13 billion in addition to the $35 billion in cuts approved earlier in this year. About $11 billion of the new cuts would come from social programs and about $2 billion from defense programs. In general, would you say you approve or disapprove of the President's proposal?" In response to the question posed in this way, 74 percent approved of budget cuts and only 20 percent disapproved (6 percent had no opinion).[101]

Kernell concludes that these results provide evidence of Reagan's remaining a persuasive force with the public.[102] This is unlikely, however. Only 36 percent of Democrats approved of Reagan's job performance, and budget matters were certainly salient at the time and central in evaluations of Reagan's performance as president. It is much more likely that the difference in the responses to the two questions was the result of Gallup raising the issue of budget deficits. In a poll taken just before the president's speech, for example, 67 percent of the public favored a balanced budget amendment to the Constitution.[103] It was the premise of using budget cuts to reduce the deficit, not the support of Ronald Reagan, that made people willing to support further reductions in spending.

GOVERNING

In the remainder of his tenure, President Reagan repeatedly went to the people regarding a wide range of policies, including the budget, aid to the Contras in Nicaragua, and defense expenditures. He traveled, made television and radio addresses, and held evening press conferences. Despite his high approval levels for much of the time, he was never again able to arouse many in his audience to communicate their support of his policies to Congress. Indeed, it was not long before observers began labeling his budgets as DOA—Dead on Arrival. Most issues hold less appeal to the public than substantial tax cuts.

Aid to the Contras. One of Reagan's principal preoccupations was to ignite concern among the American people regarding the threat of communism in Central America. At the core of his policy response to this threat was an effort to undermine the "Sandinista" government of Nicaragua through support of the opposition Contras, and he made substantial efforts to mobilize the public behind his program. Yet he consistently failed to obtain even a plurality of Americans in support of aiding the Contras. As he lamented in his memoirs:

> Time and again, I would speak on television, to a joint session of Congress, or to other audiences about the problems in Central America, and I would hope that the outcome would be an outpouring of support from Americans who would apply the same kind of heat on Congress that helped pass the economic recovery package.
>
> But the polls usually found that large numbers of Americans cared little or not at all about what happened in Central America— in fact, a surprisingly large proportion didn't even know where Nicaragua and El Salvador were located—and, among those who did care, too few cared enough about a Communist penetration of the Americas to apply the kind of pressure I needed on Congress.[104]

The data in tables 2.2–2.4 reflect the problem of which Reagan spoke. The three tables contain the responses to questions inquiring about support for aiding the Contras during Reagan's second term. No matter how pollsters worded the question, at no time did even a plurality of Americans support the president's policy of aiding the Contras. Because the questions represented in the three tables have somewhat different

TABLE 2.2
Public Support for Aid to the Contras, 1985–1986

Date	Support Aid (%)	Oppose Aid (%)	Don't Know (%)
06/85[1]	34	59	6
07/85[1]	28	64	7
03/86[3]	34	59	8
03/86[3]	30	54	16
03/86[4]	35	60	4
03/86[2]	42	53	5
03/86[5]	37	44	19
04/86[7]	33	62	5
04/86[8]	39	54	7
04/86[6]	28	65	7

SOURCES:

[1] Harris question: "Recently, President Reagan has had some serious disagreements with Congress. Now who do you think was more right—Reagan or Congress—in their differences over sending military aid to the Contra rebels in Nicaragua, which is favored by Reagan and opposed by Congress?"

[2] ABC News question: "As you may know, President Reagan has asked Congress for new military aid for the Nicaraguan rebels known as the 'Contras.' Do you agree or disagree with Reagan that Congress should approve that money?"

[3] ABC News question: "President Reagan is asking Congress for new military aid for the Nicaraguan rebels know as the 'Contras.' Do you agree or disagree with Reagan that Congress should approve that money?"

[4] ABC News question: "The House of Representatives has refused Reagan's request for $100 million in military and other aid to the Contra rebels in Nicaragua. Do you approve or disapprove of that action by the House?" [Because the question asks respondents whether they approve of the House's negative action, a response of "approve" means opposing aid to the Contras. Thus, I have reversed the results to make them consistent with the portrayal of the results from the other questions.]

[5] USA Today question: "Do you favor or oppose military aid to the Contras fighting the Sandinista government in Nicaragua?"

[6] ABC News/Washington Post question: "Do you generally favor or oppose the U.S. granting $100 million in military and other aid to the Nicaraguan rebels known as the 'Contras'?"

[7] Harris question: "Do you favor or oppose the U.S. sending $100 million in military and nonmilitary aid to the Contra rebels in Nicaragua?"

[8] Harris question: "Do you favor or oppose the U.S. sending just $30 million in nonmilitary aid to the Contra rebels in Nicaragua?"

TABLE 2.3
Public Support for Aid to the Contras, 1987

Date	Approve (%)	Disapprove (%)	Don't Know (%)
01/87	22	70	7
07/87	43	46	12
07/87	35	54	14
07/87	41	49	11
08/87	36	59	5
08/87	40	56	4
09/87	33	61	5
10/87	33	63	4

SOURCE: ABC News/*Washington Post* question: "Do you generally favor or oppose the U.S. Congress granting military aid to the Nicaraguan rebels known as the 'Contras'?"

TABLE 2.4
Public Support for Aid to the Contras, 1987–1988

Date	Approve (%)	Disapprove (%)	Don't Know (%)
01/87	28	60	12
07/87	33	51	16
07/87	40	49	12
08/87	33	49	18
10/87	35	53	12
01/88	30	58	12
03/88	39	48	14

SOURCE: CBS News/*New York Times* question: "Do you approve or disapprove of the United States government giving military and other aid to the Contras who are fighting against the government of Nicaragua?"

wording, we must be cautious about inferring trends in opinion. Nevertheless, it is difficult to conclude that Reagan's rhetorical efforts moved opinion in his direction. (The unusually low level of support in January 1987 polls is undoubtedly the result of the Iran-Contra scandal that had just broken.)

Richard Wirthlin provides additional evidence of the limits of Reagan's persuasive powers on aid to the Contras. In a memo to the president on April 20, 1985—at the height of Reagan's

popularity—Wirthlin advised against taking his case directly
to the people through major speeches. The president's pollster
told him that doing so was likely to lower his approval and
generate more public and congressional opposition than
support.[105]

In addition, a majority of the *public* always opposed Reagan's
broad policy of greater U.S. involvement in Central America
and his handling of the general issue of Central America (table
2.5). Moreover, there was no trend toward greater support for
the president on his high-priority policy.[106]

Defense spending. One of Reagan's highest priorities was increasing defense spending. He was fortunate in that support
for increased defense spending was unusually high *before* he
took office, thus his defense buildup represented an accelera-
tion of change initiated late in the Carter administration. A
number of conditions led to broad partisan support of the defense buildup, including the massive Soviet increase in their
strategic nuclear forces; a series of communist coups in Third
World countries, followed by revolutions in Nicaragua and Iran;
and the Soviet invasion of Afghanistan. American hostages held
in Iran, Soviet troops controlling a small neighbor, and communists in power in the Western Hemisphere created powerful
scenes on television and implied that American military power
had become too weak.

Nevertheless, public support for increased defense expenditures dissipated by 1982, only a year after Reagan took office
(tables 2.6 and 2.7). Indeed, in his second term, a plurality of
the public thought the United States was spending *too much*
on defense, and support for defense expenditures was decid-
edly *lower* at the end of his administration than when he took
office.[107] It is possible that the decline in support for defense
spending may have been the unintended consequence of the
military buildup that did occur.[108] However, opinion changed
by 1982, long before increased defense spending could have
influenced the nation's military security. In addition, pressures

TABLE 2.5
Public Approval of Reagan's Handling of Central America

Date	Positive (%)	Negative (%)	Unsure (%)
10/83	33	58	9
11/83	40	52	8
12/83	34	59	7
01/84	30	64	6
02/84	30	61	9
03/84	29	61	10
05/84	31	62	7
06/84	33	63	4
07/84	31	66	3
09/84	41	57	2
10/84	42	53	5
12/84	37	59	4
03/85	34	59	7
05/85	32	63	5
05/85	32	63	5
06/85	39	55	6
07/85	36	59	5
09/85	32	64	4
11/85	38	57	5
01/86	39	58	3
04/86	40	54	6
08/86	33	59	8
01/87	27	66	7
08/87	31	67	2
10/87	33	63	4
12/87	26	68	6
06/88	33	63	4

SOURCE: Harris question: "Now let me ask you about some specific
things President Reagan has done. How would you rate him on . . .
Handling the situation in Central America—excellent, pretty good,
only fair, or poor?"
NOTE: Positive = excellent/pretty good; Negative = only fair/poor.

TABLE 2.6
Public Support for Defense Spending, 1980–1987

Date	Too Little (%)	About Right (%)	Too Much (%)	Don't Know (%)
1/1980	49	24	14	13
1/1981	51	22	15	12
3/1982	19	36	36	9
3/1983	14	33	45	8
1/1985	11	36	46	7
3/1986	13	36	47	4
4/1987	14	36	44	6

SOURCE: Gallup Poll question: "There is much discussion as to the amount of money the government in Washington should spend for national defense and military purposes. How do you feel about this: Do you think we are spending too little, too much, or about the right amount?"

TABLE 2.7
Public Support for Defense Spending, 1980–1988

Date	Decrease (%)	About the Same (%)	Increase (%)
1980	11	18	71
1982	34	33	33
1984	32	32	36
1986	39	29	32
1988	35	32	33

SOURCE: National Election Study question: "Some people believe that we should be spending much less on money for defense. Others feel that spending should be greatly increased. Where would you place yourself on this scale?"

NOTE: Decrease = 1–3; About the Same = 4; Increase = 5–7 on NES's 7-point scale.

inevitably increase to spend on butter after periods of spending on guns. The point remains, however, that while Reagan wanted to continue to increase defense spending, the public was unresponsive to his wishes. As a result, Reagan suffered another disappointment, as Congress did not increase defense spending in real dollars during his entire second term.

TABLE 2.8
Public Support for Government Spending

Date	Reduce Spending (%)	Spend the Same (%)	Increase Spending (%)
1980	34	20	47
1982	41	29	33
1984	34	36	30
1986	26	28	46
1988	32	29	39

SOURCE: National Election Study question: "Some people think that government should provide fewer services, even in areas such as health and education, in order to reduce spending. Other people feel that it is important for the government to provide many more services even if it means an increase in spending. Where would you place yourself on this scale?"

NOTE: Reduce Spending = 1–3; Keep the Same = 4; Increase Spending = 5–7 on NES's 7-point scale.

Domestic spending. Limiting spending on domestic policy was at the core of Reagan's domestic policy. Because he felt "government is the problem," he was eager to limit government spending. Yet Reagan never obtained majority support for reducing spending. Indeed, support for Reagan's preference for reducing spending declined during his tenure, and in his second term pluralities actually favored *increasing* spending (table 2.8). In other words, the public was moving in the *opposite* direction from the president.[109]

Environmental protection. A hallmark of Reagan's domestic policy was his administration's antagonism toward environmental protection legislation.[110] However, the public did not follow the president's lead in this area and never wavered from its strong support for strictly enforcing laws designed to protect the environment (table 2.9).

Ideology. Presidents are also interested in influencing people's general ideological preferences. Success in affecting ideological preferences may translate into changing the premises on which citizens evaluate policies and politicians and thus can be espe-

TABLE 2.9
Public Support for Environmental Protection

Date	Favor (%)	Oppose (%)	Unsure (%)
03/11/82	83	14	3
07/09/82	85	10	5
12/27/83	84	13	3
03/08/84	88	9	3
05/16/84	84	10	6
07/02/84	85	9	6
07/20/84	84	10	6

SOURCE: Harris question: "Do you favor or oppose . . . strict
enforcement of air and water pollution controls as now
required by the Clean Air and Water Acts?"

cially significant. Ideological self-identification may also influence the kinds of political appeals to which one is attuned.

Reagan did no better in moving citizens' general ideological
preferences to the right than he did in influencing their views
of specific policies.[111] The data in table 2.10 represent how individuals characterized their own ideology and how they viewed
liberals and conservatives more generally. The readings of public opinion were taken at the time of Reagan's first election in
1980, his reelection in 1984, and at the end of his term in 1988.
It is clear that there was very little change in either dimension
between 1980 and 1988.

Taking a broader sweep, one prominent study concluded that
rather than conservative support swelling once Reagan was in
the White House, there was a movement away from conservative views almost as soon as he took office.[112] According to another scholar, "Whatever Ronald Reagan's skills as a communicator, one ability he clearly did not possess was the capacity to
induce lasting changes in American policy preferences."[113]

IRAN-CONTRA

Presidents must frequently defend both themselves and their
policies. The burden of moving public opinion in such cases is
on their opponents, who had to build support to change the

TABLE 2.10
Trends in Political Ideology

	1980 (%)	1982 (%)	1984 (%)	1986 (%)	1988 (%)
Self-Placement Scale					
Conservative	23.1	22.5	20.8	19.3	23.6
Slightly conservative	21.0	19.8	20.1	20.1	21.7
Moderate	30.6	34.9	33.4	36.9	31.3
Slightly liberal	13.5	11.7	12.9	14.2	13.1
Liberal	11.8	11.1	12.7	9.5	10.3
Mean Feeling Thermometer Ratings of					
Conservatives	62.7	53.3	59.9	58.6	61.1
Liberals	51.7	45.7	55.9	53.3	51.7

SOURCE: National Election Studies ideological self-placement question: "We hear a lot of talk these days about liberals and conservatives. Here is a 7-point scale on which the political views that people might hold are arranged from extremely liberal to extremely conservative. Where would you place yourself on this scale, or haven't you thought much about this?"

The National Election Studies "feeling thermometer" question: "I'd like to get your feelings toward some of our political leaders and other people who are in the news these days. I'll read the name of a person and I'd like you to rate that person using this feeling thermometer. You may use any number from 0 to 100 for rating. Ratings between 50 degrees and 100 degrees mean that you feel favorable and warm toward the person. Ratings between 0 and 50 mean that you don't feel too favorable toward the person. If we come to a person whose name you don't recognize, you don't need to rate that person. Just tell me and we'll move on to the next one. If you do recognize the name, but don't feel particularly warm or cold toward that person, you would rate that person at the 50 degree mark."

NOTE: In order to reduce the NES ideology scale from 7 to 5 points, "Liberal" combines those who selected themselves to be either "extremely liberal" or "liberal"; "Conservative" combines those who indicated they were either "extremely conservative" or "conservative."

status quo. The task of the White House is to *maintain* existing support. Under these circumstances, we would expect presidents to have more success than when they wish to change opinion. In other words, we would expect the president to do better on defense than on offense.

The greatest crisis of the Reagan administration began in November 1986, when the press revealed that the president had decided to sell weapons to Iran secretly in return for its aid in freeing American hostages. Many saw this move as foolish (it did not work) and contrary to long-standing U.S. policy of not negotiating with terrorists. Soon, officials also learned that National Security Council staffer Oliver North led an illegal effort to divert some of the money from the sale of missiles to funding the Contras in Nicaragua.

Clearly, the White House had some explaining to do. How convincing was it to the public? In the post-Watergate period, it is not surprising that two important questions regarding Iran-Contra were whether the president was telling the truth and whether he was involved in a cover-up of the scandal. The White House protested its innocence in four nationally televised addresses.

The first two took place on November 13 and December 2, 1986. The president's approval fell 16 percentage points in the Gallup Poll from the level he had before the speeches. He lost 6 percentage points after his March 4, 1987 speech. Only following his August 12, 1987, speech did he rise in the polls—by four percentage points. (However, after this speech, 49 percent reported that they were dissatisfied with his explanation and 39 percent thought he lied.[114])

Table 2.11 shows public responses to questions about Reagan's truthfulness. Over the period of the heart of the scandal, there was little change in public opinion and no increase in the percentage of the public who felt the president was telling the truth. Similarly, table 2.12 shows that the president did not make much headway in convincing the public that he had not engaged in a cover-up. Over the same period covered in the table, Gallup found that 75 percent of the public felt that Reagan was withholding information on Iran-Contra.[115] In addition, following both of his two 1987 speeches, the percentage of the public who felt he had made a major mistake *increased*.[116]

A second issue related to Iran-Contra was its impact on how the public viewed Reagan as a president. Table 2.13 displays public evaluations of Reagan's handling of Iran-Contra. There was very little change in the approval rates of the president's performance during the entire period, despite the four nationally televised presidential addresses on the subject. Only a third of the public approved his handling of the crisis.

TABLE 2.11
Reagan's Truthfulness on the Iran-Contra Affair

Date	Yes (%)	No (%)	Don't Know (%)
11/25/86*	40	56	4
12/02/86*	47	49	4
01/11–13/87**	42	53	5
01/18–20/87**	33	60	7
07/15/87*	34	60	6
08/12/87*	39	58	4
08/16–17/87**	42	55	3
09/19–22/87**	37	60	3

* ABC News/*Washington Post* question: "Generally speaking, do you think Reagan has been telling the public the truth about the Iran/Contra situation or not?"

** Wirthlin question: "As you may know, Ronald Reagan said he knew nothing about funding the Contra effort with money from the Iranian arms deal. From what you have heard and read, do you believe he is telling the truth?"

TABLE 2.12
Reagan's Covering Up the Iran-Contra Affair

Date	Yes (%)	No (%)	No Opinion (%)
02/26/87	38	57	5
03/05–09/87	48	48	4
05/28–06/01/87	51	47	2
06/25–29/87	50	48	2
07/11–12/87	45	49	6
07/15/87	45	49	6
08/03–05/87	43	52	5

SOURCE: ABC News/*Washington Post* question: "Do you think Ronald Reagan himself participated in an organized attempt to cover up the facts about the Iran/Contra arms affair or not?"

TABLE 2.13
Reagan's Handling of the Iran-Contra Affair

Date	Approve (%)	Disapprove (%)	No Opinion (%)
12/15–18/86	36	61	3
01/11–13/87	33	63	4
01/18–20/87	32	64	3
11/28–30/87	34	63	3

SOURCE: Wirthlin question: "Do you approve or disapprove of the way Ronald
    Reagan is handling the Iranian situation?"

Reagan never fully recovered from the scandal. His general job approval rating, which dropped 16 percentage points after the scandal was unearthed, did not rise to his pre–Iran-Contra heights until two years later, following the election of his successor.

REAGAN AS FACILITATOR

Ronald Reagan was less a public relations phenomenon than the conventional wisdom suggests. He had the good fortune to take office on the crest of a compatible wave of public opinion, and he effectively exploited the opportunity the voters had handed him. Yet when it came time to change public opinion or mobilize it on his behalf, he typically met with failure. As his press secretary Marlin Fitzwater put it, "Reagan would go out on the stump, draw huge throngs and convert no one at all."[117]

Although the public relations skills of Reagan's administration were impressive, they could not by themselves create or sustain goodwill. Despite his staff's efforts at promoting a favorable image, he fell below 50 percent approval in the polls after only ten months in office and would not obtain the approval of more than half the public again until November 1983. His average approval for his entire tenure was only 52 percent, less than that of his two successors, Bill Clinton and George H. W. Bush.[118]

Rather than serving as an example of the power of a persuasive leader, the early months of Reagan's tenure show the president brilliantly exploiting his opportunities as a facilitator. The president enjoyed favorable conditions for making appeals in his first months in office, including public anxiety over the economy and the perception of a mandate as a result of his surprising margin in the presidential election and the dramatic elevation of Republicans to majority status in the Senate. The same factors drove the Democrats into disarray as they reeled from Reagan's electoral victory and their loss of the Senate. In addition, as I discuss in chapter 4, Reagan advanced a short policy agenda that allowed him to keep a focus on his priorities and made it easier to move rapidly to exploit favorable conditions in the public.[119]

The fundamental conditions of public support in the president's legislatively crucial first year were established outside the White House. When Reagan's views matched the public mood, he effectively used the congruence to his advantage. Yet in the end, there was no persuasive magic. As one leading scholar concludes, "the supply of popular support rests on opinion dynamics over which the president may exercise little direct control."[120] Reagan was much more effective at exploiting popular support than he was in creating it in the first place.

The White House adapted adroitly to this situation. After a careful study of the Reagan administration's policy stands in 1981–1983 and the administration's internal public opinion surveys, Murray concluded that Reagan and his advisers "championed issues from their ideological agenda that fit with the current tide of mass opinion . . . and they reversed themselves whey they encountered strong majority resistance to particular policy initiatives, such as cuts in Social Security."[121]

Focused Persuasion?

The focus in this chapter has been on the president moving public opinion in his direction. When they were available, especially in the case of Ronald Reagan, I have relied on the aggregate results of national polls. In addition to national totals, the president may be especially interested in moving opinion in certain states or congressional districts, those in which he has the best chance of influencing a member of Congress. It is possible that the absence of aggregate national change may mask significant change in only a few, but critical, geographic areas.

Systematic data on opinion on policies within a state or congressional district are not available, so it is not possible to provide a definitive answer to the question of targeted impact. We can say that there is simply no evidence for this kind of effect. Moreover, even the White House lacks a mechanism for attempting to influence directly public opinion in delineated areas. How could it? In the electronic age, the bully pulpit is not a precision tool. When the president speaks, anyone can listen. In addition, even a presidential visit is unlikely to be repeated often, especially to a House district. If the White House wants to focus on a particular congressional constituency, it is much more likely to attempt quietly to mobilize campaign contributors, local elites, and interest groups than it is to employ the bully pulpit.

It is possible that despite the limitations of targeting his message, the president's rhetoric could have a disproportionate impact in certain constituencies. This is unlikely, however, as public opinion tends to swing in national trends. For example, Erikson, MacKuen, and Stimson found that public opinion tends to move similarly across a broad range of groups within the country.[122] Page and Shapiro reached the same conclusion. They found that although demographic groups may start from different levels of support, the direction and extent of opinion change within them is similar.[123] Moreover, if there is movement in some constituencies that the national totals do not capture, and these totals typically do not move in the president's direction, then there must be an even greater countermovement elsewhere. It is much more likely that the national totals have captured whatever opinion change occurs.

An alternative view is that the president primarily seeks to influence those segments of the population that may be most attuned to his appeals. Of course, there is no way for the president to segment his appeals so that only a select, but sizable, audience hears them. It is possible, however, that the president is more successful in influencing some groups than others and that the aggregate national data mask any movement that occurs among subgroups of the population, such as those most predisposed to support him. In *On Deaf Ears,* I presented a detailed analysis of disaggregated opinion on a selection of issues from the Reagan and Clinton years and found results similar to those for national totals.[124]

A Brief Comparative View

It is interesting to view the difficulties presidents have in persuading the public from a comparative perspective. Are leaders in other nations more successful in bringing about change by persuading the public? The experience of another strong conservative leader in office at about the same time as Ronald Reagan, Margaret Thatcher, suggests they are not. In a series of studies, Ivor Crewe analyzed the support for Thatcherite values, policy beliefs, and leadership style, using opinion polls by MORI, Gallup, and the British Election Surveys (1970 to 1983). He concluded that with the exception of privatization, there was no evidence that Prime Minister Thatcher converted the electorate on the central values of strong government, discipline, and free enterprise during her first term.[125] In addition, there was no increase in the Conservative vote, partisanship, or party members in the 1980s.[126] John Rentoul,[127] John Curtice,[128] and Robert Shapiro and John Young[129] report similar findings. Richard Rose reports that her average approval level in the British Gallup Poll was only 39 percent, and she never rose above 52 percent approval.[130]

Mrs. Thatcher certainly led a transformation of public policy in Britain, but she did not do so by persuading the British public of the wisdom of her views. Instead, she effectively exploited the opportunities her willing Conservative majority afforded her.

What about the greatest of British twentieth-century orators, Winston Churchill? The British wartime Ministry of Information found that events such as the capitulation of Finland in March 1940 quite understandably increased resentment of the government and the first British defeats depressed public morale. During the period of the Battle of France, Churchill delivered three of the most famous speeches in the English language to inspire his embattled nation. On May 13, three days after becoming prime minster, he offered "blood, toil, tears, and sweat." On June 4, he promised that Britain would "fight on beaches . . ." And on June 18, Churchill exhorted his fellow countrymen to "brace ourselves to our duties, and so bear ourselves that if the British Empire and its Commonwealth last for a thousand years, men will still say, 'This was their finest hour'." The prime minister's rhetoric was superb, but he was not able to stem tide of criticism of government.[131]

Indeed, it is not clear that the British people were lacking in inspiration. Even before Churchill became prime minister, defeatist and pacifist propaganda was having little effect on the public. Once at war, there was little indication that the public was reluctant to pursue the struggle against the Nazis. There were few reports of defeatist attitudes, and Hitler's peace offer did not sway the public. Much to the surprise of many leaders, the public did not require inducements such as socialism to continue to fight, nor did it demand promises for the future. The Ministry of Information realized after two or three months of heavy bombing that the public's morale would not break. "There was no mass panic, no call for peace at any price, no querulous demand for material reward in return for a continued war effort. It quickly became apparent that the individual . . . possessed reserves of strength more than sufficient to withstand the weight of attack of which the Germans were then capable." Thus, the Ministry of Information concluded in October 1941 that it was not "possible to defeat the people of Britain by any means other than extermination." In response, the Ministry ceased actively trying to influence morale in 1941—there was no need to do so.[132]

In spite of the prime minister's soaring rhetoric, the public was often dissatisfied with the government's conduct of the war until the Allies experienced military successes. Public evaluations quite sensibly reacted to events. It is true that Churchill enjoyed uniformly high job approval ratings throughout the war.[133] Yet when he led his party into an election for the first time in 1945, the public broadly rejected the Conservatives.

The official who seemed to have the greatest faith in the public's determination was none other than Churchill himself. He did not talk down to the nation and voiced his deep faith in the people.[134] There is more than humility in his later disclaimer about his pivotal role in leading the public during the Second World War. Responding to tributes on the occasion of his eightieth birthday, Churchill declared that the public's will was resolute, remorseless, and unconquerable. "I have never accepted what many people have kindly said, namely that I inspired the Nation. It was the nation and the race dwelling around the globe that had the lion heart. I had the luck to be called upon to give the roar."[135]

It is no criticism of Churchill's critical contribution to the outcome of the war to agree with George Orwell's 1944 comment that "the government has done extraordinarily little to preserve morale: it has merely drawn on existing reserves of good will."[136] Churchill was leading the British public where it wanted to go.

-o- -o- -o-

Presidents, even skilled presidents, rarely are able to lead the public and thus reshape the contours of the political landscape to pave the way for change. Instead, even the most able communicators are facilitators who depend upon the public moving at its own pace to provide opportunities to accomplish their goals. Abraham Lincoln, Franklin D. Roosevelt, and Ronald Reagan recognized and exploited such opportunities brilliantly. As Bismarck put it, "A statesman cannot create anything himself. He must wait and listen until he hears the steps of God sounding through events; then leap up and grasp the hem of his garment."[137] In a more modern idiom, John Kingdon describes the successful policy entrepreneurs as those who wait for an opportunity and then ride the wave.[138]

This conclusion about the difficulty of moving public opinion poses a direct challenge to the faith that many have in the broad premise of the potential of presidential leadership of the public. Yet it is consistent with important and wide-ranging works on public opinion, including studies by James Stimson,[139] Benjamin Page and Robert Shapiro,[140] and Benjamin Page and Marshall Bouton.[141] They find that the public's collective policy preferences generally are stable and change by large margins only in response to world events. Even on foreign policy, Page and Bouton find that there are often large gaps between public opinion and the views of leaders, and the two are not converging. Thus, there is little evidence of opinion leadership.

Strategies for governing premised on substantially increasing public support for policy proposals are prone to failure. As historian E. H. Carr put it, "the men who are popularly said to 'make history' are dealing with highly intractable material, . . . which includes the wills of their fellowmen, [which] can be moulded only in accordance with certain existing trends, and . . . the statesman who fails to understand, and refuses to comply with, those trends dooms himself to sterility."[142]

3 Leading the Public

Exploiting Existing Opinion

PRESIDENTS cannot reliably persuade the public to support their policies. They are unlikely to *change* public opinion. Is it possible, however, for the White House to exploit *existing* public opinion as a resource for changing the direction of public policy? Skilled presidents who understand the nature of public opinion may be able to use it as a resource to further their goals. At the core of this strategy is choosing the issues they emphasize and the manner in which they present their policy initiatives.

Although previous commitments, current crises, and unresolved problems left by their predecessors foist much of their agenda upon them, presidents still have substantial discretion to choose their own initiatives and the manner in which they present them to the public. From the perspective of the White House, "the key to successful advocacy is controlling the public agenda."[1] As a result, the White House invests a substantial amount of staff, time, and energy into focusing the public's attention on the issues it wishes to promote and encouraging the public to see its proposals for dealing with those issues in a positive light.[2]

Presidents may increase their chances of success by doing the following:

1. Framing proposals to emphasize their consistency with the public's existing views

2. Increasing the salience of White House initiatives that are popular with the public, and thus intensify pressure on Congress
3. Clarifying the public's wishes and showing how they are consistent with his policies
4. Defining themselves and their parties in ways that channel existing opinion on the issues into support for a party program over the longer term
5. Exploiting opinion fluidity or indifference regarding an issue

In this chapter, I explore each of these strategies for exploiting existing opinion. I also examine how factors specific to each strategy as well as general constraints on the president's ability to focus public attention inevitably limit the president's ability to take advantage of public opinion to help pave the way for change.

Framing Issues

The president is interested in not only what the public thinks about a policy but also *how* they are thinking about it. As a result, the White House attempts to influence the public's understanding of what issues are about and the questions it asks about them as it evaluates the president's positions. At its core, this effort focuses on associating the president's policies with views and values the public already holds. Structuring the choices about policy issues in ways that favor the president's programs may set the terms of the debate on his proposals and thus the premises on which the public evaluates them. As one leading adviser to Reagan put it, "I've always believed that 80 percent of any legislative or political matter is how you frame the debate."[3]

Framing and Priming

Policy issues are usually complex and subject to alternative interpretations. Both issues within the direct experience of citizens, such as poverty, health care, and racial inequality, as well as issues more remote from everyday life, such as arms control and international trade, are susceptible to widely different understandings. The crux of the decision regarding which side to support in the debate over abortion is the relative weight given to the two well-known values: the life of the unborn and right of the mother to choose to have the child. Similarly, the parties contending over the minimum wage often seem to be talking past each other. Advocates of increasing the minimum wage focus on *equity*: it is important to pay those making the lowest wages at least enough to support a minimally acceptable lifestyle. Opponents of increasing the minimum wage, on the other hand, focus on *efficiency*: raising the cost of labor puts businesses that employ low-wage earners at a disadvantage in the marketplace and may cause some employers to terminate workers in order to reduce their costs. Each side emphasizes different values in the debate in an attempt to frame the issue to its advantage.

The sheer complexity of most issues combined with the competing values that are relevant to evaluating them create substantial cognitive burdens for people. They cope by acting as cognitive misers and employing shortcuts to simplify the decisional process.[4] When people evaluate an issue or a public official, they do not search their memories for all the considerations that might be relevant; they do not incorporate all the dimensions of a policy proposal into the formulation of their preferences. The intellectual burdens would be too great and their interest in politics too limited for such an arduous task. Instead of undertaking an exhaustive search, citizens minimize their cognitive burdens by selecting the dimensions they deem to be most important for their evaluations. In this decisional process, people are likely to weigh most heavily the information and values that are most easily accessible. Recent activation is one factor that determines their accessibility.[5]

The cognitive challenges of citizens are both an opportunity and a challenge for the White House. Because individuals typically have at least two, and often more, relevant values for evaluating issue positions and because they are unlikely to canvass all their values in their evaluations, the president cannot leave to chance the identification of which values are most relevant to the issues he raises. Instead, the president seeks to influence the values citizens employ in their evaluations.

In most instances, the president does not have much impact on the values that people hold. Citizens develop these values over many years, starting in early childhood. By the time people focus on the president, their values are for the most part well established. So the president is not in a position to, say, convince people that they ought to be more generous to the poor or more concerned with the distribution of wealth in the country.

However, people use cues from elites as to the ideological or partisan implications of messages[6] (the source of a message is itself an important cue).[7] By articulating widely held values and pointing out their applicability to policy issues, events, or his own performance, the president may increase the salience (and thus the accessibility) of those values to the public's evaluations of them. In the process, the president attempts to show the public that his position is consistent with their values. Thus, if the president opposes an expansion of the federal workforce to perform a service, he will probably articulate his opposition in terms of concern for big government, an attitude already held by many in the public.

Through framing, the president attempts to define what a public policy issue is about. A *frame* is a central organizing idea for making sense of an issue or conflict and suggests what the controversy is about and what is at stake.[8] Thus, a leader might frame welfare as an appropriate program necessary to compensate for the difficult circumstances in which the less fortunate find themselves, or as a giveaway to undeserving slackers committed to living on the dole.

By defining and simplifying a complex issue through framing, the president hopes to activate and make more salient particular considerations that citizens will use for formulating their political preferences. It is not clear whether an issue frame interacts with an individual's memory so as to *prime* certain considerations, making some more accessible than others and therefore more likely to be used in formulating a political preference, or whether framing works by encouraging individuals to deliberately think about the importance of considerations suggested by a frame.[9] In either case, the frame raises the priority and weight that individuals assign to particular attitudes already stored in their memories.[10] The president's goal is to influence the attitudes and information people incorporate into their judgments of his policies and performance.[11]

For example, if the president's argument on behalf of Medicaid focuses on compassion for the poor, then those who hold such a value may be more likely to see compassion as relevant to evaluating health policy and thus be more likely to support the president's position. If, on the other hand, people see other values, such as personal responsibility or frugality, as relevant to federal health policy, they are more likely to resist the president's appeal for support.

The president may also attempt to prime perceptions of objective circumstances such as the level of economic prosperity. The White House would prefer to have citizens look on the bright side of their environments so that positive elements will play a more prominent role in their evaluations of the president and his administration.

PRESIDENTIAL FRAMING

Framing and priming have a number of advantages for the president, not the least of which is that they demand less of the public than directly persuading citizens on the merits of a policy proposal. The president does not have to persuade people to change their basic values and preferences. He does not have to convince citizens to develop expertise and acquire and process extensive information about the details of a policy proposal. In addition, framing and priming—because they are relatively simple—are less susceptible to distortion by journalists and opponents than direct persuasion on the merits of a policy proposal.[12]

Instead of trying to persuade the public directly on the merits of a proposal, then, the White House often uses public statements and the press coverage they generate to articulate relatively simple themes. Public opinion research may have identified these themes as favoring the president's positions. The goal is to frame issues and through priming raise the priority and weight that individuals assign to attitudes already stored in their memories and that will encourage them to support the president's proposals.

Attempts to frame issues are as old as the Republic.[13] Each side of a political contest usually attempts to frame the debate to its own advantage. Shafer and Claggett argue that public opinion is organized around two clusters of issues, both of which are favored by a majority of voters: social welfare, social insurance, and civil rights (associated with Democrats) and cultural values, civil liberties, and foreign relations (associated with Republicans). Each party's best strategy is to frame the choice for voters by focusing attention on the party's most successful cluster of issues.[14] Petrocik has found that candidates tend to campaign on issues that favor them in order to prime the salience of these issues in voters' decision making.[15] Similarly, an important aspect of campaigning is activating the latent predispositions of partisans by priming party identification as a crucial consideration in deciding for whom to vote.[16]

Portraying policies in terms of criteria on which there is a consensus and playing down divisive issues is often at the core of efforts to structure choices for both the public and Congress. The Reagan administration framed the 1986 Tax Reform Act as revenue-neutral, presenting the choice on the policy as one of serving special interests or helping average taxpayers. Few people would choose the former option. Federal aid to education had been a divisive issue for years before President Johnson proposed the Elementary and Secondary Education Act in 1965. To blunt opposition, he successfully changed the focus of debate from teachers' salaries and classroom shortages to fighting poverty and from the separation of church and state to aiding children. This changed the premises of congressional decision making and eased the path for the bill.[17]

Similarly, Richard Nixon articulated general revenue sharing as a program that made government more efficient and distributed benefits widely. He deemphasized the distributional aspect of the policy, which redistributed federal funds from traditional Democratic constituencies to projects favored by Republicans' middle-class constituents.[18] Dwight Eisenhower employed the uncontroversial symbol of national defense during the Cold War, even when it came to naming legislation, to obtain support for aiding education (the National Defense Education Act) and building highways (the Interstate and Defense Highway Act).

At other times, the president must try to frame choices in an atmosphere inflamed by partisanship. Independent Counsel Kenneth Starr accused President Clinton of eleven counts of impeachable offenses, perjury, obstruction of justice, witness tampering, and abuse of power. The White House fought back, accusing Starr of engaging an *intrusive* investigation motivated by a *political vendetta* against the president. The basic White House defense was that the president made a mistake (*personal failing*) in his *private* behavior, apologized for it, and was ready to move on to continue to do the people's business of governing the nation. Impeachment, the president's defenders said, was grossly *disproportionate* to the president's offense. The public found the White House argument compelling and strongly opposed the president's impeachment.

Ronald Reagan understood instinctually that his popular support was linked to his ability to embody the values of an idealized America. He continually invoked symbols of his vision of America and its past—an optimistic view that did not closely correspond to reality but did sustain public support. He projected a simple, coherent vision for his presidency that served him well in attracting adherents and countering criticism when the inevitable contradictions in policy arose. For example, he maintained his identification with balanced budgets even though he never submitted a budget that was even close to balanced and his administration was responsible for more deficit spending than all previous administrations combined. More broadly, Reagan employed the symbols of an idealized polity to frame his policies as consistent with core American values.[19]

According to Pat Buchanan, who served Reagan as the White House director of communications: "For Ronald Reagan the world of legend and myth is a real world. He visits it regularly and he's a happy man there."[20] In his 1965 autobiography, Reagan described his feelings about leaving the military at the end of World War II: "All I wanted to do . . . was to rest up awhile, make love to my wife, and come up refreshed to a better job in an ideal world."[21] The reader would never realize from this that Reagan never left Hollywood while serving in the military during the war! However, in politics, perceptions are as important as reality; consequently, many people responded positively to the president's vision of history and his place therein.

Presidents may manipulate symbols in attempts not only to lead public opinion, but also to deliberately mislead it. Perhaps the most important and effective televised address President Reagan made to the nation in 1981 was his July 27 speech seeking the public's support for his tax-cut bill. In it he went to great lengths to present his plan as "bipartisan." It was crucial that he convince the public that this controversial legislation was supported by members of both parties and therefore was, by implication, fair. Despite the fact that two days later House Democrats voted overwhelmingly against the president's proposal, Reagan described it as "bipartisan" eleven times in the span of a few minutes! No one could miss the point.

LIMITS TO FRAMING

Despite these illustrations of presidential efforts at framing, setting the terms of debate is not a silver bullet. Presidents usually fail to move the public. Bill Clinton's first major proposal as president in 1993 was a plan to stimulate the economy. The

Clinton White House wanted the public to view its plan as an effort to get the economy moving again, but congressional Republicans opposed him, defining the president's economic program in terms of wasteful pork barrel expenditures rather than spending essential for the economy. Similarly, Republicans focused public debate on the president's budget on tax increases rather than economic growth or deficit reduction.[22] Clinton tried to present the issue of taxes as one of fairness, but there is little evidence that many shared this perception. "The Clinton administration has lost control of its agenda," complained White House pollster Stan Greenberg.[23] The budget also injected tax increases into the debate over the fiscal stimulus bill, and Senate Republicans pointed to tax increases repeatedly in their successful effort to defeat it.[24] In the end, the president could not obtain the public's support: four months after the White House introduced the fiscal stimulus bill, a plurality of the public opposed it,[25] and the bill never came to a vote in the Senate.

Clinton was well aware of his inability to set the terms of the debate over his proposals. When asked why he was having such a difficult time obtaining the support of the "new" Southern Democrats, Clinton responded, "In their own districts and states, they've let the Republicans dominate the perception of what we're trying to do. . . . the Republicans won the rhetorical debate."[26] Clinton could not reach the American people—and it frustrated him. Six months after taking office the president reflected on the unexpected dimensions of his job on *Larry King Live*: "The thing that has surprised me most is how difficult it is . . . to really keep communicating what you're about to the American people."

Competing frames. Structuring choice is rarely easy. The challenge that Bill Clinton faced with his economic program is a common one for presidents: the opposition provides one or more competing frames. There is competition to set the terms of debate over issues.[27] In real life, we know very little about the terms in which the public thinks about issues. Studies that have

shown powerful framing effects typically have carefully seques-
tered citizens and restricted them to hearing only one frame,
usually in the context of a controlled experiment.[28] These
frames tend to be confined to brief fragments of arguments,
pale imitations of frames that often occur in the real world.
Studies have found that conversations that include conflicting
perspectives,[29] credible advice from other sources,[30] predispositions,[31] levels of education,[32] and relevant expertise[33] condition
the impact of framing efforts.

The early work on presidential leadership of the public employed experimental designs. In effect, the authors framed
choices as supporting or opposing the president. Lee Sigelman
ascertained public opinion on six potential responses to the
1979–1980 hostage crisis in Iran. He then asked those who opposed each option whether they would change their view "if
President Carter considered this action necessary." In each
case, a substantial percentage of respondents changed their
opinions in deference to the supposed opinion of the president.[34] In another experiment during the Reagan presidency,
Dan Thomas and Lee Sigelman posed policy proposals to
sample subjects. When informed that the president was the
source of the proposals, enthusiastic supporters of Reagan
evaluated them in favorable terms, but when the source was
withheld, Reagan supporters evaluated these same proposals
unfavorably.[35]

Not all results were as positive, however. In another study,
Lee and Carol Sigelman asked sample groups whether they
supported two proposals—a domestic policy proposal dealing
with welfare and a proposal dealing with foreign aid. Research-
ers told one of the groups that President Carter supported the
proposals, while they did not mention the president to the
other group. The authors found that attaching the president's
name to either proposal not only failed to increase support for
it, but also actually had a negative effect because those who
disapproved of Carter reacted very strongly against proposals
they thought were his.[36] More than a decade later, Jeffrey Mondak found that reference to the president in issue surveys af-

fected results only when other information was scarce. More-over, the president needed a high level of approval before his policy endorsement constituted a supportive frame.[37]

The environment in which the president usually operates is fundamentally different from that in an experiment or poll. The president's world is inhabited by committed, well-organized, and well-funded opponents. Intense disagreement among elites generates conflicting messages. John Zaller argues that attitudes on major issues change in response to changes in re-lation to the intensity of competing streams of political com-munication. When there is elite consensus, and thus only one set of cues offered to the public, opinion change may be sub-stantial. However, when elite discourse is divided, people re-spond to the issue according to their predispositions, especially their core partisan and ideological views.[38] Thus, when Paul Sniderman and Sean Theriault offered people competing frames, as in the real world, they adopted positions consistent with their preexisting values.[39]

Occasions in which elite commentary is one-sided are rare. Most issues that generate consensual elite discourse arise from external events such as surprise attacks on the United States—for example, the terrorist assaults on September 11, 2001, or its allies—for example, the invasion of Kuwait in 1990. Consensual issues also tend to be new, with few people having committed themselves to a view about them. In his examination of public opinion regarding the Gulf War, Zaller argues that the presi-dent's greatest chance of influencing public opinion is in a cri-sis (which attracts the public's attention) in which elites articu-late a unified message. At other times, most people are too inattentive or too committed to views to be strongly influenced by elite efforts at persuasion.[40]

The media is also unlikely to adopt uniformly or reliably the White House's framing of issues. In the first place, most news outlets devote little attention to a typical issue, making it diffi-cult for the president to educate the public. The press, espe-cially the electronic media, is reluctant to devote repeated at-tention to an issue even though this might be necessary to explain it adequately to the public. As a deputy press secretary in the Carter administration said: "We have to keep sending out our message if we expect people to understand. The Washington Press corps will explain a policy once and then it will feature the politics of the issue."[41]

In addition, the news is becoming more personality-centered, less time-bound, more practical, and more incident-based. About 50 percent of all news stories have no clear connection to policy issues.[42] According to ABC correspondent Sam Donaldson, "A clip of a convalescent Reagan waving from his window at some circus elephants is going to push an analytical piece about tax cuts off the air every time."[43] The television networks created distractions during President Clinton's 1997 State of the Union message when they delivered the news of the verdict in the civil suit against O. J. Simpson *during his speech*, and the front page of the *Washington Post* the next day led with the story on Simpson, not the story on the president.

Jimmy Carter voiced a complaint common to most presidents when he told reporters, "I would really like for you all as people who relay Washington events to the world to take a look at the substantive questions I have to face as a president and quit dealing almost exclusively with personalities."[44] Such criticisms have had no effect on media coverage, however. Human interest stories, scandals, conflict, and the like fill much of the news hole. As the Washington bureau chief of *Newsweek* said, "The worst thing in the world that could happen to you is for the President of the United States to choke on a piece of meat, and for you not to be there."[45] When President Bush vomited at a state dinner in Japan, television networks had a field day, running the tape of the president's illness again and again.

An important limitation on presidential framing is the increasing reluctance of journalists to let the president speak for himself. Instead, reporters increasingly feel the need to set the story in a meaningful context. The construction of such a context may entail reporting what was *not* said as well as what was said; what had occurred before; and what political implications may be involved in a statement, policy, or event. More than in the past, reporters today actively and aggressively interpret stories for viewers and readers. They no longer depend on those whom they interview to set the tone of their stories, and they now regularly pass sweeping (and frequently negative) judgments about what politicians are saying and doing.[46]

Even when the president speaks directly to the people, the media present an obstacle to his framing issues in ways that favor his positions. Commentary following presidential speeches and press conferences may influence what viewers remember and may affect their opinions.[47] Although the impact of commentary on presidential addresses and press confer- ences is unclear, it is probably safe to argue that it is a con- straint on the president's ability to lead public opinion.[48]

Increasingly the public receives news about the president in a negative context. To meet their needs for a story containing conflict, it is routine for reporters to turn to opponents of the president when he makes a statement or takes an action. Thus, it is not surprising that after his election, each president since 1976 has received more negative coverage than his predeces- sor.[49] President Clinton received mostly negative coverage dur- ing his tenure in office, with a ratio of negative to positive com- ments on network television of about two to one.[50] The trend seems to have continued in the George W. Bush presidency.[51]

The increasing negativism of news coverage of the presidents parallels the increasingly low opinions voters have of them. The media impugns the motives of presidents and presidential can- didates and portrays them as playing a "game" in which strat- egy and maneuvers, rather than the substance of public policy, are the crucial elements. This coverage fosters public cynicism and encourages citizens to view presidents and other political leaders in negative terms.[52] If politics is a game played by de- ceptive politicians, it is less attractive for a person to be influ- enced by the president's arguments.

The framing of issues in terms of strategy and wheeling-deal- ing may also undermine efforts to change the status quo by highlighting the risk of deferring to people who engage in such maneuvering. Coverage of the consideration of President

Clinton's massive health care proposal in 1993–1994 focused much more on strategy and legislative battles than on the issues of health care. Thus, the media did not mirror the president's attempts to frame the issue.[53] In addition, public support for rebuilding the health care system varied in tandem with changes in media framing.[54] In general, the media's focus on political conflict and strategy elevates the prominence of political wheeling-dealing in individuals' evaluations of policy proposals.[55]

Public awareness and knowledge. A fundamental limitation on presidential priming is the public's lack of attention to politics, which restricts its susceptibility to taking cues from political elites. Russell Neuman estimates that in the United States there is a politically sophisticated elite of less than 5 percent of the public. Another 75 percent are marginally attentive and 20 percent are apolitical. Even the marginally attentive lack the background information and rich vocabulary for quick and convenient processing of large amounts of political information. The apolitical 20 percent do not respond to political stimuli in political terms. Even in the middle, he argues, people frequently interpret political stimuli in nonpolitical terms.[56] If attempts to set the terms of debate fall on deaf ears, they are unlikely to be successful.

Among Americans, there are widely varying levels of interest in and information about politics and public policy. From one perspective, those citizens with less interest and knowledge present the most potential for presidential persuasion. Such people cannot resist arguments if they do not possess information about the implications of those arguments for their values, interests, and other predispositions. However, these people are also less likely to be aware of the president's messages, limiting the president's influence. To the extent that they do receive the messages, they will also hear from the opposition how the president's views are inconsistent with their predispositions. In addition, even if their predispositions make them sympathetic to the president's arguments, they may lack the understanding to make the connection between the president's arguments and their own underlying values. Moreover, the more abstract the link between message and value, the fewer people who will make the connection.[57]

In addition, Kuklinski and his colleagues found that people are frequently *misinformed* (as opposed to uninformed) about policy, and the less they know, the more confidence they have in their beliefs. Thus, they resist correct factual information. Even when presented with factual information, they resist changing their opinions, including those that were the objects of elite framing.[58]

On the other hand, those who pay close attention to politics and policy are likely to have well-developed views and thus be less susceptible to persuasion. Better-informed citizens possess the information necessary to identify and thus reject communications inconsistent with their values. They are also more sensitive to the implications of messages. In the typical situation of competing frames offered by elites, reinforcement and polarization of views are more likely than conversion among attentive citizens.[59]

Zaller argues that those in the public most susceptible to presidential influence are those attentive to public affairs (and thus who receive messages) but who lack strong views (and thus who are less likely to resist messages).[60] At best, such persons make up a small portion of the population. In addition, these persons will receive competing messages. There is no basis for inferring that they will be most likely to find the president's messages persuasive. Such a conclusion is especially suspect when we recognize that most attentive people have explicit or latent partisan preferences. The president is leader of one of the parties, and those affiliated with the opposition party must overcome an inherent skepticism about him before they can be converted to support his position.

Perceptions. For framing to work, people must first perceive accurately the frame offered by the president. We know very little about how people perceive messages from the president or other elites. Nor do we know much about how citizens come to understand public issues or develop their values and other predispositions that the president seeks to prime. (We also do not know whether the potential impact of frames is restricted to priming existing values or whether they may also affect understanding, which may in turn alter opinion.) There is reason to believe, however, that different people perceive the same message differently.[61] With all his personal, ideological, and partisan[62] baggage, no president can assume that all citizens hear the same thing when he speaks.

A related matter of perception is the credibility of the source. Experimental evidence supports the view that perceived source credibility is a prerequisite for successful framing.[63] The president is likely to be more credible to some people (those predisposed to support him) than to others. Many people are unlikely to find him a credible source on most issues, especially those on which opinion is divided and on which he is the leader of one side of the debate.

Nature of issues. The president faces yet other challenges to setting the terms of debate. Although there are occasions on which a president can exploit an external event such as arms control negotiations to structure choices on a single issue, he cannot rely on his environment to be so accommodating. In addition, the White House must advocate the passage of many proposals at roughly the same time, further complicating its efforts to structure choice on any single issue.

Ineptness. Attempts to structure decisions may actually hurt the president's cause if they are too heavy-handed and thus create a backlash. In 1986, Ronald Reagan was engaged in his perennial fight to provide aid to the Contras in Nicaragua. The president equated opposition to his aid program with support for the Sandinistas. More graphically, the White House's communications director, Patrick J. Buchanan, wrote an editorial in the *Washington Post* that characterized the issue in stark terms: "With the contra vote, the Democratic Party will reveal whether it stands with Ronald Reagan and the resistance or [Nicaraguan President] Daniel Ortega and the communists." These overt efforts to set the terms of debate were not successful. Instead, they irritated members of Congress and provoked charges that the White House was engaged in red baiting.[64]

Overuse. The White House can go to the well only so often. I discuss later in this chapter Ronald Reagan's effort in 1985 to frame the issue of approval of the MX missile as supporting his credibility in arms control negotiations. The next year, he faced opposition from Congress and the public over the sale of arms to Saudi Arabia. The president argued that a defeat on this highly visible foreign policy issue would undermine his international credibility and destroy his role as a mediator in the Middle East. Despite all his efforts, the president was able to garner only thirty-four votes in the Senate, then controlled by Republicans.[65]

Increasing the Salience of Popular Issues

Even if the president cannot change the public's views on issues, he may be able to influence *what* it is thinking about. Instead of seeking to change public opinion regarding an issue, presidents may make appeals on policies that already have public support in an attempt to make them more salient to the public and thus encourage members of Congress to support White House initiatives to please the public.

Brandice Canes-Wrone found that presidents are "more likely to publicize a domestic initiative the more popular it is and almost never appeal to the public about an initiative likely to mobilize popular opposition." "Only on popular domestic proposals can presidents increase their prospects for legislative success by going public." Presidents are also more likely to publicize foreign policy initiatives if a majority of the public favors them and will generally avoid going public on initiatives that face mass opposition.[66]

In 2001, George W. Bush made large tax cuts a top priority of his presidency. Although most people were not clamoring for tax cuts, the president's Republican base was enthusiastic, there was little organized opposition to the principle of the policy, many people found the prospect of lower taxes attractive, and the budget surplus in 2000 made tax cuts plausible. Bush traveled extensively to speak on behalf of his tax-cut initiative, and his travels seemed motivated more by demonstrating his support in states where he ran well in the election than in convincing more skeptical voters of the soundness of his proposals. He did not travel to California until May 29 and visited New York even later. Instead, the White House gave priority to states that Bush had won and that were represented by Democratic senators, including Georgia, Louisiana, Arkansas, Missouri, North and South Dakota, Montana, and North Carolina. The goal of these trips seemed to be to demonstrate preexisting public support in the constituencies of members of Congress who were potential swing votes. In 2003, the president seemed to be following the same strategy as he campaigned for another tax-cut proposal. His travel seemed designed to work at the margins to convince moderate senators of both parties that his tax-cut proposal enjoyed public support in their states.

Exploiting existing support for an issue by making the issue more salient to the public requires that (1) the president's initiative be popular and (2) the president has the ability to increase the salience of issues among the public. Some presidential initiatives do have public support, but many do not. Ronald Reagan's efforts to decrease government spending on domestic policy, increase it on defense policy, win support for the Contras, and reduce regulation all typically lacked majority support. Bill Clinton's proposals for stimulating the economy, reforming health care reform, intervening in Haiti, and enacting NAFTA (North American Free Trade Agreement) faced at least plurality opposition once the opposition responded to them. George W. Bush's most ambitious proposals in his second term, reforming Social Security and immigration policy and maintaining troops in Iraq, confronted a similar lack of popular support. Presidents are most likely to be advantaged when seeking to make modest alterations to existing policies.

We know little about the president's success in increasing the salience of issues, but there is reason to be cautious about attributing influence to the White House. Bill Clinton sought to start national discussions on affirmative action and Social Security, trying to develop a consensus on how to reform them. He even participated in roundtables with citizens to discuss the policies. The president's goal was laudable, but there is no evidence that he succeeded in stimulating national discussions, much less forging agreement on solutions.

Jeffrey Cohen found that presidents can influence the public's agenda through symbolic speech in State of the Union messages, at least in the short run. He also found, however, that presidents are only able to affect the public's agenda over time on foreign policy and that substantive policy rhetoric has no impact on the public's policy agenda. In general, Cohen found the president to have only a very modest impact on public opinion.[67]

Yet this influence may be even less than Cohen suggests, because presidential issue priorities in the State of the Union message may actually be a response to rather than a cause of public issue concerns. Kim Hill replicated Cohen's work to consider the possibility of reverse causality and found it operating for public concern with the economy and foreign policy, although not for civil rights.[68] B. Dan Wood found that the intensity of presidential rhetoric on the economy responds to public concerns about economy.[69] In other words, presidential issue priorities are often a response to the public rather than a cause of the public's agenda.

There are steps a president can take to increase the odds of exploiting existing support for policies. On January 27, 1998, Bill Clinton delivered one of the most anticipated State of the Union messages in modern history. News about his relationship with a White House intern, Monica Lewinsky, had broken, instantly becoming the biggest story of the day and focusing attention on how the president would handle the strain of public discussion of his personal life. Clinton showed no effects of the scandal, and never mentioned it, but he did use the occasion to promote his agenda.

The president wanted to use the new budget surplus to pay down the national debt rather than to cut taxes, as Republicans favored. He articulated the rationale for this stance in the most memorable line of his speech, which was an appeal to "save Social Security first." As one of his speechwriters put it, "The presidential pulpit had never been put to more effective use." Social Security was not a matter of great public concern at that time, but Republicans had to applaud this widely supported policy, and that gave the president the upper hand in the battle over using the budget surplus.[70]

Clinton's deft use of rhetoric is an example of a president increasing the saliency of a widely supported policy when doing so helped advance his own agenda. Stopping Republican proposals for tax cuts was not at the core of Social Security policy, but the president was able to frame the issue of using the budget surplus to pay down the national debt as being for or against the popular policy of Social Security. By showing how Social Security was relevant to paying down the national debt, the president increased the salience of the latter by making it relevant to more people, people who did not previously see debt payment as pertinent to their interests.

This strategy is the classic case of expanding the scope of conflict by making issues salient to a wider segment of the public and thus adding to a supportive coalition.[71] The primary means of making an issue relevant to more people is the inclusion of new attributes to the policy.[72] In other words, the president attempts to show that a policy that people have evaluated principally in some terms should also be evaluated in other terms. If a new group cares about the second set of attributes, it may add a crucial component to the president's coalition.

Another example of adding a popular dimension to a policy initiative occurred in 1985, when Ronald Reagan asked Congress to appropriate funds for twenty-one additional MX missiles. He had been unable to win the money he had sought in

1984, when the debate focused on the utility of the missiles as strategic weapons. He succeeded the next year, however, after the terms of the debate changed to focus on the impact of building the missiles on the arms control negotiations with the Soviet Union that had recently begun in Geneva. Senators and representatives who lacked confidence in the contribution of the MX to national security were still reluctant to go to the public and explain why they were denying American negotiators the bargaining chips they said they required. According to a senior official at the Pentagon, "By the end, we gave up on technical briefings on the missile. . . . It was all based on the unspoken bargaining chip. Without Geneva, we would have died right there."[73]

The program that the president proposed had not changed. The MX was the same missile with essentially the same capabilities in 1985 as in 1984. There is scant evidence that anyone changed his or her minds about these capabilities. Conversion was not the key to success. What had changed were the premises on which discourse on the issue occurred. The burden of proof had shifted from the administration ("MX is a useful weapon") to its opponents ("canceling the MX will not hurt the arms control negotiations") because the president had added a new, and widely supported dimension to evaluation of the MX.

Despite the success of Clinton and Reagan in these examples, it is usually difficult to frame a policy as central to the success of another, popular policy. Presidents are rarely in a position to make such claims. Indeed, as we have seen, it is generally difficult to frame issues in ways that favor the president.

ELECTIONS

Increasing the salience of popular policies may be especially useful for winning elections or increasing the president's party's representation in Congress. The Clinton White House began running ads in June 1995 to highlight its achievements, beginning with the popular Crime Bill. In the fall, it ran ads on

Republican proposals to cut Medicare and Medicaid. Other ads associated the president with popular proposals such as school uniforms, curfews for teenagers, and V-chips for televisions.[74] The president's approval ratings and his prospects for reelection began rising at this time.

Candidates in every presidential election attempt to structure the choices of voters and emphasize policies on which they have an advantage. In 1992, for example, George H. W. Bush focused on his character and foreign policy experience. In contrast, Bill Clinton emphasized domestic policy issues, particularly the economy. (Such efforts are closely related to framing voter choices, which I discuss later in this chapter.)

If candidates succeed in structuring the choices of voters around relatively clear policy alternatives by making these salient in the election, the winner may be in a position to claim a mandate. An electoral mandate—the perception that the voters strongly support the president's character and policies—can be a powerful symbol in American politics. It can accord added legitimacy and credibility to the newly elected president's proposals. Concerns for representation and political survival encourage members of Congress to support the president if they feel the people have spoken.[75] And members of Congress are susceptible to such beliefs. According to David Mayhew, "Nothing is more important in Capitol Hill politics than the shared conviction that election returns have proven a point."[76] Members of Congress also need to believe that voters have not merely rejected the losers in elections but positively selected the victors and what they stand for.

More important, mandates change the premises of decisions. Following Roosevelt's decisive win in the 1932 election, the essential question became *how* government should act to fight the Depression rather than *whether* it should act. Similarly, following Johnson's overwhelming win in the 1964 election, the dominant question in Congress was not whether to pass new social programs but how many social programs to pass and how much to increase spending. In 1981, the tables were turned; Ronald Reagan's victory placed a stigma on big government and exalted the unregulated marketplace and large defense efforts. Reagan had won a major victory even before the first congressional vote.

Winning an election does not necessarily, or even usually, provide presidents with a mandate, however. Every election produces a winner, but mandates are much less common. Even presidents who win elections by large margins often find that perceptions of support for their proposals do not accompany their victories. In the presidential elections held between 1952 and 2008, most of the impressive electoral victories (Richard Nixon's 61 percent in 1972, Ronald Reagan's 59 percent in 1984, and Dwight Eisenhower's 57 percent in 1956) did not elicit perceptions of mandates (Lyndon Johnson's 61 percent in 1964 is the exception).[77]

Candidates often appeal as broadly as possible in the interest of building a broad electoral coalition. Incumbents frequently avoid specifics on their second-term plans and attempt to increase their vote totals by asking voters to make retrospective judgments. Candidates who do not make their policy plans salient in the campaign undermine their ability effectively to claim policy mandates. Moreover, voters frequently also send mixed signals by electing majorities in Congress from the other party.

When asked about his mandate in 1960, John F. Kennedy reportedly replied, "Mandate, schmandate. The mandate is that I am here and you're not."[78] Bill Clinton could associate himself with popular initiatives in 1995–1996 to aid his reelection, but could not use this show of voter support as an indicator of public approval of initiatives he did not discuss in the campaign, especially since the public also elected a Republican Congress during his second term.

To exploit the benefits of party leadership fully, presidents need large cohorts of fellow partisans in Congress. Once members of Congress have been elected, they rarely change their party affiliation, and the few instances when they have changed have not resulted from presidential persuasion. Thus, if presidents are to alter the party composition of Congress, they must help to elect additional members of their party. One way to try to accomplish this goal is to campaign for candidates in midterm congressional elections.

In 2002, Republicans made small gains in both houses of Congress, something that had not occurred since 1934. George W. Bush was extraordinarily popular in the face of the September 11 attacks[79] and engaged in the most active midterm campaigning of any president in history. Campaigning relentlessly, he covered fifteen carefully chosen states in the last five days of the campaign alone to rally his party. The war on terrorism had shifted the public debate to national security issues that favored the Republicans and shielded the president from criticism on domestic issues that favored the Democrats. Voters did not necessarily support the Republicans on most issues, but the White House succeeded in turning the election into a referendum on a popular president[80] and the war on terrorism, at least among members of the president's party.

The most significant fact of the Republican success in the elections was the heavy turnout in Republican base. A Gallup poll taken the weekend before the election found that 64 percent of Republicans were "more enthusiastic" about voting than in the past, while only 51 percent of Democrats responded that way.[81] Most people who entered the booths did not have terrorism on their minds. More were concerned about the economy and the prospect of war with Iraq. But the minority who did have terrorism on their minds was overwhelmingly Republican, and the Democrats were not able to position themselves well on enough of the other issues to counter this strong GOP advantage. Republicans operated a finely engineered voter-mobilization effort. Aiding this grassroots mobilization were the National Rifle Association and United Seniors (an organization heavily underwritten by the pharmaceutical industry).[82] Mobilizing the president's supporters decided the midterm elections in 2002.[83]

Mobilizing supporters can be a powerful weapon for the White House, but it is not always possible to increase the sa-

lience of issues that favor the president's party and thus structure the voting choice to his advantage. Indeed, the president's
party typically loses seats in each house in midterm elections.
In 2006, for example, George W. Bush was low in the polls and
Americans had lost patience with the most salient issue—the
war in Iraq. Although the president attempted to increase the
salience of the war on terror in people's thinking about Iraq,
he had little success. On election day, Republicans lost thirty
seats in the House, six in the Senate, and, as a result, Democrats
won control of both houses of Congress.

Clarifying Opinion

Public opinion about matters of politics and policy is often amorphous. It lacks articulation and structure.
Woodrow Wilson urged leaders to interpret public opinion and
identify issues that "reflected majority will even if the majority
was not yet fully aware of it. The leader's rhetoric could translate the people's felt desires into public policy." As Jeffrey Tulis
points out, success at interpretation requires understanding
majority sentiment underlying the contradictions of factions
and discordant views, and explaining people's true desires to
them in an easily comprehended and convincing fashion.[84]

UNDERSTANDING PUBLIC OPINION

Presidents face challenges in understanding public opinion
from the day of their elections. By their very nature, elections
rarely provide clear indications of the public's thinking on
individual proposals. For presidential elections to provide majority support for specific policies, the following conditions
must be met:

1. Voters must have opinions on policies.
2. Voters must know candidates' stands on the issues.
3. Candidates must offer voters the alternatives the voters desire.

4. There must be a large turnout of voters so that the electorate represents the population.
5. Voters must vote on the basis of issues.
6. It must be possible to correlate voter support with voters' policy views.

These conditions are rarely met, if ever.[85] For this reason, it is very difficult to discern the relationship between voters' policy preferences and a president's victory at the polls.

In addition, voters may be concerned with several issues in an election, but they have only one vote with which to express their views. Citizens may support one candidate's position on some issues yet vote for another candidate because of concern for other issues or general evaluations of performance. When they cast their ballots, voters signal only their choice of candidate, not their choice of the candidates' policies. As Ken Mehlman, George W. Bush's 2004 campaign manager, put it, "This election is a choice—not a referendum."[86] The White House must be cautious in inferring support for specific policies from the results of this process, for the vote is a rather blunt instrument for expressing policy views.

Even landslide elections are difficult to interpret. For example, political scientist Stanley Kelley found that in Lyndon Johnson's victory in 1964, issues gave the president his base of support, and concerns over the relative competence of the candidates won the swing vote for him. In 1972, however, the question of competence dominated the election. Although traditional domestic issues associated with the New Deal were salient, they actually favored George McGovern, not the landslide winner, Richard Nixon.[87] In 1984, voters preferred Walter Mondale to Ronald Reagan on the issues of defense spending, aid to the Contras, environmental protection, protection of civil rights, and helping the poor and disadvantaged, but most voted for Reagan for president.[88]

Understanding public opinion does not get much easier after the president takes office. In an attempt to understand public opinion on matters of special concern to them, modern presi-

dents have commissioned their own polls. Franklin D. Roosevelt was the first to pay close attention to polls, which were just
becoming scientific during his tenure in office. All presidents
since John F. Kennedy have retained private polling firms to
provide them with soundings of American public opinion, and
in the last five administrations, pollsters have also played a significant role as high-level political advisers.[89]

Technology is not a cure-all, however. Although Americans
are usually willing to express opinions on a wide variety of
issues, we cannot interpret these responses as reflecting crystallized and coherent views. Opinions are often rife with contradictions because the public often fails to give views much
thought or consider the implications of policy stands for other
issues.[90] For example, national polls show consistently that
the American people place a very high priority on controlling
government spending. At the same time, however, majorities
favor maintaining or increasing expenditures on many domestic programs.

Policymaking is a complex enterprise, and most voters do
not have the time, expertise, or inclination to think extensively
about most issues (especially those distant from their everyday
experiences, for example, federal regulations, nuclear weapons,
and bureaucratic organization). Even closer to home, in the
summer of 2004, most Americans did not recognize that the
nation had been gaining jobs over the previous six months,
much to the chagrin of the George W. Bush administration.[91]
Adding insult to injury and despite three tax cuts in as many
years in late 2003, only a fifth of the public said that Bush's
policies had made their taxes go down, while nearly a third perceived that their taxes had gone up.[92]

Before the war with Iraq in 2003, two-thirds of the public
expressed the belief that Iraq played an important role in the
9/11 terrorist attacks. After the war, substantial percentages of
the public believed that the United States had found clear evidence that Saddam Hussein was working closely with al Qaeda,
that the United States had found weapons of mass destruction
in Iraq, and that world opinion favored the United States going

to war in Iraq.[93] All of these beliefs were inaccurate, as even the White House admitted.

On the other hand, collective public opinion has properties quite different from those of individual citizens. There is evidence that the general public holds real, stable, and sensible opinions about public policy, which develop and change in a reasonable fashion in response to changing circumstances and new information. Changes that occur are usually at the margins and represent different trade-offs among constant values.[94]

Understanding public opinion, then, is difficult, especially on new issues on which opinion is fluid. Yet on many issues, opinion is long established and stable. It is to the White House's advantage to articulate such opinion as consistent with its initiatives.

ARTICULATING OPINION

In his study of agenda setting in the national government, John Kingdon found that people in and around government believed strongly that there was such a thing as a "national mood," that they could measure it, and that it had consequences for policy.[95] Frank Baumgartner and Bryan Jones cite Brutus's advice to Cassius:

> There is a tide in the affairs of men
> Which, taken at the flood, leads on to fortune;
> Omitted, all the voyage of their life
> Is bound in shallow and in miseries,
> On such a full sea are we now afloat,
> And we must take the current when it serves
> Or lose our ventures.
>
> (William Shakespeare, *Julius Caesar*, IV, iii)

They argue that it is important for leaders to discern whether the flow of events favors their proposals and skillfully exploit the opportunity when it does.[96]

To exploit amorphous or latent opinion effectively, the president must not only recognize it but also articulate that opinion in a clear and compelling manner. Michael Nelson concludes that, above all, successful presidents require not only a strategic sense of the grain of history but also an ability to sense, define, and articulate the public mood to fulfill the historical possibilities of the time.[97] Doing so may require waiting for opinion to mature to the point that it supports White House initiatives. The most effective means of articulating newly clarified opinion may be in the form of policy proposals that encapsulate the public's views. In chapter 2, we saw that Lincoln was a master of timing and read public opinion carefully as he redefined the purpose of the Civil War. When he was confident that the public mood had shifted, he clarified opinion as he articulated a new rationale for the war.

Similarly, Franklin D. Roosevelt was well aware that Americans were ambivalent about involvement in World War II. He carefully gauged public opinion and typically relied on events to change opinion about issues such as the nature of the threat posed by the Nazis and the Japanese and the appropriate national response to it. When opinion moved in the direction he wished to go, he quickly clarified and solidified this change by announcing policies consistent with it, such as aiding the Allies in June 1940 by asking Congress for the Lend-Lease bill. As Richard Hofstadter said of Franklin D. Roosevelt, he was not able to move the public, but "he was able to give it that necessary additional impetus of leadership which can translate desires into policies."[98]

Channeling the Public

Framing and clarifying issues or increasing their salience to take advantage of existing public opinion are short-term strategies that may prove useful to the White House. Channeling the public to support a broader party program is a longer process but one that may have significant consequences for politics and public policy. Channeling involves parties and leaders signaling to voters a commonality of interests and increasing the salience of these shared interests in voting decisions.

The rise of new issues has the potential to destabilize or even destroy party coalitions, and effective leaders will recognize and channel this potential to help build a new governing coalition. The most dramatic example of such leadership in the past half century occurred after pressure from the civil rights movement, along with Lyndon Johnson's unwavering commitment and legislative acumen, resulted in the passage of the 1964 Civil Rights Act.

Republican Barry Goldwater's victory in five southern states in the presidential election that fall marked a critical stage in the transformation in the political allegiance and voting behavior of the South. Republicans, led by Richard Nixon, saw that the alienation of many southerners from their former home in the Democratic Party provided them the opportunity to engage in a "southern strategy" to win converts among conservative white southerners—and they did.

Edward Carmines and James Stimson have shown how the emergence of race as a new issue cleavage in the 1960s caused many Americans to change their party allegiances.[99] Race was the issue that pushed many conservative Democrats toward the Republican Party, but Republican leaders also attracted support by stressing patriotism, religious values, and traditional (and thus conservative) positions on social issues to attract voters alienated by the Democrats' anti-war stances and apparent sympathy for views ranging from support for greater protections for alleged criminals to a wide separation between church and state. Republicans also began stressing economic issues,[100] which the emerging white middle class in the South found especially attractive.[101] When the Supreme Court made abortion a constitutional right in *Roe v. Wade* in 1973, opposition to abortion fit seamlessly with the Republicans' emphasis and further defined the parties, attracting additional adherents and mobilizing new legions of activists.

The result was Republican domination of presidential elections for two generations after 1964. Only two Democrats won in the four decades following that election, and only one, Jimmy Carter in 1976, running on the heels of Watergate, received a majority of the vote. The changes in party identification that aided Republican candidates did not occur overnight, nor even within the period of one presidency. Nevertheless, by recognizing and exploiting the opportunity to build a new governing coalition, Republican leaders profoundly influenced the direction of public policy.

The political landscape did not change because leaders persuaded people to alter their views about race, abortion, or other issues. (It is noteworthy that grassroots organizations and local protests of ordinary people had more impact in shaping public opinion on civil rights than did elites.[102]) As Gary Jacobson put it, "as strategic vote-seekers, candidates and parties anticipate voters' potential responses to their political initiatives and so are constrained by them. . . . In adopting positions, politicians are guided by the opportunities and constraints presented by existing configurations of public opinion on political issues."[103]

Instead of changing the public's opinions, leaders acted consistent with Morris Fiorina's view that leaders can take positions that split the public in a new way without the public changing its opinions.[104] Republican leaders attracted new voters to their party by reacting to events that were not of their making, such as the war in Vietnam, urban riots, and Supreme Court decisions. They responded by articulating views with which the voters agreed and making these views more salient in voting decisions.

Exploiting Fluid Opinion

We have seen that often events, predecessors, and pressing needs of the time determine much of the White House's agenda. However, the government's attention to an issue is not solely a function of the severity of a problem.[105] Sometimes, the president may choose to advocate a policy to which the public has not been attentive. This inattention could be the result of the newness of an issue or a general lack of concern for a matter. In either case, the public is not clamoring for action and contending sides have not mobilized for action. Public indifference may signal a tolerance for a presidential initiative, providing an opportunity for the White House.

Immediately after taking office in 1963, Lyndon Johnson began his War on Poverty. Poverty was not a pressing issue in the United States at the time,[106] but such an effort animated liberals, and giving people a hand up is consistent with broad currents of American ideology. Thus, the White House launched what Jeffrey Tulis has termed a "massive rhetorical campaign" to develop a sense of urgency about poverty, and the president made it the most visible theme of his first State of the Union message.[107]

Opinion is especially likely to be open to supporting the White House on new issues. Because the public is less likely to have predispositions on such issues and thus opinion has not crystallized, the president has an opportunity to develop support before an organized opposition develops. One of Ronald Reagan's most notable proposals in national security policy was the Strategic Defense Initiative (SDI). Critics often referred to it as "Star Wars." Reagan first broached SDI in a national address on national security in March 1983, when the president was near the nadir of his approval ratings. The goal of the initiative was to protect the United States against nuclear attack, an aspiration shared by virtually everyone.

There is not much data on public opinion of SDI, but what there is shows that a majority of the people always supported the president's proposal. Moreover, the Gallup Poll found that public support for SDI increased 12 percentage points over a two-year period from 1984 to 1986. On the other hand, Reagan's own pollster, Richard Wirthlin, found that support for SDI actually *fell* during the president's second term. The president still had majority support for his initiative, which was important for the White House, but we cannot conclude that Reagan was effectively building a supportive coalition for his defensive shield.[108]

Reagan's experience on SDI reminds us that opinion changes may well be temporary. Even under unusual circumstances when people have participated in intense deliberations with fellow citizens and listened to the testimony of politicians and policy experts, research finds changes of opinion to be largely temporary.[109] Members of the public who are the easiest to sway in the short run are those without crystallized opinions. However, as issues fade into the background, the realities of daily life confront positions, or a better understanding of the implications of support for the president for basic values clarify policy options, opinions that were altered in response to presidential leadership may quickly be forgotten. This slippage is especially likely to occur in foreign policy, the area where the president's influence on public opinion may be greatest.

The president is not always advantaged on new issues. Stem cell research was not on the minds of most voters in the early summer of 2001. A Gallup poll on July 10–11, 2001, found that only 38 percent of the public was following the issue of stem cell research even "somewhat closely." More than half (56 percent) said they did not know enough to answer a question about federal funding of stem cell research. Responses to more specific questions varied greatly with the question wording. By August, however, the issue heated up and 57 percent of the public were following the debate over stem cell research at least "somewhat closely," while 78 percent felt the issue was at least "somewhat important."[110]

The precipitating factor in the change was discussion over George W. Bush's deliberations on the issue. He announced his decision in a nationally televised address on August 9, 2001, declaring that he would allow the federal government to fund research using stem cells that had been created in the past in a process that destroyed human embryos, but he would not allow funding for stem cell research that would destroy additional embryos in the future.

A few days before Bush's speech, 55 percent supported federal funding for stem cell research *and* for using embryos discarded from fertility clinics. Forty-seven percent even sup-

TABLE 3.1
Medical Research Using Stem Cells Obtained from Human Embryos

Date	Morally Acceptable (%)	Morally Wrong (%)
May 6–9, 2002	52	39
May 5–7, 2003	54	38
May 2–4, 2004	54	37
May 2–5, 2005	60	33
May 8–11, 2006	61	30
May 10–13, 2007	64	30

SOURCE: Gallup Poll

ported using embryos created in laboratories specifically for the purpose of research.[111] Initially, 60 percent of the public approved of the president's decision not to fund stem cell research that would destroy additional embryos in the future, and most of those disapproving felt he was not strict enough.[112]

The president's advantage soon faded, however. By the following May, a majority of the public felt medical research using stem cells obtained from human embryos was morally acceptable, and the percentage increased to nearly two-thirds by 2007 (see table 3.1). Four years later, 56 percent of the public felt the federal government should fund research that would use newly created stem cells obtained from human embryos.[113] Fifty-eight percent of the public disapproved of Bush's veto of a bill in 2006 that would have expanded federal funding for embryonic stem cell research.[114] By April 2007, 60 percent of the public wanted fewer or no restrictions on federal funding for stem cell research.[115]

Opinion may be fluid even on elements of highly salient ongoing policies. In September 2007, the Gallup Poll asked whether respondents favored the plan of General David Petraeus and President Bush to withdraw about 40,000 troops from Iraq by the summer of 2008, but not to make a commitment to further withdrawals until that time. Gallup also asked whether respondents supported a plan introduced by Democratic senators that called for the withdrawal of most U.S. troops within nine months. The muddled results revealed that similar and large percentages of Americans favored each plan—

and 45 percent of the public favored both plans.[116] Although the president was not able to obtain the public's support solely for his preferred option, he was able to buy himself time to pursue his policy.

On rare occasions, a crisis may hit the United States, creating new issues overnight. The onset of the Great Depression in 1929, the taking of U.S. hostages in Iran in 1975, and the terrorist attacks of September 11, 2001, are examples. In such cases, most in the public look to the White House to respond to the new problem rapidly. This deference provides the president an opportunity to build support for his policies by demonstrating competence and resolution. Franklin D. Roosevelt exploited the crisis atmosphere to obtain passage of his New Deal legislation. George W. Bush won most of what he sought for fighting the war on terrorism abroad, investigating and prosecuting terrorism at home, and reorganizing the government to enhance domestic security.

Policies not relevant to the crisis are not likely to receive support, however. Bipartisanship in one arena does not necessarily carry over to another. We have seen that the public did not defer to Roosevelt's efforts to prepare the country for entry into World War II until events made their impressions. Similarly, the politics of the war on terrorism did not fundamentally alter the consideration of domestic policy issues in 2001–2002. Those issues continued to divide the public and their representatives in Congress as they had before the September 11 attacks, as the differences between the parties emerged.[117] Moreover, the public found Herbert Hoover and Jimmy Carter wanting in their response to crises and elected their opponents in the next elections.

Focusing Attention

Increasing the salience of an issue, clarifying, framing, or channeling opinion, and taking advantage of fluid views require that the president focus the public's attention on issues of his choosing. Yet the White House faces obstacles to focusing the public's attention. In the first place, presidents must cope with an elaborate agenda established by their predecessors.[118] The president's choices of priorities usually fall within parameters set by prior commitments of the government that obligate it to spend money, defend allies, maintain services, or protect rights.[119] As Kennedy aide Theodore Sorensen observed, "Presidents rarely, if ever make decisions . . . in the sense of writing their conclusions largely on a clean slate."[120] Moreover, every administration must respond to unanticipated or simply overlooked problems that affect simultaneously the attention of the public and the priorities of Congress.

COMPETITORS FOR ATTENTION

In addition to prior commitments and unanticipated events, there are institutional competitors for the public's attention. The president communicates with the public in a congested communications environment clogged with competing messages from a wide variety of sources, through a wide range of media, and on a staggering array of subjects. Even within the domain of politics, political communications bombard Americans every day (many of which originate in the White House). The sheer volume of these communications far exceeds the attentive capacity of any individual. As Bill Clinton confided to a friend after about a year in office, "I did not realize the . . . the overriding importance of what is on the evening television news. If I am not on, or there with a message, someone else is, with their message."[121]

The media. The public's familiarity with political matters is closely related to the amount and duration of attention these affairs receive in the mass media,[122] especially in foreign affairs. The media also have a strong influence on the issues the public views as important.[123] According to Doris Graber, "Many people readily adopt the media's agenda of importance, often without being aware of it."[124] Moreover, when the media cover events, politicians comment on them and take action, reinforcing the perceived importance of these events and ensuring more public attention to them. In the words of a leading authority on the impact of television news on public opinion: "The themes and issues that are repeated in television news coverage become the priorities of viewers."[125]

Writing about matters such as U.S. interventions in Somalia and Bosnia and the abrupt end of the Gulf War, both James Baker and Colin Powell argue that media coverage creates powerful imperatives for prompt action, which makes it more difficult for the president to engage selectively in world affairs.[126] This pressure may force presidents to state policies or send troops when they would prefer to let situations develop or encourage other nations to deal with a problem. President Clinton complained that television coverage of Bosnia was "trying to force me to get America into a war."[127] In fact, the president did respond to images of atrocities in Haiti, Bosnia, and Kosovo.[128]

Television coverage may set the president's agenda even during a crisis. Pictures of Iraqi troops retreating from Kuwait on the "Highway of Death" created an impression of a bloodbath and thus influenced President Bush's decision to end the Gulf War. Bush himself described the "undesirable public and political baggage [that came from] all those scenes of carnage" appearing on television.[129] Similarly, during the 1990 invasion of Panama, the press noticed that a radio tower was standing near the center of Panama City. Reports of the tower led policy makers to order its destruction, although it had no value to the enemy.[130]

During the 1979–1980 Iranian hostage crisis, in which several dozen Americans were held hostage, ABC originated a nightly program entitled *America Held Hostage*. Walter Cronkite provided a "countdown" of the number of days of the crisis at the end of each evening's news on CBS television, a wide range of media reported countless feature stories on the hostages and their families, and the press devoted complete coverage to "demonstrations" held in front of the U.S. embassy in Tehran (often artificially created by demonstrators for consumption by Americans). This crisis dominated American politics for more than a year.

Conversely, when North Korea captured the American ship *Pueblo* in 1968, there were many more American captives, and they were held for almost as long as the hostages in Tehran. There were no television cameras and few reporters to cover the situation in North Korea, however. As a result, the incident played a much smaller role in American politics.

The president, then, is constantly in competition with the media in seeking to focus the public's attention. As Linsky concluded in his analysis of a survey of former government officials and interviews with federal policy makers: "The press has a huge and identifiable impact. . . . Officials believe that the media do a lot to set the policy agenda and to influence how an issue is understood by policymakers, interest groups, and the public."[131] Similarly, after reviewing the literature, Rogers and Dearing found that "the media agenda seems to have direct, sometimes strong, influence upon the policy agenda of elite decision makers."[132]

Recognizing the influence of the media as an agenda setter, the White House invests substantial energy and time in attempting to shape the media's own agenda.[133] It provides the press with briefings and backgrounders, press releases, and interviews and press conferences with high-level officials, including the president. It also makes efforts to coordinate the news emanating from various parts of the executive branch. Although we have rich descriptions of these efforts,[134] we know very little about their success in influencing the media.

Most examinations of presidential influence on the media's agenda have focused on the State of the Union message and found mixed results.[135] Wood and Peake broadened the focus to include all presidential rhetoric associated with the major foreign policy issues of U.S.-Soviet relations and the Arab-Israeli and Bosnian conflicts. Although most observers view the president as most influential on major foreign policy issues, the authors found that presidents are not very successful in driving media attention to these issue areas. Instead, international events and inertia drive most presidential attention to foreign policy issues.[136]

In a broader study, Edwards and Wood focused on the relationships between the president, Congress, and the media and investigated the patterns of issue attention among the president, Congress, and the media for U.S.-Soviet and Arab-Israeli relations, crime, education, and health care. They found that most of the time the president reacts, responding primarily to fluctuations in attention by the media and to events (in the case of foreign policy). In domestic policy, however, they found a more interactive relationship, which offers the president the opportunity to act in an entrepreneurial fashion to focus the attention of others in the system on major presidential initiatives, such as health care in 1993–1994.[137]

Peake replicated these studies for foreign policy using a set of lower salience issues including the Caribbean, Central America, foreign aid, and foreign trade. He found that presidents have more influence on the media's agenda when issues are low in public salience.[138] Perhaps presidents have a better chance of influencing media attention on issues that have received less attention. Eshbaugh-Soha and Peake analyzed the president's ability to influence media attention to economic issues, including the general economy, spending, inflation/unemployment, and international economic matters. They found that presidential attention to economic matters influences media attention for all four measures, but they also discovered that media attention to these matters influenced presidential attention for three of the four issues.[139]

Congress. There is no question that Congress is an important agenda setter, perhaps the central one, in the U.S. political system. Baumgartner and Jones emphasize the importance of Congress in determining and changing the national agenda.[140] Kingdon places Congress second only to the administration as a whole as an agenda setter in Washington.[141] Roy Flemming, John Bohte, and B. Dan Wood find Congress to be the major agenda setter in environmental policy.[142] The public expects Congress to take the initiative,[143] and members of Congress have strong electoral incentives to respond.

Thus, Congress is quite capable of setting its own agenda, and it generally does. One study found that Congress initiated two-thirds of the major legislative proposals in the period of 1953–1996.[144] It is not surprising, then, that when President Carter sent his large legislative program to Congress, it had to compete for space on the agenda with congressional initiatives. As a presidential aide put it, "Congress was scheduled up before most of the items arrived."[145] Similarly, most of the major legislative actions of the 1980s were congressional initiatives,[146] and the new Republican Congress in 1995 moved aggressively to govern, forcing the Clinton administration to adopt a defensive posture.

We do not know, however, how much congressional initiatives distract the public from the president's agenda. There is little doubt that Congress receives attention in the media, and individual senators and representatives have strong incentives to publicize their own activities. Because most congressional activity focuses on *its* own initiatives, Congress is inevitably a competitor for the public's attention.

The White House as competition with itself. Ironically, the White House is often its own greatest competitor. The president's complex set of public activities inevitably distracts from the administration's own agenda priorities. There are so many demands on the chief executive to speak, appear, and attend meetings that it is impossible to organize the president's schedule for very long around a focus on the administration's major goals, especially when the president has been in office for some years. Presidents make the overwhelming majority of their public statements about public policy in the context of statements about many *other* policies. In addition, the president speaks about many different issues on a regular basis and within the same news cycle.

To be effective in leading the public, the president must focus the public's attention on his policies for a sustained period of time. This requires more than a single speech, no matter how eloquent or dramatic it may be. The Reagan White House was successful in maintaining a focus on its top-priority economic policies in 1981. It molded its communication strategy around its legislative priorities and focused the administration's agenda and statements on economic policy to ensure that discussing a wide range of topics did not diffuse the president's message.[147]

Sustaining such a focus is difficult to do, however. It is even more difficult to coordinate supporters around a message.[148] After 1981, President Reagan had to deal with a wide range of noneconomic policies. Other administrations have encountered similar problems.

The White House can put off dealing with the full spectrum of national issues for several months at the beginning of a new president's term, but it cannot do so for four years; eventually it must make decisions. By the second year, the agenda is full and more policies are in the pipeline, as the administration attempts to satisfy its constituencies and responds to problems it has overlooked

A two-week period in June 1979 illustrates the White House's problem in competing with itself. At the beginning of the period, President Carter met with a congressional delegation to try to rally its support for an expected close vote on the implementation of the Panama Canal Treaty. In the course of it, Carter told two congressmen that he would "whip [Senator Kennedy's] ass" if the latter tried to run against him. This statement became a big story on the evening news, overshadowing the Panama Canal issue. Two days later, the president introduced his proposals for national health insurance. Before he could launch any campaign to obtain backing for his legislation, the president left for Vienna to sign the SALT agreements. When he returned, he addressed Congress and the nation on the subject of SALT. The president's next appearance on the news took place the following day, when he spoke at a ceremony after the completion of a solar panel for the White House hot-water system. There he urged the nation to give its attention to this important alternative to oil. Three days later, he left for a world economic conference.[149]

The degree to which unanticipated issues, including international crises, impose themselves on the president's schedule and divert attention, energy, and resources from *his* agenda will also affect the White House's success in focusing attention on priority issues.[150] As Clinton aide George Stephanopoulos put it: "On the campaign trail, you can just change the subject. But you can't just change the subject as President. You can't wish Bosnia away. You can't wish David Koresh [the leader of the Branch Davidian sect in Waco, Texas] away. You can't just ignore them and change the subject."[151] A Reagan White House aide agreed: "The hardest thing to do is not to get into a reactive mode and have your schedule dictated to you by events, rather than dictating events and having a schedule reflective of your priorities."[152]

Focusing attention on priorities is considerably easier for a president with a short legislative agenda, such as Ronald Reagan, than it is for one with a more ambitious agenda. It is also an advantage if the opposition party is in disarray and lacks alternatives to the president's agenda, a situation enjoyed by the Republicans in 1981 as the Democrats reeled from Reagan's electoral victory and their loss of the Senate.

Conversely, Bill Clinton took office with a large agenda, which he detailed in his lengthy annual State of the Union addresses.[153] In addition, Democrats had a laundry list of initiatives that George Bush had blocked, ranging from family and medical leave to motor voter registration and health care reform. He and his fellow partisans believed in activist government and were predisposed toward doing "good" and against husbanding leadership resources. But no good deed goes unpunished. The more the White House tried to do, the more difficult it was to focus the country's attention on priority issues. "I'm the most impatient person on earth," the president declared.

I've tried to do so many things that sometimes when I do things, no one notices. Most Americans don't know we did family leave or motor voter or national service or changed the environmental policy, because I was always in some other controversy that was getting more ink.[154]

As soon as I finished a task, I moved on to the next one, without doing a lot of follow-up communications.[155]

Thus, the president may be his own worst enemy in focusing the public's attention. President Clinton had an undisciplined personal style, tremendous energy, a desire to please many sides, a mind stuffed with policy ideas, and a party of interest groups clamoring for policy. As a result, he risked undermining rather than reinforcing the impact of his own words. Clinton and his advisers understood the virtue of a clear, simple agenda,[156] and the president knew that his defining issues had been overwhelmed as he had engaged in issue proliferation.[157] As he later admitted:

I gave almost no thought to how to keep the public's focus on my most important priorities, rather than on competing stories that, at the least, would divert public attention from the big issues and, at worst, could make it appear that I was neglecting those priorities.[158]

It's hard to get more than one message a day across on the evening news to the American people.[159]

The president's highest priority legislation in 1993 was health care reform, which he presented to the country in a televised address on September 22. On October 3, however, eighteen U.S. soldiers were killed on a peacekeeping mission in Somalia, and others were wounded or missing. Americans were horrified to see pictures of a dead soldier being dragged through the streets of Mogadishu. So the president returned from a trip to California to promote his health care initiative and focused on events abroad. Americans seemed to lose interest in health care at this point, and awareness of and support for the plan stopped.[160]

In addition, during this crucial period the president had to devote his full attention and all the White House's resources to obtaining passage of NAFTA, which dominated the news for weeks and which was central to his foreign policy priority of increasing international trade. Moreover, on October 11, pro-military gunmen forced the *U.S.S. Harlan County*, carrying U.S. troops as part of a United Nations plan to restore democracy in Haiti, to turn around and leave the country. Thus, national and international events sabotaged Clinton's plan to saturate the country with his message.[161]

At the same time, the White House was not able to monopolize the dialogue regarding health care reform. Democratic Representative Jim Cooper introduced his own, considerably more modest, health care proposal in the House, and Democratic Senator John Breaux introduced a similar bill in the Senate. In addition, a myriad of health care industry voices attempted to persuade the public, inundating it with a deluge of direct mail, radio spots, and advertising opposing the president's plan. One set of ads, the "Harry and Louise" ads, received substantial free media coverage as well.

New methods of mass communications and a tidal wave of special interest funding equipped anti-reform groups of even modest size with the capacity to challenge the president's bully pulpit and redefine the issue of health care. They took full advantage of their opportunities.[162] The media was only too happy to highlight the conflict between the president and his opponents.

REACHING THE PUBLIC

There is little the White House can do to limit the overall volume of messages that citizens encounter or to make the public more attentive to politics, and it has limited success in influencing the media's agenda. What it can do—in theory—is to repeat its own messages to the public so that they will break through the public's disinterest in politics and the countless distractions from it. In addition, the White House could sustain its flow of messages for the many months of the legislative cycle and concentrate its communications on the president's priorities.

It is likely that reaching the public will require frequent repetition of the president's views. According to George W. Bush, "In my line of work you got to keep repeating things over and over and over again for the truth to sink in, to kind of catapult the propaganda."[163] Given the protracted nature of the legislative process, and the president's need for public support at all stages of it, sustaining a message can be equally important as sending it in the first place. As David Gergen put it, "History teaches that almost nothing a leader says is heard if spoken only once." Administrations attempt to establish a "line of the day" so that many voices echo the same point.[164]

The lack of interest in politics of most Americans, as evidenced by the low turnouts in elections, compounds the challenge of reaching the public. We have seen that policymaking is a very complex enterprise, and most voters do not have the time, expertise, or inclination to think extensively about most issues. In fact, people generally have only a few issues that are particularly important to them and to which they pay attention.[165] The importance of specific issues to the public varies over time and is closely tied to objective conditions such as unemployment, inflation, international tensions, and racial conflict. In addition, different issues are likely to be salient to different groups in the population at any given time. For example, some groups may be concerned about inflation, others about unemployment, and yet others about a particular aspect of foreign policy or race relations.[166]

Commentary cascades from the White House. One official estimated that the White House produces as many as five million words a year in the president's name in outlets such as speeches, written statements, and proclamations.[167] Wide audiences hear only a small proportion of the president's statements, however. Comments about policy proposals at news conferences and question and answer sessions and in most interviews are also usually brief and made in the context of a discussion of many other policies at the same time. Written statements and remarks to individual groups may be focused, but the audience for these communications is modest. In addition, as Gergen puts it, nearly all of the president's statements "wash over the public. They are dull, gray prose, eminently forgettable."[168]

Perhaps the most potentially powerful tool for going public is the nationally televised address. These addresses represent the best opportunity for the president to reach the largest audience of his fellow citizens, because almost every American has access to television and many are accustomed to turning to it for news. In addition, when the president addresses the nation, he does so directly (and rapidly), without the mediation of the press. Moreover, in a televised address, the president does not appear as a partisan, but rather as a statesman, usually speaking from the dignified surroundings of the Oval Office or before a joint session of Congress.

The White House seldom realizes the full potential of these advantages, however. Presidents make most of their comments about policies in these addresses in the context of remarks about many other policies. There is little opportunity to focus on one issue area.[169] Ronald Reagan made forty-seven nationally televised addresses over his eight years in office. Most of these speeches, however, were either broad communications such as State of the Union messages or narrower reports on military interventions, summit meetings, disasters, and scandals. Only nineteen of these addresses focused on his policy proposals. Consistent with the general strategic view of the Reagan White House, the president focused these addresses on a few high-priority policies. Four sought to obtain support for aid to forces opposing communism in Central America, and four others dealt with other aspects of national security. Nine of the televised addresses centered on the budget and the economy—five of these speeches occurred in the critical months of 1981, when the bulk of the Reagan economic program passed in Congress. The only other addresses on policy proposals, a total of two, were on tax reform and drug control.

Bill Clinton made twenty-eight nationally televised addresses during his tenure. Ten of Clinton's national addresses were of a general nature, including his inaugural addresses and State of the Union messages. He also made several addresses regarding military interventions. The president made only six national addresses on legislation before Congress, four of them in 1993. The first two focused on the same issue, his economic stimulus program. Addresses on health care reform and the budget also involved issues before Congress. The president's 1994 address on a Middle Class Bill of Rights occurred after Congress had adjourned and was not focused on legislation before Congress. Instead, it was more of a desperation effort at projecting a tax-cutting image for the White House in the wake of the Republican takeover of Congress. His 1995 address on balancing the budget was also a general plan designed to co-opt the deficit reduction issue from the Republicans. In the remaining five and a half years of his presidency, he never again made a nationally televised address on legislation.

Through September 2008, George W. Bush made thirty-three nationally televised addresses, but used them even less than his predecessors to speak to the country about his initiatives. Almost all of his nationally televised addresses either were general addresses or related to the war on terrorism. Regarding other initiatives, he made one address on his decision regarding stem cell research in 2001, one on his nomination of John Roberts to the Supreme Court in 2005, one on immigration reform in 2006, and one on the Wall Street financial crisis in 2008.

Presidents not only deliver few focused televised addresses, but they also generally fail to draw an impressive audience. Scholars and other commentators have assumed that the president consistently draws a broad audience for his nationally televised speeches.[170] Although wide viewership was common during the early decades of television, when presidential speeches routinely attracted more than 80 percent of those watching television, recent presidents have seen their audiences decline to the point where less than half of the public—often substantially less—watch their televised addresses.[171]

Paradoxically, developments in technology allowed the president to reach mass audiences, yet further developments made it easier to for these same audiences to avoid listening to the White House. Cable television[172] and new networks provide alternatives that make it easy to tune out the president.

With the advent of television, presidents following Truman generally neglected radio as a medium for communication, focusing on reaching the larger audience available through television. Presidents Nixon and Ford used radio addresses on occasion, but the Reagan White House sought to capitalize on the president's fondness and experience in radio institutionalized Saturday broadcasts. With the exception of George H. W. Bush, Reagan successors have continued to use regular radio communications to the nation. The addresses have been short, however, averaging about 850 words,[173] and their audiences are typically small. Weekend media pays modest attention to them, and most broadcast and print outlets do not mention the broadcasts at all.[174]

Another way to view the extent of the president's efforts to obtain public attention is to examine his statements relative to specific pieces of legislation. Research has found that presidents on average speak publicly less than twice a month even in support of their most significant legislative initiatives, on which their legacy may be built.[175]

The first step in the president's efforts to lead the public is focusing its attention. People who are not attentive to the issues on which the president wishes to lead are unlikely to be influenced in their views on those issues. If the president's messages are to meet his coalition-building needs, the public must sort through the profusion of communications in its environment, overcome its limited interest in government and politics, and concentrate on the president's priority concerns. It is no exaggeration to conclude that focusing the public's attention is usually a substantial challenge.

❖ ❖ ❖

Although presidents are unlikely to change public opinion, there are times when the White House may exploit existing public opinion in its efforts to change public policy. The president may frame proposals to emphasize their consistency with the public's existing views, increase the salience of White House initiatives that are popular with the public, clarify the public's wishes and show how they are consistent with his policies, define themselves and their parties in ways that channel existing opinion on the issues into support for a party program, and exploit opinion fluidity or public indifference regarding an issue.

Such strategies often fail, however. The president cannot depend on framing how the public views his policies and his performance. One can sympathize with Bill Clinton when he declared, "Americans don't want me to help them understand. They just want me to do something about it."[176] Similarly, there are significant obstacles to exploiting existing opinion in other ways. In addition, it is difficult for the president to focus the public's attention. Despite the fact that rhetoric steadily flows from the White House, chief executives disperse their public remarks over a broad range of policies, and wide audiences hear only a small portion of them. The president faces strong competition for the public's attention from previous commitments of government, congressional initiatives, opposing elites, and the mass media. Equally important, presidents often compete with themselves as they address other issues. Reaching the public is a continual and sizable challenge for the president.

4 Leading Congress

Best Test Cases

NEAR THE TOP of any list of presidential responsi-
bilities would be working with Congress. According to Lyndon
Johnson, "There is only one way for a President to deal with
Congress, and that is continuously, incessantly, and without in-
terruption."[1] Since the U.S. system of separation of powers is
really one of shared powers, presidents can rarely operate independently of Congress. Although they require the cooperation
of Congress, presidents cannot depend on it. Thus, one of the
chief executive's most difficult and frustrating tasks is trying to
move Congress to support his policies.

There are hundreds, or perhaps thousands, of anecdotes that
purport to show the persuasiveness of presidents with members of Congress. Skepticism is appropriate for evaluating these
stories, however. A good example is President Johnson's efforts
at obtaining the support—or at least the neutrality—of the Senate Finance Committee chairman, Harry Byrd of Virginia, for
what became the 1964 tax cut. Byrd had resisted a tax cut because of his concern for increasing the budget deficit. Hubert
Humphrey reported in his memoirs that Johnson cajoled Byrd
into letting the tax bill out of committee, relying on Lady Bird's
charm, liquor, and his own famous "treatment."[2] Presidential
aide Jack Valenti told a different story, however. He wrote that
the president obtained the senator's cooperation by promising
to hold the budget under $100 billion.[3] Thus, we have as eyewit-

nesses two experienced political professionals who knew both Byrd and Johnson very well. Each reported on a different tactic employed by the president and each attributed Senator Byrd's response to the presidential behavior that he observed.

To confuse matters further, Henry Hall Wilson, one of the president's congressional liaison aides, indicated that both eyewitnesses were wrong. According to Wilson, when the president proudly told his chief congressional liaison aide, Lawrence O'Brien, about his obtaining Byrd's agreement to begin hearings on the tax cut on December 7, O'Brien replied, "You didn't get a thing. I already had a commitment for the seventh."[4] In other words, according to O'Brien, Johnson's efforts were irrelevant and both eyewitnesses were wrong in attributing influence to him.[5]

Clearly, we cannot rely on anecdotes to evaluate the possibilities of presidential legislative leadership. To determine whether some presidents dominated Congress, reliably obtaining its support for their policies and precluding legislative initiatives that they opposed, I turn again to an examination of best test cases. In the era of the modern presidency, there have been three periods of unusual legislative productivity in which major nonincremental policies on the president's agenda passed Congress in short order. The question for us is whether the president obtained passage of these especially significant programs by substantially altering the political landscape and convincing reluctant members of Congress to support his proposals or whether he acted as a facilitator and exploited opportunities already present in his environment to produce change.

Franklin D. Roosevelt

In 1932, Franklin D. Roosevelt did not run on a liberal platform and convince the American public to support the dramatic shifts in public policy that we now identify as New Deal programs. FDR did not mention deficit spending, gigantic federal works programs, federal housing and slum clearance, the NRA, the TVA, sharply increased income taxes on the wealthy, massive relief programs, a national labor relations board with power to enforce collective bargaining, and other central elements of the New Deal. Instead, the Democratic platform was a conservative document that differed little from the Republicans' on economic policy except for more ambitious welfare programs. The future president voiced discordant themes but generally conventional views like balancing the budget.[6]

Nevertheless, the Great Depression had thoroughly discredited his opponent, Herbert Hoover, and Roosevelt won a clear victory. Equally important, the Democrats gained large majorities in both houses of Congress.

EXPLOITING THE OPPORTUNITY

The day after his inauguration in 1933, FDR called a special session of Congress to deal with the economic crisis. All he planned to ask from Congress was to pass legislation to regulate the resumption of banking (he had closed the banks three days *after* taking office), amend the Volstead Act to legalize beer (a very popular policy),[7] and effect government economies. He expected to reassemble the legislature when he was ready with permanent and more constructive legislation.[8]

The first piece of legislation Roosevelt proposed was a bill regarding the resumption of banking. According to James Mac-Gregor Burns, "The milling representatives could hardly wait to act." Even during the forty-minute debate in the House, shouts of "Vote! Vote!" echoed from the floor. The Republican leader, Bertrand H. Snell, exclaimed in support, "The House is burning down and the President of the United States says this is the way to put out the fire."[9] The president did not have to persuade anyone to support his bill, which passed unanimously in the House after only thirty-eight minutes of debate and without a roll call vote (although few members had seen the bill—there was only one copy for the chamber)—and by a margin of 73 to

7 in the Senate, which simply adopted the House bill while waiting for printed copies. An hour later, the bill arrived at the White House for the president's signature. The whole affair took less than eight hours.[10]

The next day, the president sent Congress a proposal for spending reductions to cut the deficit. There was much more congressional resistance to this legislation, however. The prospects of benefit cuts frightened veterans' organizations, which deluged Congress with telegrams in opposition. There was open revolt against the president in Congress on his second bill. In the House, the Democratic caucus declined to support FDR because its members viewed the bill as cruel to veterans and a gift to Wall Street, and a number of liberals abandoned him. The conservative Democrats maintained parliamentary control, however, and, with the help of sixty-nine fiscally conservative Republicans, they passed the bill. Ninety Democrats, including seven party leaders, deserted the president at this early stage of his presidency. The situation was no better in the Senate, and it took the popular proposal to amend the Volstead Act to allow 3.2 beer and wine to solidify Democratic ranks. (The nominating conventions had shown more concern over prohibition than unemployment, and when the bill was on the floor, "Impatient congressmen chanted: 'Vote—vote—we want beer'.")[11] When Roosevelt had to persuade members of Congress, he found it difficult. Neither the policy of budget balancing, which reflected orthodox fiscal views, nor the president's persuasiveness was transformational.

Nevertheless, much to his surprise, the president found a situation ripe for change. Burns described it as follows:

> A dozen days after the inauguration a move of adulation for Roosevelt was sweeping the country. Over ten thousand telegrams swamped the White House in a single week. Newspaper editorials were paeans of praise. . . . A flush of hope swept the nation. Gold was flowing back to financial institutions; banks were reopening without crowds of depositors clamoring for their money; employment and production seemed to be turning upward.[12]

"I will do anything you ask," a congressman from Iowa wrote the president. "You are my leader." Even with the banks closed, "the American people were in an almost gala mood . . . reveling in a new sense of hope about the economy and about leaders who appeared actually to be doing something."[13]

Roosevelt decided to exploit this favorable environment and strike repeatedly with hastily drawn legislation. Commentators later named this period of intense activity the "Hundred Days" (a phrase that originated to describe the period between Napoleon's escape from Elba and his defeat at Waterloo). FDR had no master plan to remake America or a grand strategy for engendering change, however. He did not seek to transform policy, "but rather to revise, reform, and restore." Instead of following a visionary design, he improvised.[14] In the early years of his presidency, when he was most successful in obtaining legislative support, Congress was as often to his left as to his right. It was Congress, for example, that initiated the Federal Deposit Insurance Corporation, the National Labor Relations Act, and public housing legislation.[15] As Burns put it, "Roosevelt's main job in 1933 and 1934 was not to prod Congress into action, but to ride the congressional whirlwind."[16]

The primary result of the banking bill "was to patch up failings and shortcomings in financial institutions and in their supervision by government." Despite his critics' views that he should propose establishing a truly national banking system, FDR felt he needed to restore confidence in the system and thus offer policies that bankers themselves could support. So he focused on restoring the existing structure.[17] One historian described the bill as "an exceptionally conservative document and largely the work of bankers and Herbert Hoover's Treasury officers. It was a victory for orthodox finance and actually deflationary at a time when the times called for just the reverse in economic policy.[18]

The next month, April 1933, Roosevelt asked Congress for legislation to protect homeowners from foreclosure under a new Home Owners' Loan Corporation. Once again, he was shoring up the existing system while also strengthening the stake of the middle class in the existing order—and in the New Deal.[19] Even when he could have nationalized banking and the railroads in 1933, he did not try.[20]

Roosevelt was also not trying to transform politics. He did not employ his communications skills to appeal to the public to put pressure on their senators and representatives to support his proposals—contrary to legend. He held his first fireside chat—focused on banks—on March 12, 1933, three days after the Emergency Banking Act passed on March 9. He wanted to reassure people that their savings in the closed banks were secure and that the passage of the highly consensual policy had made it safe to return their savings to banks. FDR did not make a second fireside chat until eight weeks after the first. "Nor did he tour the country stoking backfires for his friends and against his foes; he hardly left Washington during the first hundred days."[21] He did not have to.

Robert Sherwood later declared, "No cosmic dramatist could possibly devise a better entrance for a new President—or a new Dictator, or a new Messiah—than that accorded Franklin Delano Roosevelt." Moreover, the ironic twist was that it was his enemies rather than his friends and supporters who set the stage for him. Herbert Hoover was a good act to follow.[22]

As Walter Lippmann proclaimed, "At the beginning of March, the country was in such a state of confused desperation that it would have followed almost any leader anywhere he chose to go." Will Rogers added, "The whole country is with him, just so he does something. If he burned down the capitol we would cheer and say 'well, we at least got a fire started anyhow'." Even conservatives joined in the applause as FDR displayed no evidence of radicalism, saved the old banking system, and cut government spending.[23]

In 1935–1936, the period of the Second New Deal, the White House did not engage in a consciously planned, grandly executed deployment to the left. Instead, the president responded to—and exploited—a set of trends that converged to make substantial change possible. He enjoyed broad public support, the economic hardships fostered by the Depression created an expectation of bold public leadership to restore the economy and the social order, and Democrats had increased their already huge majorities in Congress. Organized labor as well as social movements led by Huey Long, Francis Townsend, and others clamored for far-reaching change, as did newly elected Democrats who rode to office on the wave of support for the New Deal. Congress was more to FDR's left than in the previous years, pulling him in its direction. The desertion of former supporters on the right and the more organized and vocal opposition on the right also pushed the president to the left. In addition, the judicial demolition of the New Deal confirmed the president in his leftward direction.[24] After the great Democratic victory in the 1934 midterm congressional elections, Harry Hopkins declared: "This is our hour. We've got to get everything we want—a works program, social security, wages and hours, everything—now or never."[25]

Roosevelt knew he had to exploit the opportunity, and, once again, he did.[26] Yet he also realized that even under such favorable conditions his power was constrained and shared with Congress. Thus, the president refused to propose a health insurance program as part of his Social Security proposal. To minimize opposition from Congress and the medical profession, Roosevelt decided it was more important and appropriate to reduce the risk of opposition than to press forward in pursuit of his preferred policy goal.[27] Similarly, the president made compromises in Social Security that denied coverage to numerous classes of workers, including those needing it most; shirked responsibility for the elderly indigent; relied on regressive taxes and took money from the pockets of the poor; ignored sickness as a cause of unemployment in determining unemployment benefits; and did not establish national standards for unemployment compensation.[28] After several months of great legislative productivity, he declared a "breathing spell" for the rest of the year and asked Congress for little in 1936.[29]

Many viewed the Second New Deal as more conservative than the first because it relied on markets rather than on government planning. As Leuchtenburg put it, "Even the most precedent-

breaking New Deal projects reflected capitalist thinking and deferred to business sensibilities." "Roosevelt's program rested on
the assumption that a just society could be secured by imposing
a welfare state on a capitalist foundation."[30]

IMPACT OF LEADERSHIP

The most powerful incentive for members of Congress to support Roosevelt's legislative program was the appeal of the measures themselves. At the same time, as we saw in the economies
bill, the president had to worry about preserving congressional
majorities—despite the Democrats' huge margins in both
houses of Congress. He could not rely on his leadership skills
to run roughshod over the opposition and had to attract conservative Democratic and Republican votes, often yielding to
congressional pressures. He certainly had to avoid any appearance of dictating to representatives and senators and rarely got
really tough. Instead, FDR followed traditional patterns and
worked largely through the regular party leadership, with
whom he met regularly. He also had to spend long hours in his
office and on the phone seeking congressional support. When
he could not persuade members of Congress to support him,
he relied on White House aides to employ long-established
techniques such as offering patronage or pork barrel projects
to gain their votes.[31] In addition, he made appeals to the right,
such as emphasizing budget balancing to hold the confidence
of the business and financial communities[32] and appealing to
bankers with modest reforms for the banking system.

In 1933 and 1934, Roosevelt did not conceive of himself as
the leader of a new majority on the left of the political spectrum, building a new configuration of political forces. Instead,
he attempted to remain above the political fray and operate by
coaxing, consulting with, and mediating among existing leaders of major interests in American society. As Burns points out,
this brokerage approach was more passive than attempting to
change the context in which he was attempting to lead.[33]

The lasting changes in policy in the New Deal did not occur when FDR was most dominant in Congress. According to Burns, "It is significant that the enduring New Deal emerged not out of Roosevelt's 'hundred days' of 1933, when he gave a brilliant demonstration of executive leadership, but out of the 'second hundred days' of 1935, which emerged out of decades of foment, political action, and legislative as well as executive policy-making."[34]

FDR went on to serve in the White House longer than anyone else, but most of these years were not legislatively productive. Burns entitles his discussion of presidential-congressional relations in the late 1930s "Deadlock on the Potomac."[35] Either Roosevelt had lost his persuasive skills, which is not a reasonable proposition, or other factors were more significant in determining congressional support.

Burns argues that FDR had not lost his political skills. Instead, he had lost rank-and-file Democrats. In his first term, FDR led Congress by adroit and highly personal and effective handling of congressional leaders and by exploiting the sense of crisis. He dealt with the leaders with charm, tact, flexibility, astute timing, and sensitivity to their political problems. In the process, however, the president consolidated the leaders' power. He gave them a near-monopoly of access, confirming their political status and high-priority claims on administration favors. By ignoring the rank-and-file, he failed to encourage a broad organization in Congress behind New Deal programs and engendered a deep bitterness toward the White House.[36]

By 1937, despite the president's great reelection victory, his coalition was falling apart. As we will see, the president's attempt to "pack" the Supreme Court contributed to the erosion of support for the New Deal in Congress and, at the same time, was a reflection of the diversity within the Democratic Party. Although FDR governed as a party chief from mid-1935 to 1936, Burns argues that he did not build at the grass roots a party that encapsulated the liberal coalition and that was more directly responsive to national direction and centered on New Deal programs. FDR could not make the Democratic Party an instrument of the popular majority because he never made the strategic commitment that would allow a carefully considered, thorough, and long-term attempt at party reorganization. By the time of the purge of 1938, it was too late.[37] Leuchtenburg agrees about Roosevelt's failure to transform his party. Even in the 1936 election, he campaigned as the leader of a liberal crusade that was above party lines.[38]

There is no question that a party such as the one Burns advocates would have been a great asset to FDR. He criticizes Roosevelt for being "less a great creative leader than a skillful manipulator and a brilliant interpreter" who "was captive to the political forces around him rather than their shaper." Thus, the president could not lead either the public or Congress. He "lacked the necessary intellectual commitment to the right union of ends and means."[39]

Perhaps. Yet Burns premises his criticism on the view that it would have been possible for the president to transform American politics and that Roosevelt simply failed to try. In the absence of evidence to support such an hypothesis, we should remain skeptical.

Lyndon B. Johnson

The next great period of legislative productivity for a president was Lyndon Johnson's success with the 89th Congress in 1965–1966.[40] In 1964, LBJ had the good fortune to run against an opponent, Barry Goldwater, whom many in the public viewed as an extremist outside the mainstream of American politics. The election also occurred in the shadow of the traumatic national tragedy of the assassination of John F. Kennedy. Johnson won a smashing victory, and opposition to his proposals melted. As Lawrence O'Brien, his chief congressional aide, put it, Johnson's landslide "turned the tide."[41] For the first and only time since the New Deal, liberals gained majorities in both houses of Congress.

EXPLOITING THE OPPORTUNITY

Johnson did not have to convince these liberals to support policies that had been on their agenda for a generation.[42] Nor did
he have to convince the public of much. His policies were popular,[43] allowing him the luxury of emphasizing in the election
proposals such as Medicare that he knew the public already
supported so he could claim a mandate for them after the election.[44] Mark Peterson found that both congressional leaders
and White House aides felt they were working in a period of
remarkable unanimity in which, as one member of LBJ's domestic staff put it, "some of the separation got collapsed. It
seemed we were all working on the same thing."[45] Johnson even
received substantial Republican support, especially in the Senate, for some of his major initiatives, including aid to education,
Medicare, immigration, reform, clean water, and anti-poverty.
Only his aid to education and Appalachian development plan
drew widespread opposition from House Republicans.[46]

Regarding the most contentious issue of the time, civil rights,
biographer Randall Woods notes that it was Johnson's political
genius to realize that the time for change had arrived. "Lyndon
Johnson was not a man to ignore the power of circumstance,"
so he exploited the protests on voting rights, choosing the mo-
ment when the civil rights movement was peaking in its ability
to appeal to the nation's conscience to pass the Voting Rights
Act in 1965. This was a widely supported policy, however. Even
some members of Congress from the Deep South supported
it, and the Republican leadership never seriously considered
joining with southern conservatives to oppose the bill.[47]

No one understood Congress better than the Texan, and he
knew that his personal leadership could not sustain congressional support for his policies. He believed that the assassination of President Kennedy and the election of 1964 had provided him a rare window of opportunity in Congress[48] and that
he had to move rapidly to exploit it. Thus, in February 1965,
after his landslide victory, Johnson assembled the congressional liaison officials from the various departments and told

them that his victory at the polls "might be more of a loophole than a mandate," and that because his popularity could decrease rapidly they would have to use it to their advantage while it lasted.[49] Moreover, LBJ knew he would probably lose his liberal Democratic margin in the 1966 midterm elections.[50]

Johnson followed his own advice. First, he was ready to send legislation to Capitol Hill immediately after Congress convened. As he explained to one aide, "You've got to give it all you can, that first year . . . You've got just one year when they treat you right and before they start worrying about themselves."[51] To keep Congress concentrated on his proposals, he was ready to replace enacted legislation with new requests.[52]

He told his aide Jack Valenti early in his presidency, "I keep hitting hard because I know this honeymoon won't last. Every day I lose a little more political capital. That's why we have to keep at it, never letting up. One day soon . . . the critics and the snipers will move in and we will be at stalemate. We have to get all we can now, before the roof comes down."[53]

At the end of an extraordinarily productive session of Congress in 1965, he tried to push through Congress a bill providing for home rule in the District of Columbia, a feat that several presidents had attempted unsuccessfully. When asked by an aide why he was working seven days a week on the bill when the same liberal majority would be returning in January, Johnson replied that he knew the odds were greatly against his success and that it was the only chance he would have. Despite the returning liberal majority, "They'll all be thinking about their reelections. I'll have made mistakes, my polls will be down, and they'll be trying to put some distance between themselves and me. They won't want to go into the fall with their opponents calling 'em Lyndon Johnson's rubber stamp."[54]

Interviews with the former Speaker of the House Carl Albert are instructive regarding LBJ's influence in Congress. He argued that Johnson's tenaciousness and intensity in pushing legislation were his great talents. Although pressed by the interviewer for specifics on Johnson's legislative skills, Albert responded only that the president just kept pushing.[55] Russell

Renka reached a similar conclusion. After studying Johnson's legislative relations in detail, he found no special legislative touch possessed by the president. Nevertheless, Johnson moved more legislation through Congress than other contemporary presidents.[56]

Others close to Johnson agree with Albert's explanation. Johnson understood the opportunity the Eighty-ninth Congress presented to him, and he seized it, keeping intense pressure on Congress. According to Lawrence O'Brien, Congress was his obsession; no detail of the legislative process eluded him. With LBJ, "Every day, every hour it was drive, drive, drive."[57] He and his aides worked closely with representatives and senators and their staffs, "constantly cultivating and fertilizing the legislative domain."[58] He courted members of Congress, flattered them, drank with them, and generally paid attention to them. Interestingly, he did not lie or misrepresent to them and did not use information on legislators' private lives from the FBI's files to gain advantage.[59] As O'Brien put it, the White House sometimes offered the carrot but "we didn't carry any big stick."[60]

To exploit fully the favorable political environment, he pushed as much legislation as possible through Congress, keeping it in session until October 22, just two weeks before the 1966 midterm elections.[61] In those elections, the Democrats lost forty-seven seats in the House and four in the Senate. Legislating became much more difficult as a result. Sixteen months later, in March 1968, the president declared that he would not seek reelection. Johnson had lost neither his leadership skills nor his passion for change. Instead, he had lost the opportunity to exploit a favorable environment.[62] As one biographer put it, by 1968 "Congress, the hothouse that had nurtured Johnson . . . was his enemy."[63]

Even when the environment was most favorable, however, Johnson pursued a strikingly conservative approach to Medicare, certainly one of his top priorities in domestic policy. During the 1964 campaign, he promoted Medicare heavily to prime the public and Washington for its passage. The Democratic landslide delivered a clear and unambiguous mandate for a strong presidential initiative, which members of both parties in Congress accepted, conceding that the passage of Medicare was a foregone conclusion. Opposition from the American Medical Association lost its potency in the wake of Johnson's landslide. Nevertheless, the president proposed a modest program, covering only a limited number of days of hospitalization. This approach may have been a clever strategy for vesting Congress with ownership of the policy, but it fell so far short of public expectations that Wilbur Mills, the conservative Democratic chair of the House Ways and Means Committee, felt compelled to step in and add Part B to Medicare, which covers physicians and outpatient services, and Medicaid for the indigent.[64] Much like FDR in 1935, Johnson deferred to Congress—although operating in extraordinarily favorable conditions, reflecting a gifted leader's sensitivity to the limits of his influence.

The Impact of Leadership

Most would agree that John Kennedy and Lyndon Johnson had substantially different leadership styles and personal relationships with Congress. Yet leading participants in the legislative process did not view their visible differences as important for legislative success. According to Henry Hall Wilson, the White House's chief liaison aide for the House under both Kennedy and Johnson, the approach of the two presidents to the House was "practically identical."[65] Similarly, the White House liaison to the Senate for both presidents, Mike Manatos, argued that it did not make any difference on the Hill which president he represented. His members of Congress treated his appeals for support the same.[66]

Congressional leaders John McCormack, Carl Albert, Charles Halleck, and Everett Dirksen, Johnson's aides Lawrence O'Brien, Joseph Califano, and Mike Manatos, the executive branch official James Sundquist, and numerous scholars agree that had Kennedy lived and won by a large margin in 1964, he would have got much the same from Congress as Johnson did, and that the basic explanation for Johnson's phenomenal success in 1965 and 1966 was the increase in the number of liberal Democrats in Congress as a result of the elections of 1964.[67] Significantly, Kennedy and Johnson legislative liaison aides do not argue to the contrary in their published memoirs or their oral histories in the Kennedy and Johnson presidential libraries.

Arthur Schlesinger, Jr., a historian and White House aide to President Kennedy, was also skeptical about the significance of legislative skills. Comparing President Kennedy and President Johnson, he concluded:

> When Johnson lost 48 Democratic House seats in the 1966 election, he found himself, despite his alleged wizardry, in the same condition of stalemate that had thwarted Kennedy and, indeed, every Democratic President since 1938. Had the sequence been different, had Johnson been elected to the Presidency in 1960 with Kennedy as his Vice President, and had Johnson then offered the 87th Congress the same program actually offered by Kennedy, the probability is that he would have had no more success than Kennedy— perhaps even less because he appealed less effectively to public opinion. And, if Johnson had died in 1963 and Kennedy had beaten Goldwater by a large margin in 1964, then Kennedy would have had those extra votes in the House of Representatives, and the pundits of the press would have contrasted his cool management of Congress with the frenetic and bumbling efforts of his predecessor. In the end, arithmetic is decisive.[68]

Even if Johnson's legislative leadership skills did not have a systematic influence on congressional support for his policies, it is possible that they had a more restricted impact, albeit still an important one. Legislative leadership may be most significant at the margins of coalition building, that is, in gaining the last few votes needed to pass a program. Turning a sizable coalition into a victorious one after broader influences have had their impact can certainly be a critical component of leadership. Perhaps the famous Johnson Treatment made the difference in persuading members of Congress to support the historic Great Society legislation.

The evidence on the importance of legislative leadership in marginal votes is mixed. On the one hand, the White House often devotes substantial resources to obtaining votes at the margin of coalitions. Reflecting on the extraordinary economic policies passed by Congress in 1981, David Stockman declared, "I now understand that you probably can't put together a majority coalition unless you are willing to deal with those marginal interests that will give you the votes needed to win. That's where it is fought—on the margins—and unless you deal with those marginal votes, you can't win."[69]

There is reason to be cautious about accepting such a view at face value, however. For example, Russell Renka examined closely the House votes on major elements of the Great Society. A swing of twenty-three votes would have been required for the White House to have lost the closest vote (a recommittal motion sponsored by Republicans on Medicare). Renka could find no indication in the White House's files that President Johnson had done anything specifically on the issue worth twenty-three votes. Indeed, the White House did not even red-flag the Civil Rights Act of 1964, the Voting Rights Act of 1965, Medicare, or the Elementary and Secondary Education Act of 1965 for special presidential efforts as they came to the House floor. The president's intervention was not needed.[70] It is revealing that the tape recordings of his White House conversations show Johnson pleading, thanking, complimenting, and consulting but rarely trying directly to persuade a legislator, and even when he did, he employed a light touch.[71]

In an earlier study, I found that in both 1965, when Johnson had a large majority, and 1967, after the Democrats had suffered substantial losses in midterm elections, there were very few marginal victories in either chamber (victories of twenty-five votes or fewer in the House and ten votes or fewer in the Senate). In other words, there were few victories where Johnson's leadership skills could have made the difference between winning and losing. The marginal victories that did occur were generally not on major issues.[72]

Jon Bond and Richard Fleisher examined presidential success on votes decided by a margin of 10 percent or less. Controlling for the status of the president's party in each chamber, the authors found little relationship between presidential legislative leadership skills and success in winning votes.[73]

The Johnson treatment. Under ideal conditions, we would evaluate the effectiveness of presidents' legislative persuasion by measuring the extent to which they attempted to convince each member of a Congress or the same members over several Congresses. After controlling for other sources of influence, we would determine whether members of Congress on whom a president focused his persuasive skills provided more support than other members, or whether members' support over time fluctuated with the degree to which the president attempted to persuade them.

Unfortunately, there is no way to obtain data on the exercise of presidential legislative persuasion on each member of Congress. There is a substantial amount of information on the legislative activities of various presidents, however, and we know how members of Congress voted on presidential proposals.

According to the conventional wisdom, Lyndon Johnson should have received more support in Congress, *ceteris paribus*, than other presidents. Johnson was the master legislative strategist and technician, making Congress his highest priority and leaving no stone unturned in his efforts to exercise his influence. His predecessor, John Kennedy, on the other hand, had more nonlegislative concerns and lacked Johnson's fascination with the legislative process. Jimmy Carter, elected eight years after Johnson left office, lacked his predecessors' experience in Washington and was widely criticized for his maladroit handling of congressional relations from the very beginning of his term. If we cannot find clear evidence of the significance of greater success for Johnson, we are unlikely to find it for anyone.

By comparing Johnson's success in obtaining support for his policy stances with that of Kennedy and Carter, we can determine whether Johnson did better than other Democratic presidents of the same era. We can control for the factors of the size of party representation in Congress and in regions by comparing the support that similar groups gave each president. Naturally, the party of the president also plays an important role in determining the level of support given by various groups in Congress, so we must restrict formal comparisons to presidents of the same party.

Table 4.1 summarizes the records of support in the House for Kennedy, Johnson, and Carter. The data represent scores on two indices. The first, *nonunanimous support*, measures support on all votes on which the president took a stand and on which fewer than 80 percent of those voting supported the winning side. *Key votes*, on the other hand, is a more exclusive index, averaging only ten votes per year in the House and nine in the Senate. We might expect this index of presidential support to focus on issues about which the president cares the most and on which he tries the hardest, revealing differences in support that a broader index masks.

The figures in the table do not support the hypothesis that Johnson was especially persuasive in influencing representatives to support his policies. Kennedy received more support from both Northern and Southern Democrats than did Johnson, whereas Johnson received more support from Republicans. Carter's support is similar to Johnson's among Republicans, greater among Southern Democrats, and lower only among Northern Democrats (consequently, the percentages of support of all Democrats are also lower for Carter than for Johnson). One may reasonably attribute the differences in support for the two presidents among Democrats to Carter's having supported more conservative policies than Johnson.

The relationships between support for Kennedy and Johnson in the Senate (table 4.2) are similar to those in the House, except that Johnson exceeded his predecessor's support among Southern Democrats on key votes. The results for the compari-

TABLE 4.1
House Support for Democratic Presidents (%)

Kennedy, 1961–1963

	Nonunanimous Support*	Key Votes**
Democrats	73	74
Northern Democrats	85	90
Southern Democrats	54	49
Republicans	26	17

Johnson, 1964–1968

	Nonunanimous Support	Key Votes
Democrats	71	68
Northern Democrats	82	81
Southern Democrats	47	40
Republicans	27	29

Carter, 1977–1980

	Nonunanimous Support	Key Votes
Democrats	63	59
Northern Democrats	68	64
Southern Democrats	51	45
Republicans	31	29

* On roll-call votes on which the winning side was supported by fewer than 80 percent of those voting.

** As selected by Congressional Quarterly.

sons of Johnson and Carter are different, however. Carter maintained his substantial lead over Johnson in support from Southern Democrats, but he also did as well as Johnson among Northern Democrats. Interestingly, Carter obtained less support than Johnson among Republicans.

Despite Carter's relative success, one cannot ignore the fact that Johnson obtained substantially more support than Carter among Northern Democrats in the House on each of the in-

TABLE 4.2
Senate Support for Democratic Presidents (%)

Kennedy, 1961–1963

	Nonunanimous Support*	Key Votes**
Democrats	65	65
Northern Democrats	75	79
Southern Democrats	44	38
Republicans	33	32

Johnson, 1964–1968

	Nonunanimous Support	Key Votes
Democrats	56	65
Northern Democrats	65	75
Southern Democrats	36	41
Republicans	44	49

Carter, 1977–1980

	Nonunanimous Support	Key Votes
Democrats	63	64
Northern Democrats	66	70
Southern Democrats	54	50
Republicans	38	33

* On roll-call votes on which the winning side was supported by fewer than 80 percent of those voting.

** As selected by Congressional Quarterly.

dexes. This support was broad and was not concentrated only among key votes. Because Northern Democrats are always a large bloc in the House, their support is always critical to a Democratic president. Was this support due to Johnson's greater persuasiveness? Or was it due to less personal factors?

The latter explanation appears best to fit the facts. Kennedy, reputed to be less effective than Johnson with Congress,[74] obtained higher support than Johnson among Northern Democrats. Moreover, Northern Democrats, for reasons that are not clear, had been moving over the previous generation toward less support of presidents, both Democratic and Republican.

Yet other forces were at work. Johnson's average level of public approval over five years was 56 percent, whereas Carter's average over four years was only 47 percent. And Johnson won election by a landslide, whereas Carter barely prevailed over incumbent Gerald Ford.

In addition, significant modifications in the operation of Congress occurred between the administrations of Johnson and Carter—and these alterations were not the result of presidential leadership. The most visible of these changes was the dispersion of power, especially in the House.[75] Reformers democratized committees, diminishing the role of seniority as an automatic path to becoming a committee or subcommittee chair, and making the heads of committees more responsive to the desires of committee members. In the words of Representative Thomas Foley, "If I as Agriculture Committee chairman say to a member, 'I don't like your bill and I'm not going to schedule it,' I'll walk into the committee room and find a meeting going on without me."[76]

Similarly, subcommittees increased in number and in importance in handling legislation.[77] This greatly complicated the task of leadership, as was noted by Jim Wright, then House Majority Leader:

> The leadership's task must have been infinitely less complicated in the days of Mr. Rayburn and Mr. McCormack. In Mr. Rayburn's day, about all a majority leader or Speaker needed to do in order to get his program adopted was to deal effectively with perhaps 12 very senior committee chairmen. They, in turn, could be expected to influence their committees and their subcommittee chairmen whom they, in those days, appointed. . . . Well, now that situation is quite considerably different. There are, I think, 153 subcommittees. The full committee chairmen are not inviolable in their own precincts. They are not the great powers that they once were. They are dependent upon their own members for election and for the

support of their subcommittees for the program. And so, the leadership sometimes has to go beyond the committee chairmen. . . . [Therefore] we have to deal with a great many more people than was the case in Mr. Rayburn's day or Mr. McCormack's day.[78]

Members of both parties had larger personal, committee, and subcommittee staffs at their disposal, as well as new adjuncts such as the Congressional Budget Office. The number of lobbyists, independent policy analysts, and congressional work groups and caucuses, which are additional sources of expertise, also exploded. This new freedom and these additional resources, combined with more opportunities to amend legislation and more open hearings and markups, made it easier for members of Congress to inform themselves, challenge the White House (and congressional leadership), and provide alternatives to the president's policies.

There was also a heavy turnover in Congress in the 1970s, and new members brought with them new approaches to legislating. They were less likely to adopt the norms of apprenticeship, reciprocity, and specialization in their first terms than were their predecessors. Instead, the new members eagerly took an active role in all legislation,[79] placing a heavy emphasis on individualism and much less on party regularity.[80] Substantial turnover in membership also made it more difficult for leaders to develop personal relationships with members, relationships on which they might base persuasive efforts.

Thus, President Carter had more decision makers to influence than did LBJ. He could no longer rely on dealing with the congressional aristocracy and expect the rest of the members to follow. According to one assistant to Johnson, "In 1965, there were maybe ten or twelve people who you needed to corral in the House and Senate. Without those people, you were in for a tough time. Now, I'd put that figure upwards of one hundred. Believe it, there are so many people who have a shot at derailing a bill that the President has to double his effort for even routine decisions."[81] Andrew Manatos, who worked in congressional liaison for the Commerce Department, and his father, Mike, a congressional liaison aide in Lyndon Johnson's White House, wrote a report in which they concluded that the Ninety-fifth Congress (1977–78) was different from the Democratic congresses that President Johnson faced. "In the early 1960s, the 'Club' still controlled the congressional levers of power."[82] Now leaders had to persuade more people.

An aide to Carter commented on the same point:

> Take a good look at comprehensive energy. Look at how many stops it had to make in Congress. There was a great deal of committee interest but more important was the number of subcommittees who took some action. From our standpoint, it was just too complicated. It takes a real effort just to know where the legislation is, when the decisions are going to be made, and what needs to be done. There was a drop in our ability to influence outcomes in that kind of fragmented system.[83]

It is worth noting that Ronald Reagan's success in cutting social welfare expenditures in 1981 came only when he was able to bypass the decentralized decision-making process through a single vote on a massive budget proposal offered as an amendment to the House Budget Committee's budget resolution. As Reagan's lobbyist Kenneth Duberstein put it, "For most issues you have to lobby all 435 Congressmen and almost all 100 Senators."[84]

According to a lobbyist for the Department of Transportation in 1978, "Ten years ago, if you wanted a highway bill, you went to see [former House Public Works Committee chairman John] Blatnik, the Speaker, and the chairman of the Rules Committee. There would be a small collegial discussion—and all the political decisions would be made. Now there's no one person to see . . . You have to deal with everybody."[85] Speaker Tip O'Neill was just one of many who wistfully recalled the times when the party leadership could negotiate with a few other leaders who would deliver the promised votes. By the Carter years, things were different: "You don't have the discipline out there."[86]

In 1970, the House ended unrecorded teller votes (in which only the number of votes on each side is reported), and in 1973 it began electronic voting. Both changes led to an increase in the number of roll calls and thus an increase in the visibility of representatives' voting behavior. (There were 33 percent more nonunanimous roll calls on which the president took a stand per year under Jimmy Carter than under Lyndon Johnson.) This change in the rules stimulated the opposition to offer amendments on the floor and generated more pressure on House members to abandon their party, making it more difficult for the president to gain passage of legislation. Reforms that opened committee and subcommittee hearings to the public had the same effect.

Carter's program was also subject to more cross-cutting demands within Congress as a result of referrals from split and joint committees. This further complicated the president's job. A congressional liaison aide to Carter noted:

> The welfare-reform legislation was most difficult in the House. Disregarding our problems with the bill, we had a lot of trouble coordinating the lobbying effort. We had help from the departments, but on a bill like that the President has to supply the whip. The problem was in finding the horses. That bill moved to four committees in the House alone—Ways and Means, Agriculture, Education and Labor, and a special ad hoc committee on welfare reform. Within at least three of the committees, we had to deal with subcommittees—subcommittees on the budget impact as well as the legislative substance. We just didn't have the manpower. Neither did the departments. Now you tell me, how does the White House influence those kind of decisions in that many committees?[87]

Perhaps the most obvious difference between the Democratic administrations of the 1960s and Jimmy Carter's in the late 1970s is that Carter served during the period of congressional assertiveness that followed Vietnam and Watergate. The diminished deference to the president by individual members of Congress and by the institution as a whole naturally made presidential influence more problematic. As one Democratic member of Congress said in 1977, "We got such fun out of popping Nixon and Ford. We don't want to give it up and be good boys any more."[88]

Vietnam, Watergate, and a sagging economy also combined to make the public more skeptical of government policies. Anxiety over nuclear weapons, energy, and inflation replaced the optimism of the race to the moon and the idealism that fueled the war on poverty in the 1960s. For a president who desired to establish new programs, the outlook was not promising.

Carter also had the misfortune to preside during a period of substantial inflation and unemployment, whereas stable prices, sustained economic growth, and general prosperity characterized Kennedy's and Johnson's tenures. The prosperity of the 1960s provided the federal government with the funds for new policies, with little political risk. The president did not have to seek to raise taxes or ask the country to sacrifice to help the underprivileged. In the late 1970s, resources were more limited, making the passage of new welfare or health programs, for example, more difficult. When resources are scarce, presidents face internal competition for resources and must choose between policies rather than build coalitions for several policies through logrolling.

The policies of the 1970s and 1980s seemed to lack reliable bases of support. Barbara Sinclair persuasively demonstrated that coalitions in Congress, especially the Senate, became more fluid after Johnson's tenure. There were fewer members of Congress on whom a president could rely for support, and new Northern Democrats were considerably less reliable in their support of party leaders than their predecessors. Moreover, the issues of energy, environmental protection, inflation, consumer protection, and foreign and defense policy were divisive for Northern Democrats.[89]

The constant opposition he faced from the vocal and powerful liberal wing of his own party undermined Carter's ability to promote his policies. His press secretary, Jody Powell, reported that a survey of the press found that 75 percent of the critical commentary on the administration in 1977 came from Democrats, mostly liberals.[90] In 1980, the president had to deal with the challenge of Senator Edward Kennedy for the Democratic nomination for president. As Carter reflected more than a quarter century after leaving the White House, "The Democratic party was never mine. . . . I was never able to consolidate support in the Democratic party, particularly after Kennedy decided to run for president." Indeed, he could not even get a Democrat to sponsor his first piece of legislation—authority for reorganization of the executive branch.[91]

In the absence of a party consensus on policy, Carter's White House had to rely on forming discrete coalitions. Yet often the policies it proposed had no natural, organized constituency. The president himself reflected on his experience with Congress:

I think the main factor that was deleterious to the relationship was the controversial nature of the proposals that I presented to the Congress. We had to face up to some long postponed issues that I felt were in the best interests of our country to address: SALT II. The Middle East, where the Jewish lobby was aroused. Normalization with China, where the Taiwan lobby was aroused. The Panama Canal treaties . . . Energy legislation, where we aroused the animosity of both consumer groups and the oil industry. The Alaska lands bill, which had been long postponed. The environmental questions, particularly concerning Corps of Engineers projects in individual congressional districts or states. Those kinds of things were very important to me and . . . to the country. But there was nothing in any of those issues that I've just described to you that was politically beneficial to members of Congress. . . . Quite often it showed that our country had to face limits, that it had to make compromises, that it had to protect the environment in spite of opposition from some folks.[92]

An aide to Carter agreed with the president, adding, "We spent weeks and months trying to organize groups on hospital cost containment, but all the people that we wanted to feel passionately about it were insulated by insurance from the problem. The other side was able to organize influential people in the communities, the doctors and so on, the movers and shakers."[93]

It seems reasonable to conclude, then, that differences in the political and economic context of their presidencies, significant changes in the dispersion of power in Congress and the procedures and norms by which it operated, and the nature of their agendas provide at least most of the explanation of Carter's relative lack of support among Northern Democrats in comparison with Johnson's. Differences in the legislative persuasiveness of the two chief executives, on the other hand, makes little contribution to explaining congressional behavior.

Ronald Reagan

It was the Republicans' turn in 1981.[94] Although Ronald Reagan won only 51 percent of the vote in the 1980 presidential election, he beat incumbent Jimmy Carter by 10 percentage points, and the Republicans won a majority in the Senate for the first time since the 1952 election. The unexpectedly large size of Reagan's victory and the equally surprising outcomes in the Senate elections created the perception of an electoral mandate.

Unlike the other two modern mandates, 1932 and 1964, Reagan's victory placed a stigma on big government and exalted the unregulated marketplace and large defense budgets. More specifically, the terms of the debate over policy changed from which federal programs to expand to which ones to cut; from which civil rights rules to extend to which ones to limit; from how much to regulate to how little; from which natural resources to protect to which to develop; from how little to increase defense spending to how much; and from how little to cut taxes to how much. Reagan had won on much of his agenda before Congress took a single vote.

The new president also benefited from the nature of the times. Although 1981 was hardly a repeat of 1933, there was a definite sense of the need for immediate action to meet urgent problems. In its first issue after Reagan's inauguration, the *Congressional Quarterly Weekly Report* declared that "one of

Reagan's biggest advantages is the sense of both parties in Congress that the nation's problems are now very serious indeed."[95]

Similarly, David Stockman, a principal architect and proponent of Reagan's budgeting and tax proposals, remembers that when the president announced his "Program for Economic Recovery" to a joint session of Congress in February 1981, "the plan already had momentum and few were standing in the way." Reagan was "speaking to an assembly of desperate politicians who . . . were predisposed to grant him extraordinary latitude in finding a new remedy for the nation's economic ills . . . not because they understood the plan or even accepted it, but because they had lost all faith in the remedies tried before."[96] Paul Craig Roberts, a founder of supply-side economics and a principal advocate of it in the administration, recalled, "By the time Ronald Reagan entered the White House, only an incompetent administration could have lost the tax-cut battle."[97]

EXPLOITING THE OPPORTUNITY

The president's advisers recognized immediately that the perceptions of a mandate and the dramatic elevation of Republicans to majority status in the Senate provided it with a window of opportunity to effect major changes in public policy. Like LBJ, the White House knew it had to move quickly before the environment became less favorable. Thus, the president was ready with legislation, even though it was complex and hastily written.[98] Moreover, within a week of the March 30, 1981, assassination attempt on Reagan, Michael Deaver convened a meeting of other high-ranking aides at the White House to determine how best to take advantage of the new political capital the shooting had created.

The Reagan administration also knew it lacked the political capital to pass a broad program. Thus, it enforced a rigorous focus on the president's economic plan and defense spending, its priority legislation, and essentially ignored divisive social issues and tried to keep Central America on the back burner.[99] According to Max Friedersdorf, the head of Reagan's legislative liaison office, "In '81, during the whole course of the year, we only had three major votes."[100] These votes took place at wide intervals. By focusing its political resources on its priorities, the administration succeeded in using the budget to pass sweeping changes in taxation and defense policy.

It was wise for Reagan to exploit his opportunities. When the issue of the sale of AWACS planes to Saudi Arabia arose, the White House initially handled it clumsily and had to come from behind to win a victory that should never have been in doubt. It was simply preoccupied with other matters and could not devote its attention to the next item on the agenda. The going was much tougher the next year as the United States suffered a severe recession, and for the rest of his tenure, commentators frequently described Reagan's budgets as DOA: Dead on Arrival.

THE IMPACT OF LEADERSHIP

In an interview near the end of President Reagan's first two years in office, Richard Cheney, then the chair of the House Republican Policy Committee, attributed the president's success in 1981 to the results of the 1980 election, public support, the attempted assassination of the president, and Reagan's having proposed policies in which Republicans in Congress believed, not to the White House's personal dealings with members.[101] There were actually fewer Democratic defections in the House from the party's stand on Gramm-Latta II, the final vote on the budget resolution, than on any such vote in previous years. It did not matter, however, because the president had sufficient votes within his own party as a result of the election of 1980.

As it was for Lyndon Johnson, party was the dominant factor in the Reagan administration's relations with Congress. In contrasting President Reagan's difficulties with Congress in 1983–1984 with his more productive experience in 1981–1982, Tom Loeffler, the House Republican chief deputy whip, commented, "The difference is that in 1981 and 1982 the White

House was more capable of pushing the president's program through Congress simply because the makeup of the House was different."[102]

Personal appeals. The president's personal efforts at persuading members of Congress receive much attention from those who write about the president's legislative skills. These appeals take several forms, including telephone calls and private meetings in the Oval Office. Their common characteristic is that the president personally lobbies a member of Congress intimately, seeking support or at least lack of opposition on a vote.

According to Neustadt, "when the chips are down, there is no substitute for the President's own footwork, his personal negotiation, his direct appeal, his voice and no other's on the telephone."[103] Members of Congress are typically impressed when the president calls them or invites them for a personal discussion at the White House. This is a rare occurrence for most of them, and a request for support from the chief executive naturally increases their sense of self-esteem.[104] They are after all dealing directly with the president and perhaps their party leader.

Despite their potential utility, personal appeals from the president for support are not common. A legislative aide to Lyndon Johnson commented, "It was a very rare thing that he called a member of the House respecting a vote."[105] Presidents typically make personal appeals to individual legislators only after the long process of lining up votes is almost done and they need a last few votes to win on an important issue.[106] These situations usually arise only a few times a year. When they do call, presidents focus on uncommitted or weakly committed members of Congress or, to make the most of their efforts, on key members who provide cues for others.[107]

Even if the president is enthusiastic about calling for support—and not all are—his aides must be concerned about conserving the uniqueness of a presidential appeal. Calls from the president must be relatively rare to maintain their usefulness. If the president calls too often, his calls will have less impact.

In addition, members may begin to expect calls, for which the president has limited time. As one former legislative aide at the White House remarked, if a president calls a member of the House regarding a vote, 434 members cry out, "Why didn't he call me?"[108]

An aide to President Carter made the same point:

> You have to be careful when you use the president. A visit with the president or a call from the president has to be an event in the life of a senator or representative, or it loses its magic. Or they say, "Why should I give you a commitment? I want to talk to the President. John has talked to the President. And George has talked to the President. Are you taking us for granted?" You've got to be sure that you don't squander him.[109]

Ronald Reagan was quite an active president in terms of appealing for support to individual members of Congress, especially in 1981.[110] He may have been too zealous, however. Pamela J. Turner, the White House's chief lobbyist in the Senate, explained in 1984, "People now have the idea that if the president doesn't call them personally or see them, the White House doesn't care. Maybe we did our job too well in that first year."[111]

Also, the credibility of the president's staff in speaking for him will decrease the more the president speaks for himself.[112] As President Carter explained, "I would try not to get involved in that process unless the legislation was important enough to warrant my direct consideration."[113] Thus, presidential aides, not the president himself, do most direct White House lobbying.

There are other potential costs to presidential appeals. Some members of Congress may resent the application of high-level pressure on them. Moreover, representatives and senators have a natural resistance to acting as rubber stamps for the president. Speaking in 1982, then chair of the House Republican Policy Committee Richard Cheney observed, "You can lean on the guys only so many times a month. . . . Every once in a while the troops have to rear up and establish their independence."[114]

On the other hand, members of Congress may exploit a call to extract a favor from the president and say they are uncertain about an issue. When the White House calls and asks for support, representatives and senators frequently raise a question regarding some request that they have made.[115] In the words of an aide to Eisenhower, "Every time we make a special appeal to a Congressman to change his position, he eventually comes back with a request for a favor ranging in importance from one of the President's packages of matches to a judgeship or cabinet appointment for a worthy constituent."[116]

Sometimes members of Congress go to great lengths to create bargaining resources for themselves. Representative Harold Rogers, a long-time supporter of the MX missile, was absent from the vote of the House Appropriations Committee on the president's request to purchase twenty-one additional missiles. He missed the vote not because of a change of heart about the weapon, but to gain leverage with which to influence the tobacco support program, a policy of great concern to his constituents. Because the MX was important to President Reagan and the vote was close, the White House wasted no time in arranging a meeting to hear the congressman's complaint.[117]

Reagan's budget director David Stockman was quite candid about the concessions that members of Congress demanded in return for their support for the tax cut of 1981, including special breaks for holders of oil leases, real estate tax shelters, and generous loopholes that virtually eliminated the corporate income tax. "The hogs were really feeding," he declared. "The greed level, the level of opportunism, just got out of control."[118] For obvious reasons, the White House does not want to encourage this tendency among members of Congress.

There is an additional constraint on using personal appeals from the president: The White House is hesitant to have the president commit his prestige to a bill by personally lobbying and then fail.[119] To put the president on the line in a very personal way and then lose entails substantial costs for the chief executive, undermining his professional reputation within Washington and his standing with the general public. In 1987,

President Reagan went to Capitol Hill to plead with thirteen Republican senators not to vote to override his veto of a highway bill. When not one of the thirteen supported him in the final showdown, the resulting stories of the president's failure did him little good.

Appeals are inherently risky, especially when the president makes them to members of the opposition party (which is why they are rarely made), and the president wants to avoid incurring embarrassing political damage that reflects poorly on his leadership qualities. For example, two days before the vote on the second and final budget resolution in 1981, known as Gramm-Latta II, President Reagan invited to the White House all sixty-three of the Southern Democrats who had supported him on the first budget resolution. Fewer than forty even showed up, and defeat appeared certain on one of the most important votes of his administration. The president was not taking an active role in one-on-one lobbying and even left town before the vote was to take place. Then the House Rules Committee refused to propose a rule allowing a single vote of yea or nay on the budget resolution. This move aroused the Republicans' partisan energies, and victory seemed within reach. The critical budget vote actually occurred on the procedural matter of the rule. Only at this point did the president place his calls (from Los Angeles) to individual Democratic representatives.[120]

In this case, the president called fifteen Democrats and seven supported him on the vote on the rule.[121] Although we will never know whether Reagan's telephone calls were the determining factor in the decisions of these representatives, and although we must not arbitrarily dismiss the president's persuasiveness, we should be cautious of accepting the results of the vote on Gramm-Latta II as clear evidence of the impact of presidential appeals. Some of the seven who supported him might not have done so in the absence of his calls, but the president made personal appeals only to those whom his aides identified as swing votes: representatives who were fiscally conservative and inclined to support budget cuts but who remained undecided.[122] In addition, eight of the sixteen still voted against the president. The point is not that presidential appeals cannot influence votes, but that the president changed at most a few votes at the end of coalition building. Appeals are at the margins, not the core, of policy change.

Equally important, 1981 was the high point of presidential appeals in Reagan's administration. The president enjoyed favorable conditions for making appeals in his first year in office. Circumstances were not so favorable in the following years for a variety of reasons, and the president did not press as hard or as often. There was no point to his doing so when politics as usual prevailed and the president's chances of victory dimmed.

Reagan's hesitancy to intervene personally in the legislative process has puzzled some observers, who found him a curious blend of political pragmatism and ideological rigidity, passionate aggressiveness and studied passivity. Part of the explanation of these seeming contradictions is straightforward. Because the White House sensed a lack of responsiveness in Congress to the president's proposals, the president became a more passive participant in the legislative process and fell back on his ideological themes.

Given the separation of powers, presidents are not in a position to issue orders to their congressional troops. Rather, they rely on the soft sell, as President Reagan did when calling members of Congress on the eve of a budget vote in 1981: "Gee, I know it's late back there and I'm sorry to bother you. I hear you're still on the fence. If I could answer any questions, I'd be happy to. I know you've been under a lot of pressure. But I hope you can find your way clear to supporting us tomorrow."[123]

When presidents do make personal appeals for support, they may very well receive it. President Reagan, for example, appeared to have great success with his appeals on his budget and taxing proposals and the sale of AWACS planes to Saudi Arabia in 1981.[124] Yet there are also many failures.[125] Sometimes members of Congress will not even listen to their party leader. In 1984, Nancy Johnson, a freshman representative, refused to attend a private meeting with Ronald Reagan about the MX missile.[126] In one instance, the chair of the House Appropriations Committee refused even to take a call from President Johnson.[127] Another time, the Senate majority leader, Mike Mansfield, asked Johnson to talk directly to the president's old friend, Senator Richard Russell. Johnson complained to a White House legislative aide, "Well, goddamit . . . I couldn't get Dick Russell to vote with me when I was majority leader. What makes Mike think he's going to vote with me now?"[128]

In addition, what appears to be the successful use of personal appeals may actually represent the effectiveness of another factor. According to an aide to Ronald Reagan, the president's contacts with members of Congress before the tax vote of 1981 were "merely a device to keep the congressmen thinking about what could happen next year. I'm sure Mr. Reagan is charming as hell, but that isn't what is important. It's his reminding these people that they could lose their jobs next year."[129]

Four years later, the House initially rejected a tax reform bill that President Reagan very much wanted passed. After the vote, the president called many Republicans (who had overwhelmingly opposed the bill), asking for their support. He even made an unusual trip to Capitol Hill to address his party cohorts. In the end the bill passed, with the help of fifty-four Republicans who changed from opposition to support. Yet the president's personal appeals probably had less influence on Republicans than his assurances that he would veto any tax bill that reached his desk without a number of changes they desired, and the change of heart of the House minority leader, Robert Michel, who decided to support the president. By defeating the bill on the first vote, Republicans created bargaining advantages for themselves, which they used to extract explicit promises from Reagan.[130]

Despite the prestige of their office, their position as party leader, their personal persuasiveness, and their strong personalities, presidents often meet resistance from members of Congress to their appeals for support. Personal appeals by themselves are useful but unreliable instruments for passing legislation. As a result, one-on-one lobbying by the president is the exception rather than the rule. The White House conserves appeals for obtaining the last few votes on issues of special significance to it, a recognition that presidents cannot personally persuade members of Congress with any frequency.

Comparing Republican presidents. Comparing the legislative skills of Republican presidents is a difficult task. Eisenhower was supposedly bungling and ineffective, but this view had undergone significant revision.[131] Commentators often described Nixon's efforts as confrontational and negative, and so perhaps he would rate as the weakest of the four Republicans in legislative skills.[132] Gerald Ford was an experienced congressional hand, and his relationships with legislators were cordial. Ronald Reagan began his term with rave reviews for his handling of Congress, but his legislative relations soured considerably in the years that followed. Observers often commented that George H. W. Bush lacked Reagan's charisma but was a Washington insider with highly developed interpersonal skills. His son was a highly polarizing figure less oriented to cooperating with members of Congress.[133] About all that one can safely conclude is that each president was unique in his approach to Congress and that, based on their legislative skills, one should expect the lowest support for Nixon and perhaps higher support for Ford and Reagan.

Table 4.3 gives the average figures for support of Republican presidents in the House (1974 has been omitted because both Nixon and Ford served in that year). The patterns across the six presidents are fascinating, but they do not seem to relate to their legislative skills. Support by Northern Democrats steadily diminished for each succeeding president, just as it did for Democratic presidents. Southern Democratic support increased notably for Nixon and Ford over that for Eisenhower but then steadily diminished as Republicans captured seats held by conservative Democrats. In general the polarization of politics since the 1980s has led to steadily diminishing Democratic support and steadily increasing Republican support for Republican presidents. Reagan is in the middle of this trend

146

TABLE 4.3
House Support for Republican Presidents (%)

Eisenhower, 1953–1960

	Nonunanimous Support*	Key Votes**
Democrats	42	42
Northern Democrats	49	50
Southern Democrats	33	31
Republicans	64	65

Nixon, 1969–1973

	Nonunanimous Support	Key Votes
Democrats	41	36
Northern Democrats	39	31
Southern Democrats	48	46
Republicans	64	64

Ford, 1975–1976

	Nonunanimous Support	Key Votes
Democrats	35	32
Northern Democrats	29	24
Southern Democrats	48	51
Republicans	68	70

Reagan, 1981–1988

	Nonunanimous Support*	Key Votes**
Democrats	29	28
Northern Democrats	23	21
Southern Democrats	42	45
Republicans	70	72

TABLE 4.3 (*continued*)
House Support for Republican Presidents (%)

George H. W. Bush, 1989–1992

	Nonunanimous Support	Key Votes
Democrats	27	33
Northern Democrats	23	27
Southern Democrats	38	47
Republicans	73	73

George W. Bush, 2001–2007

	Nonunanimous Support	Key Votes
Democrats	20	21
Northern Democrats	17	18
Southern Democrats	30	30
Republicans	84	84

* On roll-call votes on which the winning side was supported by fewer than 80 percent of those voting.

** As selected by Congressional Quarterly.

and also in the middle of levels of support from members of both parties.

It is difficult to look across the records of these six Republican presidents and discern patterns of legislative support that are related to their legislative skills. Both our inclusive and exclusive indices of presidential support show broad patterns of congressional backing of presidents and the limited variance in support among presidents serving in the same era but with different legislative styles. There is certainly no evidence that Nixon did more poorly than we might expect from studying only the trend lines. Nor is there evidence of Reagan doing better. It is interesting that Reagan and George H. W. Bush received very similar levels of support despite substantially different personalities and leadership styles.

In the Senate (table 4.4), we find patterns of presidential support similar to those in the House. Republican support steadily

TABLE 4.4
Senate Support for Republican Presidents (%)

Eisenhower, 1953–1960		
	Nonunanimous Support*	Key Votes**
Democrats	38	37
Northern Democrats	38	35
Southern Democrats	38	39
Republicans	69	71

Nixon, 1969–1973		
	Nonunanimous Support	Key Votes
Democrats	34	38
Northern Democrats	27	29
Southern Democrats	49	58
Republicans	65	67

Ford, 1975–1976		
	Nonunanimous Support	Key Votes
Democrats	33	27
Northern Democrats	25	19
Southern Democrats	55	50
Republicans	65	59

Reagan, 1981–1988		
	Nonunanimous Support	Key Votes
Democrats	31	28
Northern Democrats	26	23
Southern Democrats	44	44
Republicans	74	75

TABLE 4.4 (*continued*)
Senate Support for Republican Presidents (%)

George H. W. Bush, 1989–1992		
	Nonunanimous	
	Support	*Key Votes*
Democrats	29	28
Northern Democrats	25	23
Southern Democrats	40	39
Republicans	75	79

George W. Bush, 2001–2007		
	Nonunanimous	
	Support	*Key Votes*
Democrats	17	27
Northern Democrats	15	24
Southern Democrats	33	45
Republicans	86	84

* On roll-call votes on which the winning side was supported by fewer than 80 percent of those voting.

** As selected by Congressional Quarterly.

increased, while Democratic support diminished for each succeeding president. Southern Democrats increased their support for Nixon and Ford and then decreased it for each of their successors. Once again, there appears to be no relationship between the support obtained by presidents and their legislative skills. Richard Nixon did no worse, indeed often better, than the old congressional hand with very different skills, Gerald Ford. There is nothing exceptional about Reagan's support. Broader forces dominated congressional reactions to presidential legislative stands.

-o- -o- -o-

Even presidents who appeared to dominate Congress were actually facilitators rather than directors of change. They understood their own limitations and explicitly took advantage of opportunities in their environments. Working at the margins, they successfully guided legislation through Congress. When their resources diminished, they reverted to the stalemate that usually characterizes presidential-congressional relations. As legendary management expert Peter Drucker put it about Ronald Reagan, "His great strength was not charisma, as is commonly thought, but his awareness and acceptance of exactly what he could and what he could not do."[134]

These conclusions are consistent with systematic research by Jon Bond, Richard Fleisher, and B. Dan Wood. They have focused on determining whether the presidents to whom we attribute the greatest skills in dealing with Congress were more successful in obtaining legislative support for their policies than were other presidents. After carefully controlling for other influences on congressional voting, they found no evidence that those presidents who supposedly were the most proficient in persuading Congress were more successful than chief executives with less aptitude at influencing legislators.[135]

Scholars studying leadership within Congress have reached similar conclusions about the limits on personal leadership. Cooper and Brady found that institutional context is more important than personal leadership skills or traits in determining the influence of leaders and that there is no relationship between leadership style and effectiveness.[136]

Presidential legislative leadership operates in an environment largely beyond the president's control and must compete with other, more stable factors that affect voting in Congress in addition to party. These include ideology, personal views and commitments on specific policies, and the interests of constituencies. By the time a president tries to exercise influence on a vote, most members of Congress have made up their minds on the basis of these other factors. Thus, a president's legislative leadership is likely to be critical only for those members of Congress who remain open to conversion after other influences have had their impact. Although the size and composition of this group varies from issue to issue, it will almost always be a minority in each chamber.

It is important to note that it is not necessary to take an extreme position to obtain a better understanding of the nature of presidential leadership. There are times, of course, when presidents do persuade some members of Congress to change their votes. A famous example of apparent large-scale change occurred over the Panama Canal treaties, ratified in 1978. In the fall of 1976, shortly before Jimmy Carter became president, forty-eight senators introduced a resolution pledging not to approve any change in the existing treaties regarding the canal. After a full-court press, Carter obtained the two-thirds vote in the Senate to ratify the new treaties.[137]

The issue for us is not whether persuasion is *ever* successful in moving a member of Congress. Instead, the question is whether persuasion is typically the key to presidential success in Congress. Examples such as the Panama Canal treaties are rare. Whatever the circumstances, the impact of persuasion on the outcome is usually relatively modest. As Calvin Mouw and Michael MacKuen concluded, "presidential influence in Congress does not rely on persuasion."[138] Although potentially important, conversion is likely to be at the margins of coalition building rather than at the core of policy change. Presidential legislative leadership is more useful in exploiting discrete opportunities than in creating broad possibilities for policy change.

5 Leading Congress
Less Favorable Contexts

CHAPTER 4 focused on periods of major change in policy that occurred under especially favorable conditions for presidents. Rather than creating opportunities for change, Franklin D. Roosevelt, Lyndon Johnson, and Ronald Reagan recognized the nature of the opportunities their environments presented them and effectively exploited these circumstances while they lasted. They adapted their agendas to the context in which they found themselves and worked intensely to push through legislation.

Most environments are not so conducive to change, however. There are great differences in the contexts of presidencies, and we should not expect every president to have the same impact on public policy. As Richard Neustadt said of Jimmy Carter, "Too much is expected of a President in Carter's shoes. . . . Washingtonians, like less attentive publics, tend to project on the Presidency expectations far exceeding anyone's assured capacity to carry through. Objectively, 1977 had little in common with 1965; still, as Carter started out the LBJ analogy filled many minds. . . . Whatever were they thinking of? Ignorance is bliss."[1]

Presidents must largely play the hands that the public deals them through its voting in presidential and congressional elections and its evaluations of the chief executive's job performance.[2] Presidents are rarely in a position to augment substantially their political resources. Since World War II, it has been common for presidents to face Congresses in which the opposition party holds a majority of the seats. In addition, there may be no slack resources, the president's own party may be split, the issues already on the national agenda may be especially controversial and resist compromise, and the president's electoral mandate may be modest or nonexistent.

Some presidents, then, face greater challenges in changing policy than do others. Having seen that facilitation rather than persuasion was the key to successful leadership in contexts favorable to the president's policies, we need to investigate presidents governing in more typical circumstances. In this chapter, I first examine the presidency of George H. W. Bush, who took office with perhaps the worst strategic position of any president in the twentieth century. Then I focus on his son, George W. Bush, who began his tenure with a tenuous majority in Congress and a loss in the popular vote for president.

These presidents did not enjoy the same level of success as their predecessors who governed in more auspicious circumstances. They did have some important achievements in Congress, however. Like Roosevelt, Johnson, and Reagan, the Bushes' success resulted from the interplay of circumstances and their skills at understanding and exploiting them. In other words, facilitative leadership was at the core of their success.

George H. W. Bush:
Leading in Unfavorable Circumstances

Following conservative icon Ronald Reagan would have been difficult for any president, especially a Republican one. Moreover, the conditions in which Reagan's successor, George H. W. Bush, found himself were not felicitous. Yet the president had successes and dealt with a number of major and contentious issues. Thus, the George H. W. Bush presidency is instructive in increasing our understanding of how presidents may make the most of the circumstances in which they serve and that are beyond their power to change.

STRATEGIC POSITION

When Bush took the oath of office on January 20, 1989, he was already fighting an uphill battle. He began his tenure with one of the worst strategic positions of any newly elected president in American history.

New presidents traditionally claim a mandate from the people, because the most effective means of setting the terms of debate and overcoming opposition is the perception of an electoral mandate, an impression that the voters want to see the winner's programs implemented. Indeed, major changes in policy, as in 1933, 1965, and 1981, virtually never occur in the absence of such perceptions.

Mandates can be powerful symbols in American politics. They accord added legitimacy and credibility to the newly elected president's proposals. Concerns for representation and political survival encourage members of Congress to support the president if they feel the people have spoken.[3] As a result, mandates change the premises of decision. As we saw in chapter 4, perceptions of a mandate in 1980 placed a stigma on big government and exalted the unregulated marketplace and large defense budgets, providing Ronald Reagan a very favorable strategic position for dealing with Congress.

George H. W. Bush was not so fortunate. The conditions of his electoral victory undermined any claims that the White House could make as to having received a mandate. The new president's popular vote percentage was a respectable but unimpressive 53 percent, and his party lost seats in both houses of Congress. He actually ran behind the winners in 379 of the 435 congressional districts. Thus, there was little basis for members of Congress inferring presidential coattails.

Other factors that might encourage the perception of a mandate were also missing in 1988. The press did not engage in the hyperbolic analyses that characterized coverage of the 1980 election results, and since Bush had led in the polls throughout the entire post-convention period, his victory lacked the psychological advantage of surprise. Furthermore, Bush emphasized continuity, not change, in his campaign and did not offer bold new initiatives.[4]

Thus, the new president's strategic position was not one in which he was able to structure the choices of Congress as being for or against a chief executive who had the support of the people.

A second important leadership resource for a president is the strength of his party in Congress. President Bush took office facing the largest opposition majority in Congress of any newly elected president in American history—Democratic advantages of ten seats in the Senate and eight-five seats in the House.

Lack of leadership resources was not Bush's only problem. The budget deficit also tightly restricted his ability to take policy initiatives, because there was very little in the way of slack resources with which to take them. The overriding concern had to be meeting the requirements of the Gramm-Rudman-Hollings legislation that was designed to balance the budget. Yet reducing expenditures is extremely difficult. Most of the budget, ranging from Social Security to payments on the national debt, falls under the heading of "uncontrollable" and is not subject to either annual review or quick fixes. In addition, Ronald Reagan cut all that was politically feasible to trim from "discretionary" domestic policy programs. Bush could not make a mark by wringing even more from them.

That left defense spending. There was no popular support for increasing the defense budget (Reagan had done that already too), especially in the Gorbachev era. At the same time, there had been no real growth in defense spending in the second Reagan term, making the Pentagon's budget difficult to reduce. Bush could do little but leave it the same until the fall of communism in Central and Eastern Europe.

In addition, problems left over from the previous administration, ranging from the budget deficit and bailing out savings and loan institutions, to cleaning up nuclear power plants and wringing corruption from federal housing programs, filled the government agenda. As a result, the president was largely re-

duced to pronouncing platitudes about a "kinder, gentler nation" and being the "education president."

Thus, Bush was in a weak position to move forward or back-
wards. The historical context of his presidency forced him into
the role of consolidating the policy shifts of his predecessor and
managing government well after the era of Ronald Reagan's
anti-government and anti-communism activism of the 1980s.
Bush political strategist Robert Teeter set the administration in
historical context when he described the 1988 election as one
that was to build on the changes Reagan had brought to government, not to change them. Once in office, Bush emphasized
continuity, as did his chief of staff, John Sununu.[5]

THE BUSH AGENDA

Such an approach fit fairly comfortably with the new president's personal agenda, which was modest. A Doonesbury car-
toon published before his inauguration had Bush on his first
day in office declaring: "So far today, I've said the Pledge and I
haven't joined the ACLU and I haven't furloughed any murder-
ers. I've delivered on my entire mandate, and it isn't even lunch
yet." At the end of Bush's first year in office, conservative columnist George Will summarized it with "Bush Promised Little;
We Got What He Promised."[6] In November 1990, John Sununu
told a conservative audience, "There's not a single piece of legislation that needs to be passed in the next two years for this
president. In fact, if Congress wants to come together, adjourn,
and leave, it's all right with us."[7]

Sununu was exaggerating, but it is true that the president
promised little. A limited agenda is not on its face illegitimate,
however, and in our analyses of presidents we ought not to
have a bias toward activism, in which we presume bold programs and "action" are good. Equally important, we should
not assume a large agenda is appropriate in all circumstances,
especially when the president is leading from a weak strategic
position.

GOVERNING TO ACHIEVE *His* GOALS

The conventional wisdom holds that one of Ronald Reagan's greatest strengths was his ability to project a vision of where he wanted the country to move. On the other hand, critics often complained that George H. W. Bush either lacked such a vision (essentially, coherent policy positions) or at least failed to effectively articulate one. This stewardship of competence without a compass, they said, detracted from his ability to build a strong image and to lead the American people and Congress.

Many criticized Gerald Ford and Jimmy Carter for exactly the same thing. Interestingly, this criticism is also reminiscent of Arthur Schlesinger, Jr.'s description of FDR, who he said was committed to people, not ideology; had "no philosophy save experiment, which was a technique; constitutionalism, which was a procedure; and humanity, which was a faith."[8] (This sounds like a "procedural presidency," which some criticized Bush for operating.[9])

Nevertheless, charges of a government adrift and of a president without moorings are serious. It is true that Bush's understated style, lack of big, new proposals, and the absence of calls to follow him on a crusade rarely inspired the public with a sense of purpose or conveyed a sense of a unifying theme and a cohesive program.

George Bush lacked rhetorical skill, and he knew it. He was uncomfortable in the "bully pulpit" but also believed that public saber rattling was counterproductive. Thus, he preferred to move incrementally toward solutions to discrete problems rather than engage in conceptual, strategic thinking and grand oratory. He went public as much as his predecessors, but he was more comfortable building consensus one-on-one, behind closed doors. Broad coalitions crafted through brokerage politics were his preferred method of problem resolution.

It is one thing to describe Bush's limitations as a public communicator. It is something quite different to attribute significance to them—and there has been more uninformed discussion here than on any area of the Bush presidency. Rhetorical skill aside, and few presidents have it, we must ask if Bush's approach was appropriate for his goals and the context in which he was operating. In general, it was.

The criticism of Bush as a public leader assumed that there was another viable choice in political strategy—that the president could have moved the public and accomplished more. Just what this "more" was, was typically left unspecified. Many conservatives agreed with columnist George Will's argument that Bush should have appealed more to the public and forced polarizing choices, losing some points off his approval ratings but solidifying a committed core of the public to serve as the base for changes in policy.[10]

The fact that there is virtually no evidence to support the proposition that presidents can successfully lead Congress by taking their cases over its head directly to the people and that Ronald Reagan attempted repeatedly to mobilize the public and succeeded only once—in a highly unusual circumstance and on a large tax cut[11]—seemed to make little impression on these critics. Indeed, they did not seem to understand their own history. One is tempted to repeat Neustadt's question, "Whatever [were] . . . they thinking of?"

The seeming lack of clarity in Bush's policy stances may have confused those accustomed to the stark positions of the Reagan administration, but they are not difficult to understand if one thinks of the president as a moderate Republican, not a zealot—a Tory who experienced conflicting impulses and who was not interested in polarizing the country to bring about substantial change.

The Buchanan Brigades of the far right were especially distressed with the president's moderation. He failed to condemn the Chinese government's repression of the democracy movement with sufficient vigor to satisfy them, and he similarly failed to support the secession movements in the Soviet Baltic states in any tangible way. Bush's support for environmental legislation, civil rights, higher taxes, Puerto Rican statehood, relaxation of high-tech exports to Eastern Europe, rights for the disabled, and a lack of restrictions on National Endowment for the Arts and his civil orientation toward homosexual groups (the Republican convention not withstanding) disappointed many on the Republican right.[12] The desertion of conservative House Republicans on the vote on the president's hard-won budget compromise in October 1990 was one of the low points of the Bush administration.

The president's stances throughout the range of public policies reflect his conflicting impulses. He supported a strong and comprehensive Clean Air Act and strengthened EPA enforcement of environmental protection regulations, but then he moderated in the face of trade-offs between the environment and jobs—much like Bill Clinton in Arkansas.

In the area of civil rights, Bush promoted the Americans with Disabilities Act, vigorous enforcement of the Voting Rights Act and the Fair Housing Act, and most of what became the 1991 Civil Rights Act. The administration tried to walk the thin line between sanctioning discrimination and endorsing big government. Thus, its opposition to special preferences for African Americans was not a function of racial prejudice but of a general antagonism to statism and a preference for personal freedom. Sensitivity to minority rights clashed with individualist inclinations.

During the Bush years, spending on social programs such as Medicaid, Elementary Education, Food Stamps, Head Start, and Child Nutrition grew much more rapidly than under Reagan (and often even than under Carter). Although Bush did not always take the lead, he negotiated reasonable compromises consistent with his views. It made sense to hammer out compromises, given the numbers in Congress. He could, of course, have made the grand gesture and ended up with a worse bill and an override of his veto. Moreover, he compromised even when it cost him politically, which it often did because the country would not credit him for a settlement and the choices were complicated and obscure and difficult to explain in a sound bite.

We find a similar moderation—and complexity—in foreign policy. The success of Operation Desert Storm was only possible because of the coalition assembled by George Bush—one unparalleled in world history—and one that would not have supported the direct overthrow of Saddam Hussein. At the end of his term, the United States deployed, for the first time in history, its armed forces for large-scale humanitarian purposes in a foreign nation (Somalia)—but only after he had exhausted the alternatives and laid the groundwork for a consensual policy.

Communism would have fallen no matter who was in the White House, but Bush deftly encouraged the dismantling of the Eastern bloc without being overly assertive and provoking a defensive backlash from the Soviet Union. The unification of Germany took discreet action and masterly skill and the ability to recognize and exploit an opportunity for achievement. The same is true of the unprecedented arms control agreements negotiated with Russia and the negotiations in the Middle East following the Gulf War.

The U.S. show of force that helped stave off the attempted coup in the Philippines also required subtle actions, not grand gestures. It is easy to forget that Central America was a hot spot in U.S. foreign policy when Bush took office, but he cooled the rhetoric and quietly helped depolarize the conflict and bring about a peaceful transition to a more democratic regime in Nicaragua.

The moderation of his policy stances led many to conclude that Bush lacked strong policy preferences. Yet the record shows that he stuck to his guns on basic economic policy, including free trade (which expanded greatly under Bush), enterprise zones, capital gains cuts, and deregulation. The 1990 budget agreement was a bold policy, and Bush made it stick in the face of enormous pressure to break it. The agreement forced Congress to find offsetting spending reductions or tax increases for every increase in spending and to meet his goal of limiting spending. The act made the most important legislative contribution to the disappearance of the federal deficit in the late 1990s, dramatically affecting net revenues and structuring the consideration of future budgets. Bush also quietly persevered and finished the costly job of bailing out the savings and loan institutions with minimal disruption to the economy.

Bush was also consistent on a wide range of other issues, including abortion, family leave, education reform, and relations with China—always in the face of strong criticism from the opposition.

Thus, the president crafted compromises in quiet negotiations over the budget, civil rights, environmental protection, and other critical areas. As a result, he made progress on numerous fronts despite his unfavorable strategic position. Bush understood both the opportunities in his environment and the most effective way of exploiting them to achieve his goals.

A REACTIVE PRESIDENCY

Nevertheless, there is only so far a president attempting to lead from a weak strategic position can go. It is difficult to overcome the lack of political resources, such as a majority party cohort in the houses of Congress. In addition, the orientation toward governing that helped Bush enjoy some success in the context in which he was operating was also inherently limited.

No matter who was president during Bush's tenure, Li Peng, Mikhail Gorbachev, Eastern European Democrats, and Manuel Noriega would have foisted much of his agenda upon him. One could argue that smaller agendas leave more time for concentration on events, especially momentous events such as those we witnessed in the early 1990s. A Tory who views his presidency as a stewardship may find such an orientation quite compatible.

Nevertheless, it is usually wise for the president to focus Congress's attention on his priority programs. Otherwise, they may become lost in the complex and overloaded legislative process. Of course, setting the agenda for Congress requires having one, and Bush had only a modest agenda. In addition, the greatest chances of success in passing legislation are at the beginning of a new president's term. Bush, however, hit the ground coasting, not running. The White House was quick to announce that there would be no One Hundred Days in the Bush administration!

Similarly, the president needs to engage the public to encourage Congress to make progress on many difficult issues. Even though the president cannot move Congress to his point of view through a few prime-time addresses, he needs to lay the groundwork for policy change. The issues on which Bush went all out and took political risks to win in Congress—the Tower and Thomas nominations, the veto override on visas for Chinese students, the war with Iraq, and the 1990 budget agreement—had a natural attraction for the media, and the press could frame the cases of Tower, Thomas, and Iraq in personal terms. As a result, the press accorded them extensive coverage. Most issues require more initiative from the White House, however.

In general, Bush was not skilled at explaining what he wanted, what he was doing, or what he had done. In addition, he made little connection between his public relations and his policy initiatives. He held more press conferences in a year than Ronald Reagan did in eight years and met frequently with reporters in informal ways as well. Yet he used these sessions to respond to journalists' inquiries rather than as part of an effort to advance his own policies.

It is also helpful to structure the choices on high-priority items on the White House's agenda. As we saw in chapter 3, framing issues in ways that favor the president's programs may set the terms of the public and congressional debate on his proposals and thus the premises on which members of Congress cast their votes. Presidents who do not attempt to set the terms of debate on important issues and structure the choices of citizens and legislators are likely to find themselves in a reactive mode. Administrations with limited agendas and passive orientations have the most potential for events and opponents to dictate the foci of their administrations and frame the choices before the country. We have also seen, of course, that there certainly is no guarantee that presidents will succeed in setting the terms of debate on public policy.[13] Nevertheless, if the president abandons the field, there is a substantial risk that his opponents will define him and his policies.

The president must also protect himself by projecting an image of someone with a concern and a direction. For example, through his public rhetoric, Ronald Reagan bought himself some protection from criticism on the budget deficit, religiosity, and family values, despite considerable variance between his stated views and his actual behavior.

The Bush White House allowed opponents to structure the issue of cuts in taxes on capital gains as a decision regarding equity ("benefits for the rich") rather than in terms of efficiency ("creating jobs"). The former had little chance of passage through a Democratic Congress, while Democrat Bill Clinton could—and did—support the latter. Bush genuinely wanted to be the "Education President," and he proposed a genuinely innovative policy to improve education in America. Yet he had little impact on the public debate about education policy and was not able to structure discussion around his proposal. This takes sustained effort and effective public relations techniques, and the Bush White House evidenced neither.

THE 1992 ELECTION

The president's weak strategic position and his restricted political strategy bore harsh consequences in the presidential election of 1992. Bush became only the fifth sitting president this century to meet defeat (the other defeated incumbents were William Howard Taft, Herbert Hoover, Gerald Ford, and Jimmy Carter). His 38 percent of the vote was the lowest for an incumbent president in eighty years. Clearly, the public, as Bill Clinton argued, wanted change. For a president who for most of his term was one of the most popular chief executives in modern times, we have to consider the election as a disaster.

The interaction between the president's strategic position and his political strategy led to his downfall. Lulled into complacency by the public's response to the Gulf War, the White House lost the election in the fall of 1991—not a year later. A president whose disposition to stay above the political fray was reinforced by his advisers, fell precipitously in polls in the autumn, a decline from which he never recovered. Nevertheless, Bush persisted in refusing to set the agenda and structure the discourse in the growing debate over economic policy, arguing that no economic initiative was needed.

The fragile coalition that put him in office in 1988 began to unravel. That coalition, the Reagan coalition, was one formed in response to hard times, but not one that could withstand them. On the one hand, Bush had to undergo a bitter primary battle with the party's right wing that opposed government intervention in the economy and displayed contempt for his moderation. On the other hand, the president's predisposition against activist government and the lack of budgetary resources undermined his efforts to attract the Reagan Democrats, who wanted government to act on their behalf when the economy soured. When the public turns to Washington, Toryism may be found wanting.

Pat Buchanan's prime-time speech opening the Republican Convention tells much of the story about the self-destructive nature of Bush's relations with the party's right wing. Although the White House had planned to stress "family values" in a positive light, Buchanan's strident speech began the proceedings on a note of intolerance that set the tone for press coverage of the convention. He vilified feminists, environmentalists, and homosexuals and tainted all that was to come (remarkably, he also drove Ronald Reagan out of prime time). Marilyn Quayle unintentionally reinforced the mean-spirited message with her own speech later in the convention.

Buchanan's oratory was at odds with the image of Bush as a man of broad and generous vision, and it moved the Bush presidency from one that had succeeded in attracting public support with the politics of inclusiveness to one that turned differences of opinion into a holy war. The exclusiveness of the Right flattened the "big tent."

The campaign started on the family values theme, but the president quickly abandoned it when the public viewed the subject as divisive. Thus, the White House lost the advantage on the "values" issue, helped Bill Clinton's ratings rise, and alienated some socially liberal Republicans and Independents. In addition, the Reagan Democrats had other things on their minds.

All elections focus ultimately around structuring the choices of voters. Candidates want voters to choose on the terms most favorable to themselves. In the broadest sense, the thrust of Bush's appeal to the electorate was trust and the nature of his appeal was fear. On the other hand, Clinton emphasized change and hope. In hard times, the challenger's message was stronger.

On a more specific level, Bush wanted to emphasize his credentials and success in foreign policy. Yet issues of anti-communism, crisis leadership, and other aspects of foreign affairs, which had dominated public evaluations of the president for most his tenure, were no longer salient in 1992.[14] The agenda had changed to economic matters.

Ronald Reagan had appealed to many conservative Democrats on the basis of valence issues, such as morality, patriotism, anti-communism, and religious values. But when the economy stagnated, economics became more salient to Democrats of all stripes. Even conservative Democrats support some government action to stimulate the economy during hard times.

By the time of the campaign, however, Republican strategists concluded that it was too late to provide a positive rationale for electing George Bush. Aside from a widely praised "agenda for American renewal" unveiled at a September 10 speech to the Detroit Economic Club, the Bush campaign placed little emphasis on an economic plan.

Instead, the strategists insisted, they needed to go negative. In other words, the reason to reelect George Bush was to avoid being governed by Bill Clinton. Thus, the campaign emphasized trust and taxes. Although the electorate displayed some responsiveness to these themes, they could not make up for the lack of a compelling positive message, a reason to support

Bush and not just oppose Clinton. And the attempts to stain Clinton confirmed the impression among many in the public that Bush was not serious about economic policy.

GEORGE H. W. BUSH IN PERSPECTIVE

In general, the presidency of George H. W. Bush was devoted to consolidating the changes of the Reagan administration and dealing with the problems it left behind rather than mobilizing a coalition behind bold new enterprises. It was a term of prudent stewardship, but not one that was oriented toward laying the groundwork for significant changes in domestic policy.

The president is in a constant state of dependency on his environment for creating favorable strategic positions from which he can exercise leadership at the margins to turn opportunities into accomplishments. Given his strategic position, President George Bush had fewer opportunities to exploit than did most presidents. He understood the weakness of his situation and that he could not improve it by persuading Democrats in Congress to vote for conservative legislation or the public to return a Republican majority in the midterm elections. Under these circumstances, he made progress on a number of fronts by pursuing moderate policies and negotiating compromises with the Democratic majority. Ultimately, however, he could not overcome the weakness of his strategic position and his orientation toward governing in it. Of course, the president also responded to the context in which he served by turning to foreign policy, where his inclinations and expertise lay and where he had greater flexibility and more opportunities to leave his mark on history.

George W. Bush:
Leading with a Tenuous Majority

The forty-third president, more than most of his predecessors over the previous half century, explicitly focused on developing and implementing a strategy for governing. Such an approach was essential if he were to succeed, because he had a more aggressive agenda than his father, seeking far-reaching changes in public policy across a broad range of issues.[15]

STRATEGIC POSITION

The early months of a new presidency represent the most important period for establishing the tone and character of the White House's relationship with Congress. It is the time of closest scrutiny and the greatest vulnerability to making major mistakes. Taking the right steps early and avoiding errors can lay the foundation for a productive working relationship. Actions taken early create lasting impressions.

We saw in chapter 3 that the early periods of new administrations most clearly etched on our memories as notable successes are those in which presidents properly identified and exploited conditions for change. Thus, the first step a new administration should take to increase the probability of success with Congress is to assess accurately its strategic position so it understands the potential for change and will not overreach or underachieve. If the White House misreads its strategic position, the president may begin his tenure with embarrassing failures in dealing with Congress. Moreover, the greater the breadth and complexity of the policy change a president desires, the more opposition he is likely to engender—and thus the stronger his strategic position must be to succeed.

George W. Bush took office after one of the closest elections in American history. The highly unusual, protracted denouement of the election and the truncated transition period of only thirty-eight days between the resolution of the election and the inauguration—about half the normal time for a shift in power—had the potential to turn the transition into a circus and undermine the new president's chances of success.

Bush received neither a majority nor even a plurality of the vote, and many (mostly Democrats) saw his victory as illegitimate, because he received more than a half-million fewer votes than Al Gore and because of the peculiar circumstances surrounding the determination of the winner of Florida's electoral votes. A Gallup poll taken just before the inauguration found that 31 percent of Americans thought Bush "won on a technicality" and 24 percent thought he "stole the election," while 45 percent said he "won fair and square." Thirty-eight percent of Americans still considered Gore to be the "real winner of the election."[16]

In light of the election results, the new president could not credibly claim a mandate from the people. Moreover, the Republicans lost seats in both houses of Congress, undermining any claim to presidential coattails. After the election, Republicans found themselves with only a very narrow majority in the House and required the vice president to break a 50–50 split in the Senate.

Bush suffered a major embarrassment when Republican Senator James Jeffords of Vermont left the party and became an Independent in the middle of 2001. Because Jeffords caucused with the Democrats, his move gave them a majority in the Senate for the rest of the congressional term. Jeffords was disappointed with the White House's refusal to support increased spending for education and other social welfare programs, and he resented the pressure it put on him to toe the party line.

Bush did have some strategic advantages. First, Democrats as well as Republicans supported at least the general goals of improving education and adding prescription drug coverage to Medicare. Second, the budget surplus (and then projected surpluses) in 2001 created the perception among members of both parties that there were resources available for tax cuts and additional expenditures. Third, as I discuss in more detail below, the president could rely on a united party, especially in the House of Representatives, that had a stake in his success.

Finally, the terrorist attacks on September 11, 2001, immediately boosted his approval ratings to record levels, and the emphasis on national unity in the weeks that followed the tragedy encouraged public support for a series of White House initiatives on anti-terrorism policy, which were to become a principal element of the president's legacy. At the same time, the

terrorist attacks and the resulting war on terrorism's dominance of the public agenda had the perverse consequence of
solving several intractable problems facing the president. As
Congress resumed its session following its summer recess in
2001, Democrats were beginning to blame the president's tax
cut for "defunding" the federal government and forcing Congress to spend the surplus provided by Social Security contributions. Congress was to have placed these funds in a "lock box,"
off limits for paying current expenses. At the same time, unemployment was climbing and news about the country's economic recession was becoming more prominent in the media.
Opponents in Congress had stalled the president's initiatives
on education and funding for faith-based charities, and the
media was reporting stories that recalcitrants in the Pentagon
were rolling Secretary of Defense Donald Rumsfeld in his efforts to reform the U.S. defense posture. After September 11,
the media focused on terrorism and preparation to wage war
in Afghanistan rather than the recession and the Social Security
lock box. The attacks also allowed the president to blame economic problems on the terrorists.

Exploiting Opportunities

It is not difficult to imagine a president elected in Bush's circumstances to move cautiously, seeking first to increase his
legitimacy with the majority of the public who did not support
his election. Some commentators saw the potential for paraly-
sis in Washington, and others (again, mostly Democrats) urged
the president to act as if he were indeed paralyzed, proposing
only policies that enjoyed bipartisan support.

Assessing the possibilities. Neither the narrowness of his election nor the nature of its resolution intimidated Bush, however.
Although his tone was one of reconciliation, he ignored those
who urged him to strike a bipartisan posture and hold off on
his major initiatives. According to author Bob Woodward, Vice
President Dick Cheney remembered that "a notion of sort of a

restrained presidency because it was such a close election, that lasted maybe 30 seconds . . . We had an agenda, we ran on the agenda, we won the election—full speed ahead."[17] Reflecting a strategic perspective, Bush concluded that he would receive the same criticism from opponents regardless of the scope of his proposals, so he might as well make big demands and compromise only when necessary. "Big steps get more followers than small steps," said Ari Fleischer, the president's press secretary.[18]

The White House correctly understood that the one policy that both unified and energized Republicans was tax cuts. Although most congressional Democrats would oppose Bush's tax proposals, a majority of the public, including Independents and even some Democrats, would support or at least tolerate them. Equally important, Congress could consider tax cuts, unlike most other major policies, under rules that prohibited a filibuster. Thus, a united, although slender, majority could prevail, and the president moved immediately to lower taxes dramatically.

In addition, congressional Republicans, who had not enjoyed unified control of the presidency and Congress for nearly half a century, were eager to govern. The overwhelmingly conservative ideology of members of the Republican caucus, especially in the House, made it easy for them to agree on shifting policy to the right, and they saw no reason to compromise with the Democrats if they did not have to. This attitude was consistent with Bush's, whose basic leadership strategy was to press for policies as close to his preferred outcomes as possible and only negotiate when absolutely necessary.

Setting priorities. New presidents are wise to resist the temptations to try to deliver on all their campaign promises immediately following their elections and to accede to the many demands that interests make on a new administration. Instead, it is important to establish priorities among legislative proposals. In addition, because the Washington community pays disproportionate attention to the first major legislative initiatives, it is especially critical to choose early battles wisely.

Setting priorities in the early weeks of a new administration is also important because during the first months in office the president has the greatest latitude in focusing on priority legislation. After the transition period, other interests have more influence on the White House agenda. Congress is quite capable of setting its own agenda and is unlikely to defer to the president for long. In addition, ongoing policies continually force decisions to the president's desk.

If the president is not able to focus Congress's attention on his priority programs, they may become lost in the complex and overloaded legislative process. Congress needs time to digest what the president sends, to engage in independent analyses, and to schedule hearings and markups. Unless the president clarifies his priorities, Congress may put the White House's proposals in a queue.

Setting priorities is also important because presidents and their staff can lobby effectively for only a few bills at a time. The president's political capital is inevitably limited, and it is sensible to focus on the issues he cares about most. Setting priorities early also can reduce intra-administration warfare over the essence of the administration.

Karl Rove, the president's wide-ranging senior adviser, maintained that Bush campaigned on six key issues: tax cuts, education standards, military upgrades and a missile defense shield, federal support for faith-based charities, partial privatization of Social Security, and Medicare reforms and prescription drug coverage for seniors.[19] If these were Bush's priorities, he did a good job of focusing on them.

First, the Bush White House made a clear choice of a large income tax cut as its highest legislative priority. This made good strategic sense for a conservative administration. The president and his advisers felt that the notable victory of enacting a major tax cut early in the administration would signal the administration's competence in governing while unifying the Republican Party for the more difficult issues ahead. Equally important, by severely limiting the government's resources, cutting taxes would set the terms of debate for nearly all the policy debates that would follow and restrain the Democrats' ability to use the budget surplus for expansion of social welfare policies.[20]

Tax cuts were not the administration's only priorities. Education reform, an overhaul of defense policy, and greater federal support for faith-based social welfare programs were also high on the list. The president not only spoke extensively about each initiative, but also went to considerable lengths to focus attention on each proposal in the early weeks of the administration. The faith-based initiative received attention in the week after the inauguration, followed in successive weeks by education, tax cuts, and defense.

The efforts of the White House to set priorities and focus on them helped to secure them a place on the national agenda. A study of the first sixty days of news coverage of the Bush and Clinton administrations found that Bush was more successful than Clinton in focusing attention on his message. Each of the five major stories about Bush was on his priority initiatives, amounting to more than a third of all stories.[21]

Husbanding resources. The George W. Bush White House rarely sent detailed legislation to Congress and took clear stands only on a select group of issues. Bush saved his intervention for the issues he found most important for spending his time, energy, and political capital. In addition, by keeping a low profile, Bush avoided appearing overbearing to congressional Republicans. As *Congressional Quarterly* reported at the end of his first term, "Overall, Bush's formula of remaining disengaged from Congress on many issues and using his political capital sparingly—but aggressively—has proven advantageous, allowing him to minimize his defeats."[22] In his first term, the president won more than 80 percent of the roll-call votes on which he took a stand in both the House and the Senate.

Even when he took stands, Bush typically did not take a personal role in negotiating details of legislation until late in the consideration of a bill. On his priority issues, he tended to focus on a few essentials, cede ground when necessary to reach his ultimate objective, and rely on Republican leaders to keep the troops in line. The president was most involved with his major tax cut bills in 2001 and 2003 and the 2002 No Child Left Behind Act, all of which the White House largely initiated. On energy and a prescription drug benefit under Medicare, he provided encouragement to act while steering clear of details. Indeed, he backed away from the Medicare debate after facing criticism early in 2003 when a leak showed he was considering proposing that only seniors who moved to privately sponsored health care plans would get a drug benefit. The White House only made a real push on Medicare in the final moments, and kept the president out of the process until the very end. It left the heavy lifting to the Republican leadership, who wanted to keep the president inoculated from conservative Republicans agitated over the huge expense of the bill. The president also stayed at the periphery of House-Senate negotiations on the 2004 intelligence bill for months and only intervened in the final weeks when success seemed attainable and after Republican leaders told him it was necessary.[23]

Moving rapidly. Presidents must not only recognize the opportunities in their environment. To succeed with Congress, they must also move rapidly to exploit those opportunities. First-year proposals have a better chance of passing Congress than do those sent to the Hill later in an administration. Thus, the White House should be ready to send its priority legislation to Capitol Hill as early as possible.

Despite a severely truncated transition, the Bush administration lost no time in sending priority bills to Congress. The president told Karl Rove during the transition that he wanted a plan for immediate action on big items because he wanted to create momentum and focus the political debate in Congress on his agenda.[24] Thus, proposals for a large cut in income taxes, education reform, and increased support for faith-based charities went to Congress in short order. Specific changes in defense policy would take longer, but the White House launched an extensive review of the nation's defense posture.

The administration was not ready with proposals for all its priority issues, however. It deferred two important items on the "big six" list. The White House delegated Social Security reform to a commission and postponed consideration of Medicare and a prescription drug benefit. Given the disappearance of the general revenue budget surplus, the lack of consensus on these issues, and the president's limited political capital, the delays appear to be sensible strategic choices rather than evidence of disorganization or lethargy.

Relying on the party. Representatives and senators of the president's party are almost always the nucleus of coalitions supporting the president's programs. Thus, leading their party in Congress is the principal task of all presidents as they seek to counter the tendencies of the executive and legislative branches toward conflict inherent in the system of checks and balances. George W. Bush was no exception, as he benefited from extraordinarily unified support from his party, especially in the House, in his first term.

The increasing uniformity of views among Republican members of Congress, especially in the House, facilitated the leadership's ability to develop and enforce a party stance on policy— and to work on behalf of the president. In addition, the rules in the House made control of the agenda by the majority party much easier than in the more decentralized Senate.

Other factors in addition to agreement on policy encouraged Republican unity. The distances between the parties in Congress increased as the range of opinion within them decreased, raising the stakes for controlling Congress and supporting the president. Congressional Republicans also wanted a record of legislative success to take to the voters. In 2003, for example, Republicans overcame their distaste for social welfare programs and supported a prescription drug program under Medicare to show that they could deliver when they had power and to give President George W. Bush a victory to aid his reelection (and hopefully theirs) in 2004.

There was virtually no Democratic input on the bill, and Republicans essentially excluded them from conference committee meetings. The Republicans passed the bill by a 216–215 vote after the leadership kept the vote open for 173 minutes (instead of the usual 15) until 2:45 A.M. while it pressured a handful of their own troops to switch their votes and put the measure over the top.[25] Of course, the administration's reluctance to compromise further alienated the opposition, and the White House won the votes of only nine House Democrats.

Finally, from his first days in office, George W. Bush was a polarizing president, eventually the most polarizing in the history of public opinion polling. The first Gallup poll of his tenure found that he had the highest level of *disapproval* of any new president since polling began.[26] Similarly, Gary C. Jacobson reported that the public's initial reception of Bush reflected the widest partisan differences for any newly elected president in polling history. In the twenty-eight Gallup and CBS/*New York Times* polls taken before September 11, 2001, Bush's approval ratings averaged 88 percent among self-identified Republicans but only 31 percent among Democrats (Independents averaged 50 percent). This 57-point difference indicates an extraordinary degree of polarization.[27] Yet this gap between the assessments of Democrats and Republicans was just the beginning. In the May 21–23, 2004, Gallup poll, the difference between his approval among Republicans (89 percent) and Democrats (12 percent) was an astounding 77 percentage points! That gap of 70 points or higher became common starting with Bush's fourth year in office.[28]

These are extreme and unprecedented levels of polarization.[29] No president, dating back to Harry Truman, has had a partisan gap above 70 points in any Gallup poll in a reelection year. Moreover, Gallup had never before found such a high proportion of partisans with such strongly opposing views of a president. In the May 21–23, 2004, poll, 64 percent of Republicans said they strongly approved of the job Bush was doing as president, while 66 percent of Democrats strongly disapproved. As Gallup put it, "Bush is the only president who has had more than 6 in 10 of his party's identifiers strongly approving of him at the same time that more than 6 in 10 of the other party's identifiers strongly disapprove of him." The only other president to have more than 60 percent of a partisan group disapproving of him was Richard Nixon in the year of his resignation, when 61 percent of Democrats strongly disapproved of him. At that time, Nixon had overall job approval ratings below 30 percent.[30]

Gallup found that 95 percent of Republicans voted for Bush in 2004—but only 7 percent of Democrats did so.[31] Jacobson's analysis of the National Election Studies found the highest level of party-line voting in the 52-year history of the National Election Studies. With partisan leaners (those who say they "lean" toward identifying with one party or the other) included, 89 percent of Democrats and 91 percent of Republicans voted for their party's candidates. If we exclude the leaners, 92 percent of Democrats voted for Kerry while 94 percent of Republicans voted for Bush.[32]

With both the Congress and the public closely divided and highly polarized, it is not surprising that the party leadership placed a priority on helping Bush succeed. To support the president, House leaders abandoned deliberation, eschewed regular order, showed a lack of concern for legislative craftsmanship, and highlighted the core value that the political ends justify the legislative means. They bent the rules, precedents, and norms of legislative behavior in ways that at least some observers felt left the institution in tatters. They regularly expanded the use of earmarks so they had chits to use to reward and punish members, losing control over a large share of discretionary spending in the process. House Republican leaders stealthily inserted significant policy changes into omnibus bills and conference reports that would not pass in an open process, and they shut out the minority. Finally, to avoid embarrassing the president, Congress adopted a passive stance toward the executive branch. It did not insist on receiving the true costs of policy initiatives—from tax cuts to Medicare prescription drugs to the war in Iraq, easing the path of passage of expensive programs. It also did not insist on extracting potentially embarrassing information from the administration, and engaged in oversight of the executive with a light touch, especially on such crucially important matters as the war in Iraq and homeland security.[33]

George W. Bush did not seek to create the conditions for a unified Republican Party, but he effectively exploited the proclivities of his fellow party members. Early in his first term, Bush concluded that it would not be possible to obtain Democratic support as he had as governor of Texas, so he made few efforts at bipartisanship. Instead, he centered his legislative strategy on maximizing unity among Republicans. As one of his senior political advisers declared, "This is not designed to be a 55 percent presidency. This is designed to be a presidency that moves as much as possible of what we believe into law while holding fifty plus one of the country and the Congress." The White House's emphasis was to find the "right" solution and ram it through the legislature.[34]

We have seen that Bush adopted a selective approach to legislative activity, taking stands on relatively few issues and often intervening late in the legislative process. The White House also typically articulated general goals for legislation and then stepped aside as the president's allies crafted the details and pushed the bill through. Moreover, the Republican House whip operation was so good that the president did not need to do much. Even when the president lost on a vote in one of the chambers, the Republican leadership was often able to remove the offending provisions in the conference committees, which they controlled.

Observers have given the president mixed marks for his efforts to lead his party more directly. On the one hand, the president was a very successful and active fundraiser for his party's congressional candidates, and campaigned actively for them when his approval levels were high. Yet in June 2005, conservative columnist Robert Novak wrote that, "in nearly four and a half years, President Bush has not progressed in handling Congress. He seems at as much of a loss in dealing with the legislative branch as the day he entered the White House." Novak claimed that Bush was not adept at turning around Republican strays. "When the House Republican leadership on occasion has given the president a list of recalcitrant members to rope in on a specific bill, he has never delivered."[35] Although this criticism may have been a bit harsh, there were other reports of the president's difficulties of convincing skeptical Republicans to support him.[36]

Capitalizing on public approval. The president stood at an unimpressive 51 percent approval in the Gallup poll that concluded on September 10, 2001. The terrorist attacks the next day provided the president an opportunity to remake his image and build a new relationship with the American people.[37] Within days (perhaps hours) of the attack, questions of the president's legitimacy or competence disappeared for most Americans in the outburst of patriotism for which the commander in chief served as the focal point. In a poll on September 11, *prior* to Bush's short nationwide address, a Gallup poll found 78 percent of Americans expressing confidence in Bush's ability to handle the situation. The September 14–15 Gallup poll showed 91 percent of Americans approving of the way the president was handling the response to the terrorist attacks—nearly a week *before* his address to a joint session of Congress. The ABC News/*Washington Post* poll on September 13 found the same level of approval.

Equally important, Americans overwhelmingly saw the president as rising to the occasion. After a shaky start, he performed well—confident, reassuring, and resolute. As R. W. Apple, Jr., wrote in the *New York Times*, Bush "sought to console the bereaved, comfort the wounded, encourage the heroic, calm the fearful, and . . . rally the country for the struggle and sacrifices ahead."[38] There was no more talk of a stature gap in the presidency.

Following the September 11 terrorist attacks, approval of Bush's job performance soared to 86 percent. This increase of 35 percentage points represents the largest rally effect ever recorded by the Gallup Poll. The second highest jump Gallup recorded in the past half-century was during the Gulf War, when approval of the president's father, George H. W. Bush, jumped by 20 percentage points after he launched Operation Desert Storm in January 1991. The president's overall job approval level rose another 4 percentage points in the September 21–22, 2001, Gallup poll, reaching 90 percent. This approval rating was one point higher than the previous high point, registered by his father at the end of hostilities in the Persian Gulf War.[39]

Shortly after September 11, the public saw Bush in a new light. Large majorities saw him as sincere, strong, and decisive, an effective manager, inspiring confidence, caring about average people, and understanding complex issues. High evaluations of his performance on terrorism, defense, and foreign policy issues undoubtedly drove the president's high overall approval. However, his impressive approval levels seem to have had a halo effect, increasing his support on unrelated issues as well. The public's evaluation of Bush's handling of issues rose substantially not only for defense and foreign affairs, but also for the economy, unemployment, energy, and the environment. He maintained the strong support he had previously achieved on education and taxes.

Although the rally in public approval of the president that began on September 11, 2001, was the most sustained in modern times, its decay was inevitable. Bush's approval ratings gradually declined, remaining above 80 percent until March 2002, above 70 percent until July 2002, and above 60 percent until January 2003. A second and more modest rally occurred after the U.S. invasion of Iraq, but the president was at about the 50 percent mark in public approval by the end of January 2004 and never again rose much above that, even after his reelection in November.

Did George W. Bush's extraordinarily high approval ratings following the terrorist attacks provide him a significant political resource in his attempts to obtain congressional support for his policies? Did the patriotic response to the attacks help him to mobilize the public on behalf of his programs? The president certainly viewed public support as a potential advantage—and was aware of its ephemeral nature, declaring, "It is important to move as quickly as you can in order to spend whatever capital you have as quickly as possible."[40]

Where the public supported his policies—on fighting the war on terrorism abroad, on investigating and prosecuting terrorism at home, and in reorganizing the government to enhance domestic security—the president ultimately won most of what he sought. Passing legislation was more difficult on the divisive domestic issues that remained on Congress's agenda, including health care, environmental protection, energy, the economy, government support for faith-based social programs, corporate malfeasance, judicial nominees, and taxes. The politics of the war on terrorism did not fundamentally alter the consideration of these issues, which continued to divide the public and their representatives in Congress as they had before. The inevitable differences between the parties emerged, exacerbated by the narrow majorities in each chamber and the jockeying for advantage in the midterm elections. The president was not able to turn public support for the war on terrorism into leverage for obtaining the passage of his domestic initiatives.

In December 2001, the president concluded quiet negotiations with the Democrats, led by Senator Edward Kennedy, and signed a bill on education reform. The president was able to claim a victory on one of his top-priority issues, even though he had given up many of the most controversial elements of his original proposal. It is significant that to accomplish even this much, the president chose to negotiate in private rather than to go public.

In 2003, the White House hoped to parlay the victory in Iraq in the spring into support for his legislative plans. His aides did not think public backing for the war would automatically transfer to an unrelated domestic policy, but they did believe that success breeds success and that a lionized wartime leader could be a leader to whom people would listen. A swell of public support, in turn, could inject some much-needed adrenaline into the president's domestic efforts[41]—or so they hoped. Such predictions were illusory, however. With Bush focused mostly on the war in Iraq, a small but crucial number of Republican moderates in the Senate broke ranks and dealt significant blows to several of his highest-profile policies, slicing in half the president's $726 billion tax-cut proposal and defeating his plan for oil drilling in the Arctic National Wildlife Refuge in Alaska.

Structuring electoral choice. One advantage that public support for his handling of the war on terrorism gave Bush was an opportunity to structure voter choice in the 2002 congressional midterm and 2004 presidential elections around terrorism, and he took full advantage of it. In the month preceding the 2002 congressional elections, Bush engaged in the most active midterm campaigning of any president in history. In the end, the Republicans gained seats in both houses of Congress, maintaining the majority in the House and regaining it in the Senate. The historic nature of these gains (exceeded only once—in 1934—during the previous century) generated considerable commentary about the president's public leadership.

Bush campaigned relentlessly, covering fifteen carefully chosen states in the last five days of the campaign alone, and he rallied his party. The most significant reason for the Republican success in the elections was the heavy turnout in Republican base. Bush was successful in preaching to the choir rather than to the unconverted. A Gallup poll taken the weekend before the election found that 64 percent of Republicans were "more enthusiastic" about voting than in the past, while only 51 percent of Democrats responded that way.[42] On the other hand, the Democrats failed to rally—they had little to rally around, lacking both a message and a messenger. Voters did not necessarily support the Republicans on the issues, but the White House succeeded in turning the election into a referendum on a popular president.[43]

Most people who entered the booths did not have terrorism on their minds. More were concerned about the economy and the prospect of war with Iraq. But the minority who did have terrorism on their minds was overwhelmingly Republican, and the Democrats were not able to position themselves well on enough of the other issues to counter this strong GOP advantage. The war on terrorism had shifted the public debate to national security issues that favored the Republicans and shielded the president from criticism on domestic issues that favored the Democrats.

Despite the Republican success, perspective is important. The election was very close. The *Washington Post* reported that a change of 41,000 votes in only two states out of 77 million cast nationwide would have kept the Senate in Democratic hands. As political analyst Charlie Cook put it, "This was a year of very close races that, for the most part, broke toward Republicans but in no way reflected a significant shift in the national direction."[44]

In addition, the Republicans enjoyed several advantages, including the amount of money raised,[45] the quality of their candidates,[46] the partisan proclivities of competitive House seats,[47] and even Bush's lack of coattails in 2000, and they benefited from the redistricting following the 2000 census.[48]

Cook found no Republican wave except perhaps in Georgia. Instead, he concluded that the basics of getting out the vote decided the midterm elections in 2002.[49] Indeed, the Republicans operated a finely engineered voter-mobilization effort. In Georgia, the state with the biggest Republican successes, the party implemented a meticulous organizational plan that included computer analysis, training programs for volunteers, and a voter registration drive followed by massive mailing, telephone, and neighborhood canvasses in the closing days of the campaign. The president visited as late as November 2 to energize the Republican ranks. Aiding this grassroots mobilization were the National Rifle Association and United Seniors (an organization heavily underwritten by the pharmaceutical industry).[50]

In 2004, Bush succeeded in turning the election into a referendum on the challenger rather than on the incumbent. The Republicans attacked Senator John Kerry early and relentlessly, focusing on his character and arguing that he lacked the strength, decisiveness, and reliability to prosecute the war on terrorism. They also stressed terrorism much more than other issues, because it was almost the only policy on which Bush had an advantage over his challenger. The facts that Kerry was not an especially effective candidate, was prone to self-inflicted wounds and slow to respond to critics, and that Republican efforts to turn out the base continued to be effective also helped Bush win despite his modest support among Americans. Although the president received a five-point bounce in his approval rating after his election, his 53 percent rating was the lowest of any of the last seven presidents who won election while serving as president in the first poll conducted after their elections.

FALL FROM GRACE

In both his policies and his politics, Bush was a divider, not a uniter.[51] Such an approach was reasonably successful when the country was tolerant of his policy experimentation, there was slack in the budget, and he was high in the polls. When his party was united, the president could obtain much of what he sought from Congress.

None of these conditions characterized the president's second term. The president was well below 50 percent approval in the polls for almost all of it, there was widespread dissatisfaction with the direction of the country, the war in Iraq, the state of the economy, and other areas of policy, and the budget deficit showed no sign of disappearing. Equally important, the president had lost the public's trust.

Republican unity frayed over social issues, immigration, the government's performance on issues ranging from Iraq to Hurricane Katrina, and the general growth of both the government and the budget. At least some of Bush's fellow partisans were less willing to accord him the benefit of the doubt. Most significantly, Democrats won majorities in both houses of Congress following the 2006 midterm election campaign in which they focused on the president's performance, particularly the war in Iraq.

The president's fall from the public's grace was also a reaction to years of attempts to persuade the public to support his party and his policies. Bush pushed arguments for his policies to the limit (his detractors alleged he made exaggerated claims, manipulated information, and misled the public, most notably regarding the war in Iraq), and challenged his critics' patriotism. Appealing to core voters about the war in Iraq helped to win the 2002 and 2004 elections, but it increased partisan divisions by implying that opponents were practically traitors. At one point, the administration equated the terrorist threat to fascism and smeared critics of the war as "appeasers." At least partially as a result, large segments of the public no longer trusted the president and the discourse of politics was often harsh, leaving Bush with little margin for error when events turned against him.

Equally important, the president seemed to lose his strategic sense. As we will see in chapter 6, he began his second term by misreading his strategic position, grossly overestimating his political capital, and launching the most extensive public relations campaign in the history of the presidency in an effort to reform Social Security. It was a classic example of an attempt to persuade the public, employing the same public relations techniques, party apparatus, and allied groups that were responsible for his reelection. The president's most vigorous effort to alter public opinion was a significant failure. Not only was the public unresponsive to his appeals for support, but the more the president talked, the less the public supported his ideas. As a result, Congress quietly dropped consideration of the president's proposals.[52]

The effort to reform Social Security is especially interesting because it came on the heels of the presidential election. Republican strategists concluded that there was little pliability in the electorate, so they could not substantially broaden their electoral coalition. Instead, they focused most of their efforts in 2004 on energizing their partisan base and encouraging turnout rather than on changing the preferences of the electorate.[53]

Social Security reform was not Bush's only experience with failing to move the public. The other major initiative of his second term was reforming immigration policy. Although he was steadfast in raising the issue and defending his proposal, he was not able to convince either the general public or his own party to support it. It is not clear why public unresponsiveness to the president should have surprised the White House, because in Bush's first term, he failed to change public opinion, and thus increase his leverage with Congress, on such core issues as tax cuts and the war in Iraq.[54] In these cases, however, the public's initial proclivities (cutting people's taxes and fighting perceived enemies are not inherently unpopular policies) and united support from his party provided all the resources he required to get his way.

The administration's experience with attempting to move public opinion or Congress on Social Security and immigration once again raised serious questions about the efficacy of presidential persuasion. When Bush changed his strategy from exploiting opportunities to persuading a resisting public and members of Congress, he met with failure—even with those in his own party. When the public and Congress were not already inclined to support him, for whatever reasons, he could not convince them to change their minds.

George W. Bush in Perspective

Without a mandate and with a substantial minority of the public viewing his election as illegitimate, the George W. Bush presidency commenced under difficult circumstances. In his first term, however, the president surprised many observers, who underestimated both his character and his political skills. The White House made unusually focused efforts to govern strategically and effectively exploited the context in which it was attempting to govern by focusing on priorities, husbanding its resources, moving rapidly to exploit opportunities, relying on a unified and effectively led party in Congress, capitalizing on public support, and structuring voters' choices at the polls. The public's enthusiastic response to the president's stewardship in the war on terrorism kept him high in the polls for much of his first term and was a critical factor in his reelection and the Republicans' success in congressional elections.

By recognizing and effectively exploiting the opportunities in his environment, George W. Bush won major changes in public policy, including substantial tax cuts, the No Child Left Behind Act, and the addition of prescription drug coverage to Medicare. The budget surplus (and then projected surpluses) in 2001 created the perception among members of both parties of resources available for tax cuts. Democrats as well as Republicans supported at least the general goals of improving education and adding prescription drug coverage to Medicare. The president also obtained several important pieces of legislation related to the war on terrorism, including the USA Patriot Act, the new Department of Homeland Security, and congressional support for the wars in Afghanistan and Iraq. The shock of the September 11 attacks and widespread agreement that Saddam Hussein possessed weapons of mass destruction and was poised to use them against the United States undermined the potential of an effective opposition to the war in Iraq.

Despite its sensitivity to its strategic position and its discipline in exploiting it in Bush's first term, the administration faced the familiar frustrations of contemporary presidents. It was not able to increase its political capital through persuasion, as the public was unresponsive to the president's pleas for support and a polarized Congress provided little potential for conversion. Even Republicans abandoned the president when it was no longer to their advantage to support him. When the president misread the opportunities for change in his environment, he overreached and met with embarrassing failure. Ultimately, the public awarded Democrats majorities in both houses of Congress in a dramatic rejection of the president's performance.

-o- -o- -o-

Although the potential for policy change in the Bush administrations was considerably less than in the early 1930s, mid-1960s, or early 1980s, the key to understanding the successes these presidents did experience is no different than for the periods of more historic levels of legislative productivity: the president's understanding of his strategic position, especially recognizing the possibilities for change in the environment, and fashioning strategies that most effectively exploited the opportunities that existed.

Some political commentators imply that all the president has to do to obtain the support of the public or Congress is to reach into his inventory of leadership skills and employ the appropriate means of persuasion, but such a view is naive. The president's strategic position dominates the persuasive presidency. Successful leadership is not the result of the dominant chief executive of political folklore who restructures the contours of the political landscape, altering his strategic position to pave the way for change. Rather than creating the conditions for important shifts in public policy, effective leaders are the less heroic facilitators who work at the margins of coalition building to recognize and exploit opportunities in their environments.

6 Reassessing Leadership

PRESIDENTIAL POWER is *not* the power to persuade. Presidents cannot reshape the contours of the political landscape to pave the way for change by establishing an agenda and persuading the public, Congress, and others to support their policies. Instead, successful presidents facilitate change by recognizing opportunities in their environments and fashioning strategies and tactics to exploit them.

If presidents cannot use persuasion to create opportunities for change, we should reassess the role of the chief executive within the American political system. To begin, we should adjust our expectations of presidential leadership and not presume that persuasion will be at the core of engendering change. Moreover, properly understanding the potential of leadership should give us a renewed appreciation for compromise and democratic constraints.

Some, especially those who desire significant changes in public policy, may find the role of facilitator unsatisfactory. Yet the nature of the American system is such that presidents will not bring about major changes in public policy through persuasion. Although it may be appealing to explain major changes in terms of personalities, the political system is too complicated, power too decentralized, and interests too diverse for one person, no matter how extraordinary, to dominate. As Neustadt observed, "If the President envisages substantial innovations, whether conservative or liberal, then almost everything in modern history cries caution to such hopes unless accompanied by crises with potential for consensus."[1]

Moreover, we should not undervalue the facilitating skill required to recognize and exploit opportunities. Not everyone who occupies the Oval Office will be adept at building coalitions for new policies. Facilitators are not unskilled leaders. Instead, they are leaders who depend on their environments for providing opportunities that they can exploit to accomplish their objectives. When the various streams of political resources converge to create opportunities for major change, facilitators are critical to engendering significant alterations in public policy.

It takes considerable skill to fashion strategies and tactics to exploit opportunities. To repeat, facilitators are not merely conduits who grasp opportunities that appear and ask people to do what they already want to do. Change is not inevitable, and facilitators, as we have seen throughout this book, make things happen that otherwise would not. In essence, *facilitators can make crucial contributions to transforming policy without performing transformational leadership.*

Lessons for Scholars

Understanding the nature and possibilities of leadership puts us in a better position to evaluate both the performance of presidents and the opportunities for change. Equally important, we have a better sense of where to look for explanations of the success and consequences of presidential leadership.

To better understand the presidency and the engines of change, we should focus less exclusively on the president and devote more attention to the context in which the president seeks to lead. If there are significant limits on presidential persuasion, it follows that major changes in public policy require more than just the "right" person in the job and will not necessarily turn on a president's leadership qualities.

The president's dependency on existing opportunities implies a critical interdependence between leaders and followers, which we miss when we focus only on the pinnacle of power. Moreover, there are many influences on followers and potential followers and many obstacles to influencing them. The president is an important agenda setter,[2] for example, but there are other key influences on the agenda as well.[3] Thus, we need to devote more attention to thinking about politics from the bottom up as well as the top down and to the context in which the president seeks to lead.

It does not follow, of course, that we never should attribute failures of presidential leadership to the White House or that presidents have no control over the outcome of their relations with other political actors. The president may be a vital centralizing force, providing direction and energy for the nation's policymaking.

I do not suggest, then, that we ignore presidents as individuals. Instead, we need to think more clearly about how presidents actually marshal resources to bring about change. Exploiting opportunities requires a different set of skills than creating them. It calls for presidents with the analytical insight necessary to evaluate their strategic positions correctly and the ability to take advantage of the possibilities in their environments.

In addition, a successful president requires the commitment, resolution, and strength to take full advantage of opportunities that arise. We would benefit from work that explores *systematically* the contribution of presidential energy, perseverance, and resiliency to presidential success.

If exploiting opportunities to steer true believers is more critical to engendering change than persuading the skeptical, much less converting the opposition, it follows that we should focus more on maintaining and managing coalitions and less on the verbal dexterity or interpersonal persuasiveness that is hypothetically necessary to expand coalitions and thus transform the political landscape.

Sustaining and channeling coalitions should encourage research on agenda setting, a topic that has played a modest role
in scholarship on the presidency. Presidents come to office with
an electoral platform. Yet they continually add to their agenda,
often in response to unforeseen events. How skillful are chief
executives at energizing their coalitions to support these new
agenda items?

At the same time, there are a number of possible means or
venues of presidential leadership that require our attention. For
example, Stephen Skowronek has called our attention to the
role presidents may play in reconstituting the terms of discourse and thus structuring the choices of citizens and legislators,[4] arguing that "to establish a common sense of the times
. . . is the primal act of leadership." His sweeping view of presidential history leads him to conclude, "All presidents change
American politics, but rarely do they change it even roughly in
the manner they intended."[5]

For example, the typical political effect of such high-impact
presidents as James Polk, Theodore Roosevelt, Lyndon Johnson, and George W. Bush has been "schismatic." Thus, he argues, "the political world seldom conforms to definitions and
formulas; no matter how tight, skilled, or hands-on the controls
exerted, events can be orchestrated to set terms only for so
long." The president's opponents are unlikely to accept his
terms of debate and "relentlessly and ruthlessly" provide an
alternative view.[6] Skowronek is correct about the importance of
the terms of discourse, but we lack systematic understanding of
the influence presidents may have on them and need to devote
more attention to the topic.

Similarly, Jeffrey Tulis[7] and David Zarefsky,[8] among others,
have suggested that the impact of rhetoric may be in realms
other than that of the general public. The real influence of rhetoric may be on elite debate, journalistic coverage, and congressional deliberation. Unfortunately, we know almost nothing
about such impacts.

In chapter 3, I identified several means by which presidents
might increase their chances of success in leading the public.

We know little about them, however. We need systematic studies of efforts to frame policy proposals and their consequences;
the ability of the White House to increase the salience of its
initiatives, clarify the public's wishes and show how they are
consistent with its policies; define themselves and their parties
in ways that channel existing opinion on the issues into support for a party program over the longer term; and exploit the
public's opinion fluidity or indifference regarding an issue.

If presidents typically operate at the margins of coalition
building and exercise their legislative skills primarily to exploit
rather than create opportunities for leadership, we should devote more effort to examining other influences on Congress,
such as ideology, party leadership, and public opinion, and less
on personal skills. Personalizing politics can distract our attention from factors that play a larger role in explaining presidential success in Congress and greatly oversimplify our understanding of executive-legislative relations.

Finally, if presidents cannot persuade, exercising discretionary authority may be a key to success. It is perhaps ironic that,
finding the potential of persuasiveness limited, some scholars
are returning to a focus on the president's discretionary authority—the power to command.[9] In this regard, the revolution that
Neustadt launched has come full circle.

Lessons for Presidents

The stakes of understanding the potential of persuasiveness are especially high for the White House. Because
presidents are not in strong positions to create opportunities
for legislative success, recognizing those that already exist is
particularly significant. Indeed, it may be the most important
skill of all. Analyzing the prospects for change properly is difficult, however. The adoption of a core governing strategy of
changing public opinion based on a belief in the potential of
persuasive leadership may encourage presidents to underesti-
mate their opponents and eschew necessary compromises in

the mistaken belief that they can move the public. Presidents—and the country—often endure self-inflicted wounds when they fail to appreciate the limits of their influence.

To illustrate the problem of presidential overreach, I examine some famous examples of the White House's attempts at persuasion.

FDR's Court-Packing Plan

In February 1937, shortly after his landslide reelection and at the height of his powers, Franklin D. Roosevelt surprised the nation by proposing a plan to increase the size of the Supreme Court. His motivation was transparent: to add members who would support New Deal policies. It is telling that after the election, the president was so confident of his public support and his ability to channel it to support his initiatives that he did not consult with major groups of supporters, such as leading liberals or leaders of labor unions and farm organizations, on his proposal and ignored information on the public's fundamental support for the Court.[10]

According to historian William Leuchtenburg, "FDR's message generated an intensity of response unmatched by any legislative controversy of this century, save perhaps for the League of Nations episode," and the president's opponents, who seemed to include Vice President Garner, enjoyed widespread support. Nevertheless, the president persisted, believing he had the country's support.[11]

The story of the battle is a complicated one, and Roosevelt claimed success (a more responsive Court) even though his bill failed to pass. However we interpret the White House's success in achieving its immediate goal, there is little doubt that the entire episode was a costly one for the president. As Leuchtenburg put it, "Never again would FDR be as predominant, either on Capitol Hill or at the polling places, as he was when 1937 began."[12] The Court battle became a rallying point around which latent opposition to the New Deal could coalesce[13] and helped to weld together a bipartisan coalition of anti–New Deal senators. "For the first time Southern Congressmen in large numbers deserted the leader and the opposition found an issue on which it could openly take the field. Things were never quite the same again."[14] Senators from both sides of the aisle soon organized a conservative bloc strong enough to deal Roosevelt his first serious setback in four years. The bloc was composed of the irreconcilable Democrats, Republicans, and, most important, previously loyal moderate Democrats—and the uncrowned leader of this group was Vice President Garner.[15]

The battle over the Court also deeply divided the Democratic Party, precipitating factional wars in states. These conflicts in turn led to a series of episodes, notably the purge campaign of 1938, that rubbed brine into the wounds. Some members of Congress who broke with FDR in 1937 never again would accord him the same degree of loyalty they had in his first term. Similarly, the dispute produced divisions among reformers of many types, undermining the bipartisan support for the New Deal and confirming for Republican progressives their suspicions that New Dealers were interested in self-aggrandizement and concentrating power in Washington. Finally, the attempt to pack the Court helped to cause the middle-class backing Roosevelt had mobilized in the 1936 campaign to ebb away.[16]

As a result, the Court struggle helped to blunt the most important drive for social reform in American history and squandered the advantage of Roosevelt's triumph in 1936. The conservative coalition handed FDR a series of rebuffs during the special session of Congress in the autumn of 1937 and in the regular session the following year, and the prospects for reform diminished considerably. Years later, Henry Wallace reflected: "The whole New Deal really went up in smoke as a result of the Supreme Court fight." At the end of the session, one reporter inquired, "How did the President slide so far—so fast?"[17]

By 1939, Congress was handling the president more roughly than it had in his first term and began moving aggressively to dismantle the New Deal. It slashed relief spending, killed appointments, eliminated what was left of the undistributed profits tax, and killed agencies with weak constituencies.

Roosevelt was able to stave off other changes and occasionally won some battles, but his relations with Congress had changed from cooperation to stalemate.[18]

The Court fight also had implications for American foreign policy, for it distracted Roosevelt from the growing crisis in Europe, rekindled Americans' fear of executive power, and weakened the president's power at a time when he needed it most.[19] Robert Dallek argues that FDR accepted a mandatory law of neutrality in good part because he wished to avoid a congressional debate that could forestall action on judicial reform. He was in a weak position to ask for executive discretion in foreign affairs when critics were accusing him of seeking to destroy the Constitution and the courts.[20]

BILL CLINTON'S HEALTH CARE REFORM

Bill Clinton declared health care reform as the cornerstone of his new presidency. On September 22, 1993, the president delivered a well-received national address on the need for reform of health care. Two months later, he sent a 1,342-page proposal to Congress. The administration based its massive health care reform plan on the underlying, and unquestioned, assumption within the White House that the president could sell his plan to the public and thus solidify congressional support. Because the administration believed it could persuade the public, Clinton and his aides felt they could focus on developing their preferred option in health care policy in 1993. In the process, they discounted centrist opinion and underestimated how opponents could criticize their plan as big government. The president was not able to sustain the support of the public for health care reform, however.[21]

Moreover, even as the bill's fortunes soured, the White House refused to compromise. As Lawrence Jacobs and Robert Shapiro put it, "The White House's unquestioned faith that the president could rally Americans produced a rigid insistence on comprehensive reforms." In the end, Clinton's proposal did not pass—or even come to a vote in either house of Congress. The president and his aides had greatly overestimated their ability to persuade the public to support their proposal.[22]

This is not the lesson that Clinton learned, however. Indeed, the premise of the power of the presidential pulpit was so strong that each downturn in the bill's progress prompted new schemes for going public rather than a reconsideration of the fundamental framework of the bill or the basic strategy for obtaining its passage.[23] Ultimately, the president concluded that health care reform failed because "I totally neglected how to get the public informed. . . . I have to get more involved in crafting my message—in getting across my core concerns."[24] In other words, his strategy was not inappropriate, only his implementation of it. The premise of the potential of presidential persuasion seems to be nonfalsifiable.

In the 1994 midterm elections, the Democrats lost majorities in both the House and the Senate for the first time in four decades. The administration's health care proposal was the prime example of the Republicans' charge that the Democrats were ideological extremists who had lost touch with the wishes of Americans. Summing up the health care reform debacle, Jacobs and Shapiro concluded that the "fundamental political mistake committed by Bill Clinton and his aides was in grossly overestimating the capacity of a president to 'win' public opinion and to use public support as leverage to overcome known political obstacles—from an ideologically divided Congress to hostile interest groups."[25]

George W. Bush's Social Security Reform

On November 4, 2004, two days after the presidential election, George W. Bush painted his second-term vision in bold, aggressive strokes during a press conference at the White House. One central thrust of his second term would be to spend the political capital he felt he had earned in the election to reform Social Security. Rather than winding down its 2004 campaign effort, the administration launched an extensive public relations effort to convince the public, and thus Congress, to support the president's reform proposal.

Even before the inauguration, the White House announced plans to reactivate Bush's reelection campaign's network of donors and activists to build pressure on lawmakers to allow workers to invest part of their Social Security taxes in the stock market. As Treasury Secretary John W. Snow put it, the "scope and scale goes way beyond anything we have done."[26] The same architects of Bush's political victories, principally political strategists Karl Rove at the White House and Ken Mehlman, who was the Bush-Cheney campaign manager, at the Republican National Committee (RNC), would be masterminding the new campaign.

Mehlman declared that he would use the campaign apparatus—from a national database of 7.5 million e-mail activists, 1.6 million volunteers, and hundreds of thousands of neighborhood precinct captains—to build congressional support for Bush's plans, starting with Social Security. "There are a lot of tools we used in the '04 campaign, from regional media to research to rapid response to having surrogates on television," he said. "That whole effort will be focused on the legislative agenda."[27]

In addition to their own efforts, White House and RNC officials worked closely with the same outside groups that helped Bush win reelection in 2004, especially Progress for America. Thus, corporations, the financial services industry, conservative think tanks, much of the Washington trade association community, and GOP lobbyists and consultants prepared to spend $200 million or more on lobbying, television advertising, grassroots campaigning, letter-writing, and phone calls to help the president obtain passage of his priority domestic policy proposals, the most important of which was personal accounts under Social Security.[28]

White House allies also launched a market-research project to figure out how to sell the plan in the most comprehensible and appealing way, and Republican marketing and public relations gurus were building teams of consultants to promote it. The campaign intended to use Bush's campaign-honed techniques of mass repetition, sticking closely to the script, and the politics of fear to build support—contending that a Social Security financial crisis was imminent. There would be campaign-style events to win support and precision targeting of districts where lawmakers could face reelection difficulties. The White House would also use hard-hitting television ads to discredit its opponents and build support for the president's plan.[29]

At the end of President Bush's "60 Stops in 60 Days" campaign to promote his Social Security proposals, the Treasury Department reported on its Web site that 31 administration officials had made 166 stops outside the beltway, visiting 40 states and 127 cities, and had given more than 500 radio interviews in 50 states. Administration officials also placed opinion columns in newspapers with circulation totaling 7.94 million during this period, and they participated in 61 town hall meetings with 30 members of Congress in their constituencies.[30]

All this effort did not succeed in convincing the public to support the president or his Social Security proposal. So the president kept on stumping in an effort to reverse the dwindling public support for his plan. The continuation of the campaign-style trips underscored the challenge facing Bush, and they did not advance the president's cause.

What was probably the largest and best-organized public relations effort to sell a policy in the history of the Republic ended with a whimper—and in failure. Neither the public nor Congress supported the president's plan.[31] Instead, the president's efforts contributed to the unraveling of Republican cohesiveness in Congress and reinforced the growing perception among the public that he was not up to the job of president. When the Pew Research Center asked a national sample in February 2005 to describe the president in one word, a plurality of the respondents chose a negative term like "arrogant," "incompetent," or "idiot." Only 34 percent chose a positive term like "honest," "integrity," or "leader."[32] A year later, the same organization found that the single word most frequently associated with George W. Bush was "incompetent," followed closely by "idiot" and "liar."[33]

OVERREACH

Franklin D. Roosevelt, Bill Clinton, and George W. Bush overestimated the prospects for change on Supreme Court appointments, health care policy, and Social Security, respectively, overreached, and failed to achieve their goals. (In his memoirs, Clinton admits that he overestimated the pace and amount of change Americans could digest.[34]) In these cases, the president's assumption that he could achieve his goals through persuasion led to much greater problems than the failure to achieve immediate policy goals. It also weakened each administration in the long term.

Implications for Governing

A study in 2007 found that 77 percent of Americans felt there was a leadership crisis in the United States.[35] Given our new understanding of the nature of presidential leadership, it is appropriate to consider the broad implications of the limitations of presidential persuasion for basic strategies of governing.

If persuasion is problematic, is compromise an option? In the context of polarized politics, might presidents conclude that they cannot govern by adopting an inclusive orientation to policymaking and reaching out to a diminishing middle of the electorate? We have seen that sometimes George W. Bush attempted to persuade the public to support his policies. Often, however, he apparently concluded that there was little potential for persuasion in a context of polarized politics. Thus, he sought to transform policy on the basis of a 50 percent plus 1 majority.[36] Rather than seeking compromise with his opponents by bringing them into an inclusive coalition and supporting legislation broadly acceptable to the electorate, the president sought to defeat the opposition, creating winners and losers in a zero-sum game. Was that strategy his only option?

Similarly, do the limitations on presidential persuasion inevitably create incentives for polarizing politics in order to mobilize a president's base? In the 2004 presidential election, Republican political strategist Matthew Dowd argued to Karl Rove that the presidential election was "about *motivation* rather than *persuasion*."[37] Thus, the campaign focused on mobilizing its base rather than convincing undecided voters. In the process, the White House alienated large percentages of the country, reinforcing partisan polarization and making future efforts at persuasion even more difficult. Was there another strategy for Bush to win reelection in the context of polarized politics?

Answering such questions will be difficult. We do know, however, that there is a widespread desire to change basic features of our politics, including the tendency for civility to lose out to conflict, compromise to deadlock, deliberation to sound bites, legislative product to campaign issues, and public confidence to cynicism. A richer understanding of the true potential of leadership is a critical step in addressing these characteristics of contemporary politics.

Notes

Chapter 1: Power as Persuasion

1. New York: Simon & Schuster, 1992.

2. See *Lincoln at Gettysburg*, pp. 37–39, 86–87, 89, 101, 103, 120, and 145–47, for Wills's comments on Lincoln's impact on thinking about equality. In his other writing, however, Wills is much more ambivalent about the nature of leadership, especially in *Certain Trumpets* (New York: Simon & Schuster, 1994), in which he argues that followers are as important as leaders. See also "What Makes a Good Leader," *Atlantic Monthly*, April 1994, pp. 63–80.

3. Gabor Boritt, *The Gettysburg Gospel: The Lincoln Speech That Nobody Knows* (New York: Simon & Schuster, 2006), p. 123, chap. 6, 265–72.

4. See Desmond S. King and Stephen Tuck, "De-centering the South: America's Nationwide White Supremacist Order after Reconstruction" (paper, University of Oxford, November 2005) on the racism in the North as well as the South shortly after the Civil War; and Desmond S. King, *Separate and Unequal: Black Americans and the US Federal Government* (New York: Oxford University Press, 1995) on the role the federal government played in maintaining racist policies.

5. Quoted in Rich Jaroslovsky, "Manipulating the Media Is a Specialty for the White House's Michael Deaver," *Wall Street Journal*, January 5, 1984, p. 44.

6. Gallup poll, August 5–8, 2003. In a Gallup poll of January 28–29, 1987, only 32 percent of the public felt the Reagan administration had made progress in solving the problems of education.

7. Michael K. Deaver, *A Different Drummer: My Thirty Years with Ronald Reagan* (New York: HarperCollins, 2001), p. 154.

8. James MacGregor Burns, *Leadership* (New York: Harper & Row, 1978), p. 2.

9. Barbara Kellerman, "Leadership as a Political Act," in Barbara Kellerman, ed., *Leadership: Multidisciplinary Perspectives* (Englewood Cliffs, NJ: Prentice-Hall, 1984), p. 70.

10. Gary A. Yukl, *Leadership in Organizations*, 6th ed. (Upper Saddle River, NJ: Pearson Prentice Hall, 2006).

11. Richard E. Neustadt, *Presidential Power and the Modern Presidents* (New York: Free Press, 1990), p. 11.

12. Edward S. Corwin, *The President, Office and Powers, 1787–1957*, 4th rev. ed. (New York: New York University Press, 1957).

13. Clinton L. Rossiter, *The American Presidency*, 2nd ed. (New York: Harcourt, Brace, 1960).

14. Neustadt, *Presidential Power*, p. 10.

15. Ibid., p. 37. Italics in original.

16. Much of my own work has followed this path. See, for example, George C. Edwards III, *On Deaf Ears: The Limits of the Bully Pulpit* (New Haven, CT: Yale University Press, 2003); *At the Margins: Presidential Leadership of Congress* (New Haven, CT: Yale University Press, 1989); *The Public Presidency* (New York: St. Martin's, 1983); *Implementing Public Policy* (Washington, DC: Congressional Quarterly, 1980); and *Presidential Influence in Congress* (San Francisco: W. H. Freeman, 1980).

17. Neustadt, *Presidential Power*, p. 4.

18. Ibid., p. 32.

19. *Leadership*. Also see, for example, James MacGregor Burns, *Transforming Leadership* (New York: Grove Press, 2003); and James MacGregor Burns and Susan Dunn, *The Three Roosevelts: The Leaders Who Transformed America* (London: Atlantic Books, 2001). The dust jacket of the latter work claims that these three leaders "reshaped dramatically the political, social, and moral landscape of the United States."

20. Burns, *Leadership*, pp. 4, 20, 455; *Transforming Leadership*, chap. 2.

21. See, for example, *Leadership*, pp. 13, 20, 33–34, 39–40, 43–44, 68–69, 454.

22. Quoted in David McCullough, *Truman* (New York: Simon & Schuster, 1992), pp. 584–85.

23. Joseph Cooper and David W. Brady, "Institutional Context and Leadership Style: The House from Cannon to Rayburn," *American Political Science Review* 75 (June 1981): 411–25. See also David W. Rohde and Kenneth A. Shepsle, "Leaders and Followers in the House of Rep-

resentatives: Reflections on Woodrow Wilson's Congressional Government," *Congress and the Presidency* 14 (Autumn 1987): 111–13; and Barbara Sinclair, "Party Leadership and Policy Change," in Gerald C. Wright, Jr., Leroy N. Rieselbach, and Lawrence C. Dodd, eds., *Congress and Policy Change* (New York: Agathon, 1986).

24. Sidney Hook, *The Hero in History* (Boston: Beacon, 1943).

25. James MacGregor Burns, *Roosevelt: The Lion and the Fox* (New York: Harcourt, Brace and World, 1956), pp. 399–402, 487.

26. Ibid., pp. 401–2.

27. David Brooks, "Heroes and History," *New York Times*, July 17, 2007.

28. See, for example, Fred I. Greenstein, *The Presidential Difference: Leadership Style from FDR to George W. Bush* (Princeton, NJ: Princeton University Press, 2004).

29. The fullest treatment of his sweeping view of the presidency is in Stephen Skowronek, *The Politics Presidents Make: Leadership from John Adams to George Bush* (Cambridge, MA: Harvard University Press, 1993). See also his remarks at the Annual Meeting of the American Political Science Association, 2006.

30. Skowronek, *The Politics Presidents Make*.

CHAPTER 2: Leading the Public: Best Test Cases

1. Theodore C. Sorensen, *Kennedy* (London: Hodder and Stoughton, 1965), p. 392.

2. Sidney Blumenthal, *The Permanent Campaign* (New York: Simon & Schuster, 1982), p. 24. See also pp. 297–98.

3. Recent prominent examples are Frank Luntz, *Words that Work* (New York: Hyperion, 2007); George Lakoff, *Don't Think of an Elephant* (White River, VT: Chelsea Green Publishing, 2004); and Jeffrey Feldman, *Framing the Debate: Famous Presidential Speeches and How Progressives Can Use Them to Change the Conversation (and Win Elections)* (New York: Ig Publishing, 2007).

4. See, for example, Theodore J. Lowi, *The Personal President* (Ithaca, NY: Cornell University Press, 1985).

5. David Gergen, *Eyewitness to Power: The Essence of Leadership* (New York: Simon & Schuster 2000), p. 210.

6. Ibid., p. 348.

7. Blumenthal, *The Permanent Campaign*, p. 284. See also James A. Baker III, *"Work Hard, Study . . . and Keep Out of Politics!"* (New York: G. P. Putnam's Sons, 2006), p. 174.

8. Lawrence R. Jacobs and Robert Y. Shapiro, *Politicians Don't Pander* (Chicago: University of Chicago Press, 2000), pp. 45, 106, 136.

9. See Martin J. Medhurst, *The Prospect of Presidential Rhetoric* (College Station: Texas A&M University Press, 2007), for an overview of this literature.

10. George C. Edwards III, "Presidential Rhetoric: What Difference Does It Make?" in Martin J. Medhurst, ed., *The Future of the Rhetorical Presidency* (College Station: Texas A&M University Press, 1996).

11. Quoted in Victor Gold, "George Bush Speaks Out," *The Washingtonian*, February 1994, p. 41.

12. Ronald Reagan, *An American Life* (New York: Simon & Schuster, 1990), p. 471.

13. Richard J. Carwardine, *Lincoln* (Essex, UK: Longman 2003), pp. xiii, 304.

14. See, for example, Douglas L. Wilson, *Lincoln's Sword: The Presidency and the Power of Words* (New York: Knopf, 2006); Phillip Shaw Paludan, *"The Better Angels of our Nature": Lincoln, Propaganda and Public Opinion in the North During the American Civil War* (Fort Wayne, IN: The Lincoln Museum, 1992); Garry Wills, *Lincoln at Gettysburg: The Words that Remade America* (New York: Simon & Schuster, 1992).

15. Michael Kempner, "Five Best Books on Public Relations," *Wall Street Journal*, November 25, 2006, p. P10. Kempner is the president and CEO of MWW Group public relations. The Lincoln book is Ronald C. White, Jr., *The Eloquent President* (New York: Random House, 2005).

16. Carwardine, *Lincoln*, pp. xiii, 47, 193–98, 218, 306.

17. Quoted in Michael Burlingame and John R. Turner Ettlinger, eds., *Inside Lincoln's White House: The Complete Civil War Diary of John Hay* (Carbondale: Southern Illinois University Press, 1997), p. 135.

18. Carwardine, *Lincoln*, p. 306.

19. Ibid., pp. xiii, 260, 273, 292, 306, 310.

20. Ibid., pp. 249, 261–62.

21. Ibid., pp. 86, 193, 205, 219, 249. See also Gary Wills, *Certain Trumpet: The Call of Leaders* (New York: Simon & Schuster, 1994), p. 16.

22. Paludan, *"The Better Angels of our Nature,"* pp. 13–15.

23. See Paludan, *"The Better Angels of our Nature."*

24. Carwardine, *Lincoln*, pp. 249, 257–80; Paludan, *"The Better Angels of our Nature,"* pp. 6–9, 15–16.

25. Carwardine, *Lincoln*, pp. 202, 211–13, 291.

26. David Herbert Donald, *Lincoln* (New York: Simon & Schuster, 1995), pp. 14–15.

27. Abraham Lincoln, Letter to Albert G. Hodges, April 4, 1864, *The Collected Works of Abraham Lincoln*, vol. 7, ed. Roy P. Basler (New Brunswick, NJ: Rutgers University Press, 1953), p. 281.

28. Quoted in Donald, *Lincoln*, p. 332.

29. Carwardine, *Lincoln*, pp. 249–50.

30. Doris Kearns Goodwin, "FDR's Fireside Chats," *Media Studies Journal* 14 (Winter 2000): 76.

31. Donald A. Ritchie, *Electing FDR: The New Deal Campaign of 1932* (Lawrence: University Press of Kansas, 2007), pp. 172, 176.

32. William E. Leuchtenburg, *Franklin D. Roosevelt and the New Deal, 1932–1940* (New York: Harper & Row, 1963), pp. 6–7, 267–72; Arthur M. Schlesinger, Jr., *Crisis of the Old Order* (Boston: Houghton Mifflin, 1957), p. 293; James MacGregor Burns, *Roosevelt: The Lion and the Fox* (New York: Harcourt, Brace and World, 1956), pp. 131–33, 358–66.

33. Hadley Cantril, *Public Opinion, 1935–1946* (Princeton, NJ: Princeton University Press, 1951), pp. 409–10. The Gallup Poll reported similar results for the January to March 1941 period when Congress considered the bill, which the president signed on March 11. Moreover, FDR did not propose the bill until he felt he had the public's support. See note 65.

34. Matthew A. Baum and Samuel Kernell, "From 'Dr. New Deal' to 'Dr. Win-the-War': Assessing the Constituency Foundations of Franklin Roosevelt's Popular Support." Paper presented at the annual meeting of the Midwest Political Science Association, Chicago, April 15–17, 1999, pp. 17–18. See also Wesley C. Clark, *Economic Aspects of a President's Popularity* (Philadelphia: University of Pennsylvania Press, 1943).

35. Burns, *Roosevelt: The Lion and the Fox*, pp. 271, 337; Cantril, *Public Opinion, 1935–1946*, pp. 756.

36. Kristi Andersen, *The Creation of a Democratic Majority 1928–1936* (Chicago: University of Chicago Press, 1979).

37. Richard Hofstadter, *The American Political Tradition* (New York: Vintage, 1954), p. 316.

38. Arthur M. Schlesinger, Jr., *The Coming of the New Deal* (Boston: Houghton Mifflin, 1958), p. 558.

39. Ole R. Holsti, *Public Opinion and American Foreign Policy* (Ann Arbor: University of Michigan Press, 1996), pp. 53, 200; John Ruggie Gerard, "The Past as Prologue? Interests, Identity, and American Foreign Policy," *International Security* 21 (Summer 1997): 98; Hadley Cantril, *The Human Dimension: Experiences in Policy Research* (New Brunswick, NJ: Rutgers University Press, 1967), p. 44; Schlesinger, *The Coming of the New Deal*, pp. 525–26, 528, 530; Burns, *Roosevelt: The Lion and the Fox*, p. 284.

40. Elvin T. Lim, "The Lion and the Lamb: De-Mythologizing Franklin Roosevelt's Fireside Chats," *Rhetoric and Public Affairs* 6 (Fall): 437–64.

41. See Elmer E. Cornwell, Jr., *Presidential Leadership of Public Opinion* (Bloomington: Indiana University Press, 1965), pp. 262–63. Cornwell reports the other instances of FDR pointedly discussing pending legislation as Social Security, holding company legislation, and some other items on April 28, 1935; a program he had just sent to Congress to cope with the then-current recession on April 14, 1938; and wartime economic stabilization legislation on April 28, 1942. See also Schlesinger, *The Coming of the New Deal*, p. 559.

42. Gregory A. Caldeira, "Public Opinion and the U.S. Supreme Court: FDR's Court-Packing Plan," *American Political Science Review* 81 (December 1987): 81–82. See also William Lasser, *Benjamin V. Cohen: Architect of the New Deal* (New Haven, CT: Yale University Press, 2002), p. 163.

43. Matthew A. Baum and Samuel Kernell, "Economic Class and Popular Support for Franklin Roosevelt in War and Peace," *Public Opinion Quarterly* 65 (Summer 2001): 198–229.

44. Douglas L. Kriner, "Examining Variance in Presidential Approval: The Case of FDR in World War II," *Public Opinion Quarterly* 70 (Spring 2006), pp. 33, 43.

45. See the poll results in Cantril, *Public Opinion, 1935–1946*, pp. 587–89.

46. *Fortune* poll, listed in Cantril, *Public Opinion, 1935–1946*, p. 587.

47. Burns, *Roosevelt: The Lion and the Fox*, pp. 262. See also pp. 255, 263.

48. Robert Dallek, *Franklin D. Roosevelt and American Foreign Policy, 1932–1945* (New York: Oxford University Press, 1979), pp. 71, 95–97, 101–8, 127–28, 152–53, 159–60; Leuchtenburg, *Franklin D. Roosevelt and the New Deal, 1932–1940*, pp. 215–26; Burns, *Roosevelt: The Lion and the Fox*, pp. 251, 255–60, 356.

49. Holsti, *Public Opinion and American Foreign Policy*, pp. 15–16, 189.

50. See Steven Casey, *Cautious Crusade: Franklin D. Roosevelt, American Public Opinion, and the War Against Nazi Germany* (New York: Oxford University Press, 2001). See also Burns, *Roosevelt: The Lion and the Fox*, pp. 251, 255.

51. John C. Donovan, "Congressional Isolationists and Roosevelt Foreign Policy," *World Politics* 3 (April 1951): 316.

52. Samuel I. Rosenman, *Working with Roosevelt* (New York: Harper and Brothers, 1952), pp. 166–68. See also Burns, *Roosevelt: The Lion and the Fox*, pp. 318–19.

53. Burns, *Roosevelt: The Lion and the Fox*, p. 388.

54. See Dorothy Borg, *The United States and the Far Eastern Crisis of 1933–1938* (Cambridge, MA: Harvard University Press, 1964), chap. 13; Travis B. Jacobs, "Roosevelt's 'Quarantine' Speech," *Historian* 24 (August 1962): 483–502; Leuchtenburg, *Franklin D. Roosevelt and the New Deal, 1932–1940*, pp. 226–27; Norman Graebner, ed., *Ideas and Diplomacy: Readings in the Intellectual Tradition of American Foreign Policy* (New York: Oxford University Press, 1964), p. 562; Dallek, *Franklin D. Roosevelt and American Foreign Policy, 1932–1945*, pp. 150–52. But see Leila Sussman, "Mass Political Letter Writing in America," *Public Opinion Quarterly* 23 (Summer 1959): p. 210; Manfred Landecker, *The President and Public Opinion* (Washington, DC: Public Affairs Press, 1968), pp. 118.

55. Leuchtenburg, *Franklin D. Roosevelt and the New Deal, 1932–1940*, pp. 284, 291–95; Burns, *Roosevelt: The Lion and the Fox*, pp. 392–93, 396–97; Dallek, *Franklin D. Roosevelt and American Foreign Policy, 1932–1945*, pp. 112–13, 115, 124, 154–55, 168, 179, 183, 188, 201, 210, 211, 219, 227, 229, 231–32, 253, 264, 267, 272, 278, 291.

56. Leuchtenburg, *Franklin D. Roosevelt and the New Deal, 1932–1940*, pp. 300, 304; Robert Shogan, *Hard Bargain* (New York: Scribner, 1995); Burns, *Roosevelt: The Lion and the Fox*, pp. 263, 389, 458; Dallek, *Franklin D. Roosevelt and American Foreign Policy, 1932–1945*, pp. 261, 286.

57. *Fortune* poll, November 1939.

58. Gallup poll, February 6, 1940.

59. Gallup poll, July 22, 1941. See also Dallek, *Franklin D. Roosevelt and American Foreign Policy, 1932–1945*, pp. 248–49, 277.

60. Gallup poll, November 25, 1941.

61. Quoted in Burns, *Roosevelt: The Lion and the Fox*, p. 458.

62. Robert A. Divine, *Roosevelt and World War II* (Baltimore, MD: Johns Hopkins University Press, 1969), pp. 42–43; Bernard C. Cohen, *The Public's Impact on Foreign Policy* (Boston: Little Brown, 1973), pp. 71–72; Dallek, *Franklin D. Roosevelt and American Foreign Policy, 1932–1945*, p. 261.

63. Dallek, *Franklin D. Roosevelt and American Foreign Policy, 1932–1945*, pp. 289, 310–12.

64. Ibid., pp. 267, 287–89. See also pp. 285, 292.

65. Ibid., pp. 228, 257, 286.

66. Adam J. Berinsky, "Assuming the Costs of War: Events, Elites, and American Public Support for Military Conflict," *Journal of Politics* 69 (November 2007): 975–97.

67. Burns, *Roosevelt: The Lion and the Fox*, pp. 380, 399–400.

68. Cantril, *The Human Dimension*, pp. 44, 76.

69. Holsti, *Public Opinion and American Foreign Policy*, pp. 18–19, 91; Cantril, *The Human Dimension*, pp. 44, 76.

70. Holsti, *Public Opinion and American Foreign Policy*, p. 187.

71. Dallek, *Franklin D. Roosevelt and American Foreign Policy, 1932–1945*, pp. 284–85, 289.

72. Baker, *"Work Hard, Study . . . and Keep Out of Politics!"* p. 174.

73. This section is based on George C. Edwards III, *On Deaf Ears: The Limits of the Bully Pulpit* (New Haven, CT: Yale University Press, 2003), chap. 3.

74. Martin Anderson, *Revolution: The Reagan Legacy* (Stanford, CA: Hoover Institution Press, 1990), p. 7.

75. Ibid., pp. xviii–xix.

76. Haynes B. Johnson, *Sleepwalking Through History: America in the Reagan Years* (New York: Norton, 1991), p. 49. Johnson (p. 79) also argued that Reagan's election as governor of California in 1966, during the period of discord over the war in Vietnam, civil rights, and campus unrest, occurred because "through Reagan the public had a vehicle to express resentment at both national disorder and political leadership."

77. William A. Niskanen, *Reaganomics* (New York: Oxford University Press, 1988), p. 22.

78. James A. Stimson, *Public Opinion in America: Moods, Cycles, and Swings* (Boulder, CO: Westview, 1991), pp. 64, 126–27.

79. Benjamin I. Page and Robert Y. Shapiro, *The Rational Public* (Chicago: University of Chicago Press, 1992), pp. 127, 136.

80. James A. Davis, "Changeable Weather in a Cooling Climate," *Public Opinion Quarterly* 56 (Fall 1992): 261–306.

81. William G. Mayer, *The Changing American Mind* (Ann Arbor: University of Michigan Press, 1992), p. 123.

82. Tom W. Smith, "Liberal and Conservative Trends in the United States since World War II," *Public Opinion Quarterly* 54 (Winter 1990): 479–507.

83. Martin P. Wattenberg, *The Rise of Candidate-Centered Politics* (Cambridge, MA: Harvard University Press, 1991), chap. 4.

84. *Los Angeles Times* poll, October 12–15, 1984; Martin P. Wattenberg, *The Decline of American Political Parties, 1952–1984* (Cambridge, MA: Harvard University Press, 1986), p. 154.

85. Quoted in Samuel Kernell, *Going Public*, 3rd ed. (Washington, DC: CQ Press, 1997), p. 145.

86. Ibid., p. 146.

87. There was a 1 percentage point increase in approval between the Gallup polls on April 10–13, 1981, and May 8–14, 1981.

88. Kernell, *Going Public*, p. 146.

89. Wirthlin poll, June 12–14, 1981.

90. Kernell, *Going Public*, p. 147.

91. Yankelovich, Skelly, and White, May 4–12, 1981.

92. NBC News/Associated Press poll, May 18–19, 1981.

93. Quoted in "Tax Cut Passed by Solid Margin in House, Senate," *Congressional Quarterly Weekly Report*, August 1, 1981, p. 1374. See also Kernell, *Going Public*, pp. 150–51.

94. Kernell, *Going Public*, pp. 169–70. See also p. 146.

95. M. Stephen Weatherford and Lorraine M. McDonnell, "Ronald Reagan as Legislative Advocate: Passing the Reagan Revolution Budgets in 1981 and 1982," *Congress and the Presidency* 32 (Spring 2005): 16–17; Kernell, *Going Public*, p. 149.

96. Quoted in William Greider, "The Education of David Stockman," *Atlantic* (December 1981): 51.

97. David Stockman, *The Triumph of Politics* (New York: Harper & Row, 1986), pp. 208–9, 214–15, 251, 253, 260–61, 264–65. See also "White House's Lobbying Apparatus . . . Produces Impressive Tax Vote Victory," *Congressional Quarterly Weekly Report*, August 1, 1981, pp. 1372–73.

98. Laurence I. Barrett, *Gambling with History* (New York: Penguin, 1984), pp. 160–61; Greider, "The Education of David Stockman," p. 50.

99. Marc A. Bodnick, "'Going Public' Reconsidered: Reagan's 1981 Tax and Budget Cuts, and Revisionist Theories of Presidential Power," *Congress and the Presidency* 17 (Spring 1990): 13–28.

100. See "Reagan's Legislative Strategy Team Keeps His Record of Victories Intact," *National Journal*, June 26, 1982, p. 1130.

101. *Gallup Report*, November 1981, no. 194, pp. 3–8.

102. Kernell, *Going Public*, p. 152.

103. Gallup poll, September 18–21, 1981.

104. Reagan, *An American Life*, p. 479. See also p. 471.

105. Memo from Richard Wirthlin to Ronald Reagan, April 20, 1985. My thanks to Lawrence R. Jacobs and Robert Y. Shapiro for sharing a copy of the memo.

106. Edwards, *On Deaf Ears*, pp. 54–55.

107. Larry M. Bartels, "The American Public's Defense Spending Preferences in the Post–Cold War Era," *Public Opinion Quarterly* 58 (Winter 1994): 479–508; Seymour Martin Lipset, "Beyond 1984: The Anomalies of American Politics," *PS* 19 (1986): 229; Mayer, *The Changing American Mind*, pp. 51, 62, 133. See also "Defense," Gallup Report, May 1987, pp. 2–3; "Opinion Outlook," *National Journal*, June 13, 1987, p. 1550; CBS News/*New York Times* Poll, October 27, 1987, table 15.

108. See Christopher Wlezien, "Dynamics of Representation: The Case of U.S. Spending on Defense," *British Journal of Political Science* 26 (January 1996): 81–103.

109. For data on more specific expenditures, see Edwards, *On Deaf Ears*, pp. 60–64.

110. See, for example, Robert F. Durant, *The Administrative Presidency Revisited* (Albany: SUNY Press, 1992); Dan B. Wood, "Principals, Bureaucrats, and Responsiveness in Clean Air Enforcement," *American Political Science Review* 82 (March 1988): 213–34.

111. See, for example, John A. Fleishman, "Trends in Self-Identified Ideology from 1972 to 1982: No Support for the Salience Hypothesis,"

American Journal of Political Science 30 (1986): 517–41; Martin P. Wattenberg, "From a Partisan to a Candidate-Centered Electorate," in Anthony King, ed., *The New American Political System* (Washington, DC: American Enterprise Institute, 1990), pp. 169–71; Wattenberg, *The Rise of Candidate-Centered Politics*, pp. 95–101.

112. Stimson, *Public Opinion in America*, pp. 64, 126–27.

113. Mayer, *The Changing American Mind*, p. 127.

114. ABC News/*Washington Post* poll, August 12, 1987.

115. "Do you feel that President Reagan has told the public everything he knows about the Iran-Contra affair or that he is holding back certain information?" in polls of January 16–19, 1987, and August 24–September 2, 1987.

116. ABC News/*Washington Post* polls of March 5–9 and August 12, 1987.

117. Quoted in R. W. Apple, "Bush Sure-Footed on Trail of Money," *New York Times*, September 29, 1990, p. 8.

118. George C. Edwards III, *Presidential Approval* (Baltimore, MD: Johns Hopkins University Press, 1990).

119. See, for example, Baker, *"Work Hard, Study . . . and Keep Out of Politics!"* pp. 132–33, 136–37, 148, 171.

120. Kernell, *Going Public*, p. 169.

121. Shoon Kathleen Murray, "Private Polls and Presidential Policymaking: Reagan as a Facilitator of Change," *Public Opinion Quarterly* 70 (Winter 2006): 477–98.

122. Robert S. Erikson, Michael B. MacKuen, and James A. Stimson, *The Macro Polity* (New York: Cambridge University Press, 2002), pp. 219, 369.

123. Page and Shapiro, *The Rational Public*, chap. 7.

124. Edwards, *On Deaf Ears*, chap. 9.

125. Ivor Crewe, "Values: The Crusade that Failed," in Dennis Kavanagh and Anthony Seldon, eds., *The Thatcher Effect: A Decade of Change* (Oxford: Oxford University Press, 1989), p. 241. See also Ivor Crewe, "Has the Electorate Become Thatcherite?" in Robert Skidelsky, *Thatcherism* (London: Chatto and Windus, 1988); Ivor Crewe and Donald Searing, "Ideological Change in the British Conservative Party," *American Political Science Review* 82 (June 1988): 361–84.

126. Ivor Crewe and Donald Searing, "Mrs. Thatcher's Crusade: Conservatism in Britain, 1972–1986," in B. Cooper, Allan Kornberg,

and William Mishler, eds., *The Resurgence of Conservatism in Anglo-American Democracies* (Durham, NC: Duke University Press, 1988).

127. John Rentoul, *Me and Mine: The Triumph of the New Individualism* (London: Unwin Hyman, 1989), p. 158.

128. John Curtice, "Interim Report: Party Politics," in Roger Jowell, Sharon Witherspoon, and Lindsay Brook, *British Social Attitudes: The 1987 Report* (Aldershot Hants: SCPR\Gower, 1986), chap. 8, 171–82. See also John Curtice, "Political Partisanship," in Roger Jowell, Sharon Witherspoon, and Lindsay Brook, *British Social Attitudes: The 1986 Report* (Aldershot Hants: SCPR\Gower, 1986), chap. 3, 39–53.

129. Robert Y. Shapiro and John T. Young, "Public Opinion and the Welfare State: The United States in Comparative Perspective," *Political Science Quarterly* 104 (Spring 1989): 59–89.

130. Richard Rose, "A Crisis of Confidence in British Party Leaders?" *Contemporary Record* 9 (Autumn 1995): 278.

131. Ian McLaine, *Ministry of Morale; Home Front Morale and the Ministry of Information in World War II* (London: George Allen and Unwin, 1979), pp. 59–60, 72.

132. Ibid., pp. 55, 94, 102, 107, 123, 136, 141, 217.

133. British Institute of Public Opinion (Gallup) Polls, 1938–1946, archived at the University of Essex.

134. McLaine, *Ministry of Morale*, pp. 99, 138–39, 220.

135. Sir Winston Churchill, Speech to Parliament, November 30, 1954.

136. Sonia Orwell and Ian Angus, eds., *The Collected Essays, Journalism and Letters of George Orwell*, vol. 2 (London: Secker & Warburg 1970), p. 168.

137. Quoted in A.J.P. Taylor, *Bismarck: The Man and the Statesman* (New York: Alfred A. Knopf, 1955), p. 115.

138. John W. Kingdon, *Agendas, Alternatives, and Public Policies*, 2nd ed. (New York: Longman, 2003), p. 181.

139. Stimson, *Public Opinion in America: Moods, Cycles, and Swings*.

140. Page and Shapiro, *The Rational Public*.

141. Benjamin I. Page with Marshall M. Bouton, The *Foreign Policy Disconnect: What Americans Want from Our Leaders but Don't Get* (Chicago: University of Chicago Press, 2006).

142. E. H. Carr, *Conditions of Peace* (New York: Macmillan, 1942), p. 6.

CHAPTER 3: Leading the Public:
Exploiting Existing Opinion

1. Martha Joynt Kumar, *Managing the President's Message: The White House Communications Operation* (Baltimore, MD: Johns Hopkins University Press, 2007), p. 9.

2. A key source on these activities is Kumar, *Managing the President's Message.*

3. Quoted in Gerald M. Boyd, "'General Contractor' of the White House Staff," *New York Times*, March 4, 1986, sec. A, p. 22.

4. See, for example, Daniel Kahneman, Paul Slovic, and Amos Tversky, *Judgment Under Uncertainty: Heuristics and Biases* (New York: Cambridge University Press, 1982); Arthur Lupia, "Shortcuts versus Encyclopedias: Information and Voting Behavior in California Insurance Reform Elections," *American Political Science Review* 88 (March 1994): 63–76; Herbert A. Simon, "A Behavioral Model of Rational Choice," *Quarterly Journal of Economics* 69 (February 1955): 99–118; Samuel L. Popkin, *The Reasoning Voter* (Chicago: University of Chicago Press, 1991); Paul M. Sniderman, Richard Brody, and Philp E. Tetlock, *Reasoning and Choice* (New York: Cambridge University Press, 1991).

5. E. Tory Higgins and Gary A. King, "Accessibility of Social Constructs: Information-Processing Consequences of Individual and Contextual Variation," in Nancy Cantor and John F. Kihlstrom, eds., *Personality, Cognition, and Social Interaction* (Hillsdale, NJ: Erlbaum, 1981); Robert S. Wyer, Jr., and Jon Hartwick, "The Recall and Use of Belief Statements as Bases for Judgments," *Journal of Experimental Social Psychology* 20 (January 1984): 65–85; Thomas K. Srull and Robert S. Wyer, Jr., *Memory and Cognition in Their Social Context* (Hillsdale, NJ; Erlbaum, 1989); Thomas K. Srull and Robert S. Wyer, Jr., "The Role of Category Accessibility in the Interpretation of Information about Persons: Some Determinants and Implications," *Journal of Personality and Social Psychology* 37 (10, 1979): 1660–72; Thomas K. Srull and Robert S. Wyer, Jr., "Category Accessibility and Social Perception: Some Implications for the Study of Person Memory and Interpersonal Judgments," *Journal of Personality and Social Psychology* 38 (6, 1980): 841–56; Richard R. Lau, "Construct Accessibility and Electoral Choice," *Political Behavior* 11 (March 1989): 5–32.

6. Philip E. Converse, "The Nature of Belief Systems in Mass Publics," in David E. Apter, ed., *Ideology and Discontent* (New York: Free Press, 1964).

7. John R. Zaller, *The Nature and Origins of Mass Opinion* (New York: Cambridge University Press, 1992), pp. 42–48; James H. Kuklinski and Norman Hurley, "On Hearing and Interpreting Messages: A Cautionary Tale of Citizen Cue-Taking," *Journal of Politics* 56 (August 1994): 729–51; Jeffrey Mondak, "Source Cues and Policy Approval: The Cognitive Dynamics of Public Support for the Reagan Agenda," *American Journal of Political Science* 37 (February 1993): 186–212.

8. See, for example, William A. Gamson and Andre Modigliani, "The Changing Culture of Affirmative Action," in Richard D. Braungart, ed., *Research in Political Sociology,* vol. 3 (Greenwich, CT: JAI Press, 1987), p. 143; William A. Gamson and Andre Modigliani, "Media Discourse and Public Opinion on Nuclear Power: A Constructionist Approach," *American Journal of Sociology* 95 (July 1989): 1–37; William A. Gamson, *Talking Politics* (Cambridge, UK: Cambridge University Press, 1992); Donald R. Kinder and Lynn M. Sanders, *Divided by Color: Racial Politics and Democratic Ideals* (Chicago: University of Chicago Press, 1996); and Zhongdang Pan and Gerald M. Kosicki, "Framing Analysis: An Approach to News Discourse," *Political Communication* 10 (1, 1993): 55–75.

9. For the latter view that framing does not work by altering the accessibility to different considerations, see James N. Druckman, "On the Limits of Framing Effects: Who Can Frame?" *Journal of Politics* 63 (November 2001): 1041–66. See also Thomas E. Nelson, Rosalee A. Clawson, and Zoe M. Oxley, "Media Framing of a Civil Liberties Conflict and Its Effect on Tolerance," *American Political Science Review* 91 (September 1997): 567–84; and Joanne M. Miller and Jon A. Krosnick, "News Media Impact on the Ingredients of Presidential Evaluations: Politically Knowledgeable Citizens Are Guided by a Trusted Source," *American Journal of Political Science* 44 (April 2000): 301–15.

10. Over the past generation, the research on public opinion has produced a large number of studies showing the impact of framing on people's opinions. For evidence of the impact of framing effects, see Stanley Feldman and John Zaller, "The Political Culture of Ambivalence: Ideological Responses to the Welfare State," *American Journal of Political Science* 36 (February 1992): 268–307; Donald R. Kinder and Lynn M. Sanders, "Mimicking Political Debate with Survey Questions: The Case of White Opinion on Affirmative Action for Blacks," *Social*

Cognition 8 (1, 1990): 73–103; Donald R. Kinder and Lynn M. Sanders, *Divided by Color: Racial Politics and Democratic Ideals* (Chicago: University of Chicago Press, 1996); Thomas E. Nelson and Donald R. Kinder, "Issue Frames and Group-Centrism in American Public Opinion," *Journal of Politics* 58 (November 1996): 1055–78; Nelson, Clawson, and Oxley, "Media Framing of a Civil Liberties Conflict and Its Effect on Tolerance"; Thomas E. Nelson, Rosalee A. Clawson, and Zoe M. Oxley, "Toward a Psychology of Framing Effects," *Political Behavior* 19 (September 1997): 221–46; Thomas E. Nelson and Zoe M. Oxley, "Issue Framing Effects on Belief Importance and Opinion," *Journal of Politics* 61 (November 1999): 1040–67; John Zaller and Stanley Feldman, "A Simple Theory of the Survey Response: Answering Questions versus Revealing Preferences," *American Journal of Political Science* 36 (August 1992): 579–616; Amos Tversky and Daniel Kahneman, "The Framing of Decisions and the Psychology of Choice," *Science* 211 (30 January 1981): 453–58; Dennis Chong, "How People Think, Reason, and Feel about Rights and Liberties," *American Journal of Political Science* 37 (August 1993): 867–99; William G. Jacoby, "Issue Framing and Public Opinion on Government Spending," *American Journal of Political Science* 44 (October 2000): 750–67; Daniel Kahneman and Amos Tversky, "Choices, Values, and Frames," *American Psychologist* 39 (April 1984): 341–50; Daniel Kahneman and Amos Tversky, "Rational Choice and the Framing of Decisions," in Hillel J. Einhorn and Robin M. Hogarth, eds., *Rational Choice: The Contrast between Economics and Psychology* (Chicago: University of Chicago Press, 1987); Jon A. Krosnick and Donald R. Kinder, "Altering the Foundations of Support for the President through Priming," *American Political Science Review* 84 (June 1990): 497–512; Joseph N. Cappella and Kathleen Hall Jamieson, *Spiral of Cynicism: The Press and the Public Good* (New York: Oxford University Press, 1997); John H. Aldrich, John Sullivan, and Eugene Borgida, "Foreign Affairs and Issue Voting: Do Presidential Candidates Waltz Before a Blind Audience?" *American Political Science Review* 83 (March 1989): 123–41; W. Russell Neuman, Marion K. Just, and Ann N. Crigler, *Common Knowledge: News and the Construction of Political Meaning* (Chicago: University of Chicago Press, 1992); Nicholas A. Valentino, Vincent L. Hutchings, and Ismail K. White, "Cues that Matter: How Political Ads Prime Racial Attitudes During Campaigns," *American Political Science Review* 96 (March 2002): 75–90; Thomas E. Nelson, "Policy Goals, Public Rhetoric, and Political Attitudes," *Journal of Politics* 66 (May 2004): 581–

605; Nicholas J. G. Winter, "Beyond Welfare: Framing and the Racialization of White Opinion on Social Security," *American Journal of Political Science* 50 (April 2006): 400–20.

11. There is some evidence that the president's rhetoric can prime the criteria on which the public evaluates him. See James N. Druckman and Justin W. Holmes, "Does Presidential Rhetoric Matter? Priming and Presidential Approval," *Presidential Studies Quarterly* 34 (December 2004): 755–78.

12. For a good discussion of this point, see Lawrence R. Jacobs and Robert Y. Shapiro, *Politicians Don't Pander* (Chicago: University of Chicago Press, 2000), pp. 49–52.

13. See, for example, William B. Riker, *The Art of Political Manipulation* (New Haven, CT: Yale University Press, 1986); William B. Riker, *The Strategy of Rhetoric: Campaigning for the American Constitution* (New Haven, CT: Yale University Press, 1996); William B. Riker, "The Heresthetics of Constitution Making: The Presidency in 1787, with Comments on Determinism and Rational Choice," *American Political Science Review* 78 (March 1984): 1–16.

14. Byron E. Shafer and William J. M. Claggett, *The Two Majorities: The Issue Context of Modern American Politics* (Baltimore, MD: Johns Hopkins University Press, 1995). See also James N. Druckman, Lawrence R. Jacobs, and Eric Ostermeier, "Candidate Strategies to Prime Issues and Image," *Journal of Politics* 66 (November 2004): 1180–1202.

15. John R. Petrocik, "Divided Government: Is It All in the Campaigns," in Gary W. Cox and Samuel Kernell, eds., *The Politics of Divided Government* (Boulder, CO: Westview Press, 1991); John R. Petrocik, "Issue Ownership in Presidential Elections, with a 1980 Case Study," *American Journal of Political Science* (August 1996): 825–50.

16. Andrew Gelman and Gary King, "Why Are American Presidential Election Campaign Polls So Variable When Votes Are So Predictable"? *British Journal of Political Science* 23 (Part 4, 1993): 409–51.

17. See, for example, Carl Albert, interview by Dorothy Pierce McSweeny, April 13, 1969, interview 3, transcript, pp. 8–9, Lyndon Johnson Library, Austin, Texas.

18. See, for example, Richard P. Nathan et al., *Revenue Sharing: The Second Round* (Washington, DC: Brookings Institution, 1977).

19. David Gergen, *Eyewitness to Power: The Essence of Leadership* (New York: Simon & Schuster 2000), p. 348.

20. Quoted in Steven V. Roberts, "Return to the Land of the Gipper," *New York Times*, March 9, 1988, p. A28.

21. Ronald Reagan, *Where's the Rest of Me? The Autobiography of Ronald Reagan* (New York: Karz, 1965), p. 138.

22. Bob Woodward, *The Agenda: Inside the Clinton White House* (New York: Simon & Schuster, 1994), pp. 243, 247–48.

23. "Pollster: Mistakes Made," *Bryan–College Station Eagle*, May 23, 1993, p. A8.

24. "Democrats Look to Salvage Part of Stimulus Plan," *Congressional Quarterly Weekly Report*, April 24, 1993, p. 1002.

25. George C. Edwards III, *On Deaf Ears: The Limits of the Bully Pulpit* (New Haven, CT: Yale University Press, 2003), pp. 35–36.

26. Jann S. Wenner and William Greider, "President Clinton," *Rolling Stone*, December 9, 1993, p. 43.

27. See Stephen Skowronek, "Leadership by Definition: First Term Reflections on George W. Bush's Political Stance," *Perspectives on Politics* 3 (December 2005): 818.

28. An exception to the experimental nature of framing studies is Jacoby, "Issue Framing and Public Opinion on Government Spending." He employed NES data to present both frames to the same sample. Even here, however, the framing occurred in the context of an interview in which different frames were presented at different times.

29. James N. Druckman and Kjersten R. Nelson, "Framing and Deliberation: How Citizens' Conversations Limit Elite Influence," *American Journal of Political Science* 47 (October 2003): 729–45.

30. James N. Druckman, "Using Credible Advice to Overcome Framing Effects," *Journal of Law, Economics, and Organization* 17 (April 2001): 62–82.

31. Donald P. Haider-Markel and Mark R. Joslyn, "Gun Policy, Opinion, Tragedy, and Blame Attribution: The Conditional Influence of Issue Frames," *Journal of Politics* 63 (May 2001): 520–43.

32. Gregory A. Huber and John S. Lapinski, "The 'Race Card' Revisited: Assessing Racial Priming in Policy Contests," *American Journal of Political Science* 50 (April 2006): 421–40.

33. James N. Druckman and Kjersten R. Nelson, "Framing and Deliberation."

34. Lee Sigelman, "Gauging the Public Response to Presidential Leadership," *Presidential Studies Quarterly* 10 (Summer): 427–33. See also Pamela Johnston Conover and Lee Sigelman, "Presidential Influence and Public Opinion: The Case of the Iranian Hostage Crisis," *Social Science Quarterly* 63 (June 1982): 249–64.

35. Dan Thomas and Lee Sigelman, "Presidential Identification and Policy Leadership: Experimental Evidence on the Reagan Case," in George C. Edwards III, Steven A. Shull, and Norman C. Thomas, eds., *The Presidency and Public Policy Making* (Pittsburgh: University of Pittsburgh Press, 1985).

36. Lee Sigelman and Carol K. Sigelman, "Presidential Leadership of Public Opinion: From 'Benevolent Leader' to Kiss of Death?" *Experimental Study of Politics* 7 (3, 1981): 1–22.

37. Jeffrey J. Mondak, "Source Cues and Public Approval: The Cognitive Dynamics of Public Support for the Reagan Administration," *American Journal of Political Science* 37 (February 1993): 186–212.

38. Zaller, *The Nature and Origins of Mass Opinion*, p. 99, chap. 9. See also Adam J. Berinsky, "Assuming the Costs of War: Events, Elites, and American Public Support for Military Conflict," *Journal of Politics* 69 (November 2007): 975–97.

39. See Paul M. Sniderman and Sean M. Theriault, "The Structure of Political Argument and the Logic of Issue Framing," in Willem E. Saris and Paul M. Sniderman, eds., *Studies in Public Opinion: Attitudes, Nonattitudes, Measurement Error and Change* (Princeton, NJ: Princeton University Press, 2004). Also see Paul M. Sniderman, "Taking Sides: A Fixed Choice Theory of Political Reasoning," in Arthur Lupia, Mathew D. McCubbins, and Samuel L. Popkin, eds., *Elements of Reason: Understanding and Expanding the Limits of Political Rationality* (New York: Cambridge University Press, 2000); James N. Druckman, "Political Preference Formation: Competition, Deliberation, and the (Ir)relevance of Framing Effects," *American Political Science Review* 98 (November 2004): 671–86.

40. John Zaller, "Elite Leadership of Mass Opinion: New Evidence from the Gulf War," in W. Lance Bennett and David L. Paletz, eds., *Taken by Storm: The Media, Public Opinion, and U.S. Foreign Policy in the Gulf War* (Chicago: University of Chicago Press, 1994), pp. 186–209.

41. Quoted in Michael B. Grossman and Martha J. Kumar, *Portraying the President* (Baltimore, MD: Johns Hopkins University Press, 1981), p. 26.

42. Thomas E. Patterson, *Doing Well and Doing Good* (Cambridge, MA: Shorenstein Center, 2000), pp. 2–5.

43. Sam Donaldson, quoted in "Washington Press Corps," *Newsweek*, May 25, 1981, p. 90.

44. President Carter, quoted in Michael Baruch Grossman and Martha Joynt Kumar, "Carter, Reagan, and the Media: Have the Rules Really Changed or the Poles of the Spectrum of Success?" Paper presented at the Annual Meeting of the American Political Science Association, New York, September 3–6, 1981, p. 8.

45. Quoted in Grossman and Kumar, *Portraying the President*, p. 43.

46. Thomas E. Patterson, *Out of Order* (New York: Knopf, 1993), pp. 16–21, 113–15; Matthew Robert Kerbel, *Edited for Television* (Boulder, CO: Westview, 1994), pp. 111–12; Kevin G. Barnhurst and Catherine A. Steele, "Image-Bite News: The Visual Coverage of Elections on U.S. Television, 1968–1992," *Press/Politics* 1n 2 (Winter 1997): 40–58; S. Robert Lichter and Richard E. Noyes, *Good Intentions Make Bad News*, 2nd ed. (Lanham, MD: Rowman and Littlefield, 1996), pp. 116–26; Richard Nadeau, Richard G. Niemi, David P. Fah, and Timothy Amato, "Elite Economic Forecasts, Economic News, Mass Economic Judgments, and Presidential Approval," *Journal of Politics* 61 (February 1999): 109–35; "Campaign 2000 Final: How TV News Covered the Election Campaign," *Media Monitor* 14 (November/December 2000).

47. Dwight F. Davis, Lynda Lee Kaid, and Donald L. Singleton, "Information Effects of Political Commentary," *Experimental Study of Politics* 6 (June 1977): 45–68; Lynda Lee Kaid, Donald L. Singleton, and Dwight F. Davis, "Instant Analysis of Televised Political Addresses: The Speaker versus the Commentator," in Brent D. Ruben, ed., *Communication Yearbook I* (New Brunswick, NJ: Transaction Books, 1977), pp. 453–64; John Havick, "The Impact of a Televised State of the Union Message and the Instant Analysis: An Experiment." Unpublished paper, Georgia Institute of Technology, 1980.

48. David L. Paletz and Robert M. Entman, *Media—Power—Politics* (New York: Free Press, 1981), p. 70.

49. Patterson, *Doing Well by Doing Good*, pp. 10, 12.

50. *Media Monitor*, May/June 1995, pp. 2–5; Thomas E. Patterson, "Legitimate Beef: The Presidency and a Carnivorous Press," *Media Studies Journal* 8 (Spring 1994): 21–26. However, compare Andras Szanto, "In Our Opinion . . .: Editorial Page Views of Clinton's First Year," *Media Studies Journal* 8 (Spring 1994): 97–105; Lichter and Noyes, *Good Intentions Make Bad News*, p. 214.

51. Stephen J. Farnsworth and S. Robert Lichter, *The Mediated Presidency: Television News and Presidential Governance* (Lanham, MD: Rowman and Littlefield, 2006), pp. 40–45, chap. 4; Stephen J. Farns-

worth and S. Robert Lichter, *The Nightly News Nightmare: Television's Coverage of U.S. Presidential Elections, 1988–2004,* 2nd ed. (Lanham, MD: Rowman and Littlefield, 2007), chap. 4. See also Jeffrey E. Cohen, *The Presidency in the Era of 24-Hour News* (Princeton, NJ: Princeton University Press, 2008), chaps. 5–6.

52. Patterson, *Out of Order,* p. 22, chap. 2; Cappella and Jamieson, *Spiral of Cynicism;* Jacobs and Shapiro, *Politicians Don't Pander,* p. 231; Dhavan V. Shah, Mark D. Watts, David Domke, and David P. Fan, "News Framing and Cueing of Issue Regimes: Explaining Clinton's Public Approval in Spite of Scandal," *Public Opinion Quarterly* 66 (Fall 2002): 339–70.

53. Jacobs and Shapiro, *Politicians Don't Pander,* pp. 176–82, 214–15; Kathleen Hall Jamieson and Joseph N. Cappella, "The Role of the Press in the Health Care Reform Debate of 1993–1994," in Doris Graber, Denis McQuail, and Pippa Norris, eds., *The Politics of News, The News of Politics* (Washington, DC: CQ Press, 1998).

54. Jacobs and Shapiro, *Politicians Don't Pander,* pp. 232–55.

55. Cappella and Jamieson, *Spiral of Cynicism.*

56. W. Russell Neuman, *The Paradox of Mass Politics; Knowledge and Opinion in the American Electorate* (Cambridge, MA: Harvard University Press, 1986), pp. 170, 172, 177–78, 186.

57. Converse, "The Nature of Belief Systems in Mass Publics"; William G. Jacoby, "The Sources of Liberal-Conservative Thinking: Education and Conceptualization," *Political Behavior* 10 (Winter 1988): 316–32; Robert C. Luskin, "Measuring Political Sophistication," *American Journal of Political Science* 31 (November 1987): 856–99; Neuman, *The Paradox of Mass Politics;* Edward G. Carmines and James A. Stimson, "The Two Faces of Issue Voting," *American Political Science Review* 74 (March 1980): 78–91; Zaller, *The Nature and Origins of Mass Opinion,* p. 48.

58. James H. Kuklinski, Paul J. Quirk, Jennifer Jerit, David Schwieder, and Robert F. Rich, "Misinformation and the Currency of Democratic Citizenship," *Journal of Politics* 62 (August 2000): 790–816.

59. Zaller, *The Nature and Origins of Mass Opinion,* pp. 102–13.

60. Zaller, "Elite Leadership of Mass Opinion"; Zaller, *The Nature and Origins of Mass Opinion.*

61. See, for example, James H. Kuklinski and Norman L. Hurley, "On Hearing and Interpreting Political Messages: A Cautionary Tale of Citizen Cue-Taking," *Journal of Politics* 56 (August 1994): 729–51.

62. See Edwards, *On Deaf Ears*, chap. 9; Larry Bartels, "Beyond the Running Tally: Partisan Bias in Political Perceptions," *Political Behavior* 24 (June 2002): 117–50; and Brian J. Gaines, James H. Kuklinski, Paul J. Quirk, Buddy Peyton, and Jay Verkuilen, "Same Facts, Different Interpretations: Partisan Motivation and Opinion on Iraq," *Journal of Politics* 69 (November 2007): 957–74, on how partisanship biases processing perceptions, interpretations, and response to the political world.

63. Druckman, "On the Limits of Framing Effects: Who Can Frame?" See also Miller and Krosnick, "News Media Impact on the Ingredients of Presidential Evaluations"; and James N. Druckman, "Using Credible Advice to Overcome Framing Effects," *Journal of Law, Economics, and Organization* 17 (April 2001): 62–82.

64. "Reagan Loses Ground on 'Contra' Aid Program," *Congressional Quarterly Weekly Report*, March 8, 1986, pp. 535–36.

65. Steven V. Roberts, "Senate Upholds Arms for Saudis, Backing Reagan," *New York Times*, June 6, 1986, sec. A, pp. l, 10. The thirty-four votes did sustain the president's veto, however.

66. Brandice Canes-Wrone, *Who Leads Whom? Presidents, Policy, and the Public* (Princeton, NJ: Princeton University Press, 2006), p. 80, chaps. 3–4.

67. Jeffrey E. Cohen, *Presidential Responsiveness and Public Policy-Making* (Ann Arbor: University of Michigan Press, 1997).

68. Kim Quaile Hill, "The Policy Agendas of the President and the Mass Public: A Research Validation and Extension," *American Journal of Political Science* 42 (October 1998): 1328–34.

69. B. Dan Wood, *The Politics of Economic Leadership* (Princeton, NJ: Princeton University Press, 2007), chap. 3.

70. Michael Waldman, *POTUS Speaks* (New York: Simon & Schuster, 2000), p. 216.

71. See E. E. Schattschneider, *The Semisovereign People: A Realist's View of Democracy in America* (New York: Holt, Rinehart and Winston, 1960).

72. See Bryan D. Jones and Frank R. Baumgartner, *The Politics of Attention: How Government Prioritizes Problems* (Chicago: University of Chicago Press, 2005), chap. 3; Bryan D. Jones, *Reconceiving Decision-Making in Democratic Politics* (Chicago: University of Chicago Press, 1994), chap. 4.

73. Quoted in "MX Debate: It's Not Over," *New York Times*, March 30, 1985, pp. 1, 8. See also "Senate Hands Reagan Victory on MX

Missile," *Congressional Quarterly Weekly Report*, March 23, 1985, pp. 515–23.

74. Bill Clinton, *My Life* (New York: Knopf, 2004), p. 682; Kumar, *Managing the President's Message*, p. 42.

75. George C. Edwards III, *At the Margins: Presidential Leadership of Congress* (New Haven, CT: Yale University Press, 1989), chap. 8; David Peterson, Lawrence J. Grossback, James A. Stimson, and Amy Gangl, "Congressional Response to Mandate Elections," *American Journal of Political Science* 47 (June 2003): 411–26.

76. David R. Mayhew, *Congress: The Electoral Connection* (New Haven, CT: Yale University Press, 1974), 70–71.

77. For an analysis of the perceptions of mandates, see Edwards, *At the Margins*, chap. 8; Peterson, Grossback, Stimson, and Gangl, "Congressional Response to Mandate Elections."

78. Quoted in Everett Carll Ladd, *The Ladd Report #1* (New York: W. W. Norton, 1985), 3.

79. See George C. Edwards III, *Governing by Campaigning: The Politics of the Bush Administration*, 2nd ed. (New York: Longman, 2007), chap. 4.

80. William Schneider, "A Popularity Contest," *National Journal*, November 16, 2002, p. 3346.

81. William Schneider, "The Bush Mandate," *National Journal*, November 9, 2002, 3358; Adam Nagourney and Janet Elder, "Positive Ratings for the G.O.P., If Not Its Policy," *New York Times*, November 26, 2002, pp. A1, A22.

82. Peter H. Stone and Shawn Zeller, "Business and Conservative Groups Won Big," *National Journal*, November 9, 2002, p. 3355.

83. Gary C. Jacobson, "Terror, Terrain, and Turnout: Explaining the 2002 Midterm Election," *Political Science Quarterly* 118 (Spring 2003): 1–22; Charlie Cook, "A Landslide? That Talk Is Mostly Just Hot Air," *National Journal*, November 9, 2002, 3346–47.

84. See Jeffrey Tulis, "The Two Constitutional Presidencies," in Michael Nelson, *The Presidency and the Political System* (Washington, DC: CQ Press, 1984), pp. 78–79.

85. See, for example, George C. Edwards III, *The Public Presidency* (New York: St. Martin's, 1983), 18–23.

86. Quoted in Robert Draper, *Dead Certain: The Presidency of George W. Bush* (New York: Free Press, 2007), p. 234.

87. Stanley Kelley, Jr., *Interpreting Elections* (Princeton, NJ: Princeton University Press, 1983), 72–125.

88. Martin P. Wattenberg, *The Rise of Candidate-Centered Politics: Presidential Elections of the 1980s* (Cambridge, MA: Harvard University Press, 1991), chaps. 5–6.

89. See Kathryn Dunn Tenpas and James A. McCann, "Testing the Permanence of the Permanent Campaign: An Analysis of Presidential Polling Expenditures, 1977–2002," *Public Opinion Quarterly* 71 (Fall 2007): 349–66; Diane J. Heith, *Polling to Govern: Public Opinion and Presidential Leadership* (Palo Alto, CA: Stanford University Press, 2004); Lawrence R. Jacobs and Robert Y. Shapiro, "Issues, Candidate Image, and Priming: The Use of Private Polls in Kennedy's 1960 Presidential Campaign," *American Political Science Review* 88 (September 1994): 527–40; Lawrence R. Jacobs and Robert Y. Shapiro, "The Rise of Presidential Polling: The Nixon White House in Historical Perspective," *Public Opinion Quarterly* 59 (Summer 1995): 163–95; Robert M. Eisinger, *The Evolution of Presidential Polling* (Cambridge, UK: Cambridge University Press, 2003); and Shoon Kathleen Murray and Peter Howard, "Variations in White House Polling Operations," *Public Opinion Quarterly* 66 (Winter 2002): 527–58.

90. See Stanley Feldman and John Zaller, "The Political Culture of Ambivalence: Ideological Responses to the Welfare State," *American Journal of Political Science* 36 (February 1992): 268–307.

91. AP/Ipsos Poll, June 7–9, 2004.

92. CBS News/*New York Times* Poll, September 28–October 1, 2003.

93. Steven Kull, Clay Ramsay, and Evan Lewis, "Misperceptions, the Media, and the Iraq War," *Political Science Quarterly* 118 (Winter 2003–2004): 569–98.

94. Benjamin I. Page and Robert Y. Shapiro, *The Rational Public* (Chicago: University of Chicago Press, 1992); James A. Stimson, *Public Opinion in America: Moods, Cycles, and Swings* (Boulder, CO: Westview, 1991).

95. John W. Kingdon, *Agendas, Alternatives, and Public Policies*, 2nd ed. (Boston: Little, Brown, 1995), pp. 146–50.

96. Frank Baumgartner and Bryan D. Jones, *Agendas and Instability in American Politics* (Chicago: University of Chicago Press, 1993), pp. 236–37.

97. Michael Nelson, "The President and the Court: Reinterpreting the Court-packing Episode of 1937," *Political Science Quarterly* 103 (Summer 1988): 272.

98. Richard Hofstadter, *The American Political Tradition* (New York: Vintage, 1954), p. 316.

99. Edward G. Carmines and James A. Stimson, *Issue Evolution: Race and the Transformation of American Politics* (Princeton, NJ: Princeton University Press, 1989).

100. Mark Smith, *The Right Talk: How Conservatives Transformed the Great Society into the Economic Society* (Princeton, NJ: Princeton University Press, 2007).

101. Byron E. Shafer and Richard Johnston, *The End of Southern Exceptionalism* (Cambridge, MA: Harvard University Press, 2006).

102. Taeku Lee, *Mobilizing Public Opinion: Black Insurgency and Racial Attitudes in the Civil Rights Era* (Chicago: University of Chicago Press, 2002).

103. Gary C. Jacobson, *A Divider, Not a Uniter: George W. Bush and the American Public*, 2nd ed. (New York: Longman, 2007), p. 36.

104. Morris P. Fiorina, *Culture War? The Myth of a Polarized America*, 2nd ed. (New York: Longman, 2006).

105. Jones and Baumgartner, *The Politics of Attention*, p. 241.

106. David Zarefsky, *President Johnson's War on Poverty: Rhetoric and History* (University: University of Alabama Press, 1986), p. 24.

107. Jeffrey K. Tulis, *The Rhetorical Presidency* (Princeton, NJ: Princeton University Press, 1987), pp. 161–72. See also Zarefsky, *President Johnson's War on Poverty*, for a discussion of the administration's framing of the issue.

108. Edwards, *On Deaf Ears*, pp. 57–59.

109. Kuklinski et al., "Misinformation and the Currency of Democratic Citizenship"; Robert C. Luskin, James S. Fishkin, and Roger Jowell, "Considered Opinions: Deliberative Polling in Britain," *British Journal of Political Science* 32 (July 2002): 455–87.

110. Gallup poll, August 3–5, 2001.

111. Ibid.

112. Gallup poll, August 10–12, 2001.

113. Gallup poll, August 5–7, 2005.

114. Gallup poll, July 21–21, 2006.

115. Gallup poll, April 13–15, 2007.

116. Gallup poll, September 24–27, 2007.

117. See Edwards, *Governing by Campaigning*, chap. 5.

118. See Charles O. Jones, *The Presidency in a Separated System*, 2nd ed. (Washington, DC: Brookings Institution, 2005), chap. 5.

119. On continuity in foreign policy despite changes in the occupant of the presidency, see William J. Dixon and Stephen M. Gardner, "Presidential Succession and the Cold War: An Analysis of Soviet-

American Relations, 1948–1988," *Journal of Politics* 54 (February 1992): 156–75.

120. Quoted in John C. Donovan, *The Politics of Poverty,* 2nd ed. (Indianapolis, IN: Pegasus, 1973), p. 111.

121. Woodward, *The Agenda,* p. 313.

122. Page and Shapiro, *The Rational Public,* pp. 12–13.

123. Fay Lomax Cook, Tom R. Tyler, E. G. Goetz, M. T. Gordon, D. Protess, D. Leff, and H. L. Molotch, "Media and Agenda-Setting: Effects on the Public, Interest Group Leaders, Policy Makers, and Policy," *Public Opinion Quarterly* 47 (Spring 1983): 16–35; James W. Dearing and Everett M. Rogers, *Agenda Setting* (Thousand Oaks, CA: Sage, 1996); William Gonzenbach, *The Media, the President, and Public Opinion: A Longitudinal Analysis of the Drug Issue, 1984–1991* (Mahwah, NJ: Lawrence Erlbaum, 1996); Shanto Iyengar, Mark D. Peters, and Donald R. Kinder, "Experimental Demonstrations of the 'Not-So-Minimal' Consequences of Television News Programs," *American Political Science Review* 76 (December 1982): 848–58; Michael Bruce MacKuen and Steven Lane Coombs, *More than News* (Beverly Hills, CA: Sage, 1981), chaps. 3–4; Maxwell McCombs and George Estrada, "The News Media and the Pictures in Our Heads," in Shanto Iyengar and Richard Reeves, eds., *Do the Media Govern? Politicians, Voters, and Reporters in America* (Thousand Oaks, CA: Sage, 1997); Maxwell McCombs and Donald Shaw, "The Evolution of Agenda Setting Research: Twenty-five Years in the Marketplace of Ideas," *Journal of Communication* 43 (Spring 1993): 58–67; David L. Protess and Maxwell McCombs, eds., *Agenda Setting: Readings on Media, Public Opinion, and Policymaking* (Hillsdale, NJ: Lawrence Erlbaum, 1991); James P. Winter and Chaim H. Eyal, "Agenda-Setting for the Civil Rights Issue," *Public Opinion Quarterly* 45 (Fall 1981): 376–83; Doris A. Graber, "Agenda-Setting: Are There Women's Perspectives?" in Laurily Epstein, ed., *Women and the News* (New York: Hastings House, 1978), pp. 15–37; Jacobs and Shapiro, *Politicians Don't Pander,* pp. 232–33.

124. Doris A. Graber, *Mass Media and American Politics,* 7th ed. (Washington, DC: CQ Press, 2005), p. 194.

125. Shanto Iyengar, *Is Anyone Responsible?* (Chicago: University of Chicago Press, 1991), p. 2. See also Iyengar, Peters, and Kinder, "Experimental Demonstrations of the 'Not-So-Minimal' Consequences of Television News Programs"; Larry M. Bartels, "Messages Received: The Political Impact of Media Exposure," *American Political*

Science Review 87 (June 1993): 267–85; and Dhavan V. Shah, Mark D. Watts, David Domke, David P. Fan, and Michael Fibison, "News Coverage, Economic Cues, and the Public's Presidential Preferences, 1984–1996," *Journal of Politics* 61 (November 1999): 914–43. There is also evidence that presidential approval is influenced by elite opinion, as brought to the public's attention in the mass media. See Richard A. Brody, *Assessing the President* (Stanford, CA: Stanford University Press, 1991).

126. James A. Baker III, *The Politics of Diplomacy* (New York: Putnam, 1995), p. 103; Colin Powell, *My American Journey* (New York: Ballantine, 1995), pp. 418, 550, 573. See also Eytan Gilboa, "Television News and U.S. Foreign Policy," *Press/Politics* 8 (Fall 2003): 97–113.

127. Quoted in Morris, *Behind the Oval Office* (New York: Random House, 1997), p. 245.

128. Carl M. Cannon, "From Bosnia to Kosovo," *National Journal*, April 3, 1999, p. 881.

129. Quoted in Powell, *My American Journey*, p. 507.

130. Ibid., p. 418.

131. Martin Linsky, *Impact: How the President Affects Federal Policymaking* (New York: Norton, 1986), p. 87.

132. Everett M. Rogers and James W. Dearing, "Agenda-Setting Research: Where Has It Been, Where Is It Going?" in Doris A. Graber, ed., *Media Power in Politics*, 3rd ed. (Washington, DC: CQ Press, 1994), p. 91.

133. See George C. Edwards III and Stephen J. Wayne, *Presidential Leadership*, 8th ed. (New York: Wadsworth, 2009), chap. 5.

134. Kumar, *Managing the President's Message*; Grossman and Kumar, *Portraying the President*; John A. Maltese, *Spin Control: The White House Office of Communications and the Management of Presidential News* (Chapel Hill: University of North Carolina Press, 1992); Mark J. Rozell, *The Press and the Ford Presidency* (Ann Arbor: University of Michigan Press, 1992); Mark J. Rozell, *The Press and the Bush Presidency* (Westport, CT: Praeger, 1996).

135. Sheldon Gilberg, Chaim Eyal, Maxwell McCombs, and David Nicholas, "The State of the Union Address and the Press Agenda," *Journalism Quarterly* 57 (Winter 1980): 584–88; Wayne Wanta, Mary Ann Stephenson, Judy VanSlyke Turk, and Maxwell E. McCombs, "How President's State of Union Talk Influenced News Media Agendas," *Journalism Quarterly* 66 (Autumn 1989): 537–41.

136. B. Dan Wood and Jeffrey S. Peake, "The Dynamics of Foreign Policy Agenda Setting," *American Political Science Review* 92 (March 1998): 173–84.

137. George C. Edwards III and B. Dan Wood, "Who Influences Whom? The President, Congress, and the Media," *American Political Science Review* 93 (June 1999): 327–44. See also Jacobs and Shapiro, *Politicians Don't Pander*, pp. 201–2.

138. Jeffrey S. Peake, "Presidential Agenda Setting in Foreign Policy," *Political Research Quarterly* 54 (March 2001): 69–86.

139. Matthew Eshbaugh-Soha and Jeffrey S. Peake, "Presidents and the Economic Agenda," *Political Research Quarterly* 58 (March 2005): 127–38.

140. Baumgartner and Jones, *Agendas and Instability in American Politics.*

141. Kingdon, *Agendas, Alternatives, and Public Policies*, pp. 34–42.

142. Roy B. Flemming, John Bohte, and B. Dan Wood, "One Voice Among Many: The Supreme Court's Influence on Attentiveness to Issues in the United States, 1947–1990," *American Journal of Political Science* 41 (October 1997): 1,224–50.

143. See, for example, Adam Clymer, "Majority in Poll Expect Congress to Cut Spending," *New York Times*, November 17, 1985, sec. 1, p. 1.

144. George C. Edwards III and Andrew Barrett, "Presidential Agenda Setting in Congress," in Jon R. Bond and Richard Fleisher, eds., *Polarized Politics: Congress and the President in a Partisan Era* (Washington, DC: CQ Press, 2000).

145. Quoted in Paul C. Light, *The President's Agenda: Domestic Policy Choice from Kennedy to Carter* (Baltimore, MD: Johns Hopkins University Press, 1982), p. 54. See also Robert Shogan, *Promises to Keep* (New York: Thomas Y. Crowell, 1977), p. 205.

146. See, for example, Jacqueline Calmes, "The 99th Congress: A Mixed Record of Success," *Congressional Quarterly Weekly Report* 44 (October 25, 1986), p. 2647; Edwards, *On Deaf Ears*, pp. 145–47.

147. Mark Hertsgaard, *On Bended Knee: The Press and the Reagan Presidency* (New York: Farrar, Straus, and Giroux, 1988), pp. 107–8; Larry Speakes, *Speaking Out* (New York: Scribner's, 1988), p. 301.

148. Jacobs and Shapiro, *Politicians Don't Pander*, p. 140, agree with this point.

149. Grossman and Kumar, *Portraying the President*, pp. 99–100; see also p. 314.

150. See an interview with Bill Clinton by Jack Nelson and Robert J. Donovan, "The Education of a President," *Los Angeles Times Magazine*, August 1, 1993, p. 39. See also Clinton, *My Life*, p. 556.

151. Quoted in Thomas L. Friedman and Maureen Dowd, "Amid Setbacks, Clinton Team Seeks to Shake Off the Blues," *New York Times*, April 25, 1993, sec. 1, p. 12.

152. Quoted in Dick Kirschten, "For Reagan Communication Team . . . It's Strictly One Week at a Time," *National Journal*, March 8, 1986, p. 594.

153. See, for example, Michael Waldman, *POTUS Speaks*, pp. 42–43.

154. Quoted in Wenner and Greider, "President Clinton,"p. 80. See also Clinton, *My Life*, pp. 467–68, 481, 518–19, 556, 671.

155. Clinton, *My Life*, p. 556.

156. Woodward, *Agenda*, p. 241; comments by Clinton White House chiefs of staff Leon Panetta and Erskine Bowles on the importance of focusing the president's message in Terry Sullivan, ed., *The Nerve Center: Lessons in Governing from the White House Chiefs of Staff* (College Station: Texas A&M University Press, 2004), pp. 56–57.

157. Thomas L. Friedman, "Scholars' Advice and New Campaign Help the President Hit His Old Stride," *New York Times*, November 17, 1993, p. A10; Nelson and Donovan, "The Education of a President," p. 14.

158. Bill Clinton, *My Life*, pp. 467, 514, 521. See also "Excerpts from Clinton's Question and Answer Session in the Rose Garden," *New York Times*, May 28, 1993, p. A10; and David S. Broder and Dan Balz, "Clinton Finds Change Harder than Expected," *Washington Post*, May 14, 1993, p. A11.

159. Nelson and Donovan, "The Education of a President," p. 14.

160. Quoted in "For Health Care, Time Was a Killer," *New York Times*, August 29, 1994, p. A8.

161. Clinton, *My Life*, p. 556; Jacobs and Shapiro, *Politicians Don't Pander*, pp. 114, 142.

162. Jacobs and Shapiro, *Politicians Don't Pander*, p. 124, chap. 4.

163. "Remarks by President Bush in a Conversation on Strengthening Social Security," Greece, New York, March 24, 2005.

164. Gergen, *Eyewitness to Power*, pp. 54, 186. Also see Kumar, *Managing the President's Message*, chaps. 2–3.

165. Converse, "The Nature of Belief Systems in Mass Publics," pp. 206–61.

166. Charles W. Ostrom, Jr. and Dennis M. Simon, "The President's Public," *American Journal of Political Science* 32 (November 1988): 1096–1119.

167. Gergen, *Eyewitness to Power*, p. 54. See also Kumar, *Managing the President's Message*, chap. 1.

168. Gergen, *Eyewitness to Power*, p. 54.

169. See Edwards, *On Deaf Ears*, pp. 130–31, 140–42; Edwards, *Governing by Campaigning*, pp. 82–84.

170. John E. Mueller, *War, Presidents, and Public Opinion* (New York: Wiley, 1973); Lyn Ragsdale, "The Politics of Presidential Speech-making, 1949–1980," *American Political Science Review* 78 (December 1984): 971–84; Roy L. Behr and Shanto Iyengar, "Television News, Real World Cues, and Changes in the Public Agenda," *Public Opinion Quarterly* 49 (Spring 1985): 38–57; Lyn Ragsdale, "Presidential Speech-making and the Public Audience," *Journal of Politics* 49 (August 1987): 704–36; Dennis M. Simon and Charles W. Ostrom, "The Impact of Televised Speeches and Foreign Travel on Presidential Approval," *Public Opinion Quarterly* 53 (Spring 1989): 58–82; Paul Brace and Barbara Hinckley, "Presidential Activities from Truman through Reagan: Timing and Impact," *Journal of Politics* 55 (May 1993): 382–98; Jeffrey E. Cohen, *Presidential Responsiveness and Public Policy-Making* (Ann Arbor: University of Michigan Press, 1997).

171. Joe S. Foote, "Ratings Decline of Presidential Television," *Journal of Broadcasting and Electronic Media* 32 (Spring 1988): 225–30; A. C. Nielsen, *Nielsen Newscast* (Northbrook, IL: Nielson, 1975); Edwards, *On Deaf Ears*, chap. 8; Edwards, *Governing by Campaigning*, pp. 86–94.

172. Matthew A. Baum and Samuel Kernell, "Has Cable Ended the Golden Age of Presidential Television?" *American Political Science Review* 93 (March 1999): 99–114.

173. Lee Sigelman and Cynthia Whissell, "'The Great Communicator' and 'The Great Talker' on the Radio: Projecting Presidential Personas," *Presidential Studies Quarterly* 32 (March 2002): 137–46.

174. Beverly Horvit, Adam J. Schiffer, and Mark Wright, "The Limits of Presidential Agenda Setting; Predicting Newspaper Coverage of the Weekly Radio Address," *Press/Politics* 13 (January 2008): 8–28.

175. Andrew Barrett, "Gone Public: The Impact of Presidential Rhetoric in Congress," unpublished Ph.D. dissertation, Texas A&M University, 2000.

176. Quoted in Bob Woodward, *The Choice* (New York: Simon & Schuster, 1996), p. 315.

Chapter 4: Leading Congress: Best Test Cases

1. Lyndon Johnson quoted in Doris Kearns, *Lyndon Johnson and the American Dream* (New York: Harper & Row, 1976), p. 226.

2. Hubert H. Humphrey, *The Education of a Public Man: My Life and Politics* (Garden City, NY: Doubleday, 1976), pp. 290–93.

3. Jack Valenti, *A Very Human President* (New York: Norton, 1975), pp. 196–97. See also Russell D. Renka, "Bargaining with Legislative Whales in the Kennedy and Johnson Administration." Paper presented at the annual meeting of the American Political Science Association, Washington, DC, August 1980, p. 20.

4. Transcript, Henry Hall Wilson Oral History Interview, April 11, 1973, by Joe B. Frantz, p. 16, Lyndon B. Johnson Library, Austin, TX.

5. For another example of the unreliablity of "eyewitness" accounts, see Robert Dallek, *An Unfinished Life: John F. Kennedy, 1917–1963* (Boston: Little, Brown, 2003), pp. 318–19.

6. William E. Leuchtenburg, *Franklin D. Roosevelt and the New Deal, 1932–1940* (New York: Harper & Row, 1963), pp. 9–12; Donald A. Ritchie, *Electing FDR: The New Deal Campaign of 1932* (Lawrence: University Press of Kansas, 2007).

7. Ritchie, *Electing FDR*, pp. 110, 122, 146.

8. James MacGregor Burns, *Roosevelt: The Lion and the Fox* (New York: Harcourt, Brace and World, 1956), pp. 166–68. See also Arthur M. Schlesinger, Jr., *The Coming of the New Deal* (Boston: Houghton Mifflin, 1958), p. 8; William E. Leuchtenburg, *Franklin D. Roosevelt and the New Deal, 1932–1940*, p. 48.

9. Burns, *Roosevelt: The Lion and the Fox*, pp. 166–67.

10. Schlesinger, *The Coming of the New Deal*, pp. 7–8; Leuchtenburg, *Franklin D. Roosevelt and the New Deal, 1932–1940*, pp. 43–44.

11. Burns, *Roosevelt: The Lion and the Fox*, pp. 167–68; James MacGregor Burns and Susan Dunn, *The Three Roosevelts: The Leaders Who Transformed America* (London: Atlantic Books, 2001), p. 258;

Schlesinger, *The Coming of the New Deal*, pp. 10–11; Leuchtenburg, *Franklin D. Roosevelt and the New Deal, 1932–1940*, pp. 9, 45–46.

12. Burns, *Roosevelt: The Lion and the Fox*, pp. 166–68.

13. Burns and Dunn, *The Three Roosevelts*, 255.

14. Ibid., p. 258. See also Burns, *Roosevelt: The Lion and the Fox*, pp. 143–45, 155–56, 171, 234–44, 323; Arthur M. Schlesinger, Jr., *The Politics of Upheaval* (New York: Houghton Mifflin, 1960), p. 654, chap. 35.

15. Schlesinger, *The Coming of the New Deal*, pp. 554–55; *Leuchtenburg, Franklin D. Roosevelt and the New Deal, 1932–1940*, pp. 117, 124, 131, 134, 158; Burns, *Roosevelt: The Lion and the Fox*, pp. 175, 185, 190–91, 221, 225–26.

16. Burns, *Roosevelt: The Lion and the Fox*, p. 185.

17. Schlesinger, *The Coming of the New Deal*, pp. 5, 10; Burns and Dunn, *The Three Roosevelts*, pp. 256, 258.

18. Leuchtenburg, *Franklin D. Roosevelt and the New Deal, 1932–1940*, pp. 43–48.

19. Schlesinger, *The Coming of the New Deal*, pp. 297–98; Leuchtenburg, *Franklin D. Roosevelt and the New Deal, 1932–1940*, p. 165.

20. Burns, *Roosevelt: The Lion and the Fox*, p. 243.

21. Burns and Dunn, *The Three Roosevelts*, p. 258.

22. Robert E. Sherwood, *Roosevelt and Hopkins: An Intimate History* (New York: Harper and Brothers, 1948), p. 40.

23. Schlesinger, *The Coming of the New Deal*, p. 13.

24. Burns, *Roosevelt: The Lion and the Fox*, pp. 220, 224–26, 234, 239.

25. Quoted in Sherwood, *Roosevelt and Hopkins*, p. 65.

26. Burns, *Roosevelt: The Lion and the Fox*, pp. 223–24.

27. Lawrence R. Jacobs, "The Promotional Presidency and the New Institutional Toryism: Public Mobilization, Legislative Dominance, and Squandered Opportunities," in George C. Edwards III and Desmond S. King, eds., *The Polarized Presidency of George W. Bush* (Oxford: Oxford University Press, 2007).

28. Leuchtenburg, *Franklin D. Roosevelt and the New Deal, 1932–1940*, pp. 132, 165, 180.

29. Burns, *Roosevelt: The Lion and the Fox*, pp. 226, 234.

30. Leuchtenburg, *Franklin D. Roosevelt and the New Deal, 1932–1940*, pp. 163, 165.

31. Schlesinger, *The Coming of the New Deal*, pp. 553–56; Burns, *Roosevelt: The Lion and the Fox*, pp. 175, 186–88, 223–24.

32. Burns and Dunn, *The Three Roosevelts*, pp. 257–58; Schlesinger, *The Politics of Upheaval*, pp. 212–13, 385–86; Leuchtenburg, *Franklin D. Roosevelt and the New Deal, 1932–1940*, pp. 37, 93, 138, 163, 165, 244; Julian E. Zelizer, "The Forgotten Legacy of the New Deal: Fiscal Conservatism and the Roosevelt Administration, 1933–1938," *Presidential Studies Quarterly* 30 (June 2000): 331–58.

33. Burns, *Roosevelt: The Lion and the Fox*, pp. 182–84, 193–94, 197–98, 375. See also Leuchtenburg, *Franklin D. Roosevelt and the New Deal, 1932–1940*, p. 84.

34. James MacGregor Burns, *Leadership* (New York: Harper & Row, 1978), p. 396.

35. Burns, *Roosevelt: The Lion and the Fox*, pp. 310–15, 321, 337–52, 366–70.

36. Ibid., pp. 346–50.

37. Ibid., pp. 311, 376–80, 402.

38. Leuchtenburg, *Franklin D. Roosevelt and the New Deal, 1932–1940*, p. 190.

39. Burns, *Roosevelt: The Lion and the Fox*, p. 403.

40. Some of this section is based on material in George C. Edwards III, *At the Margins: Presidential Leadership of Congress* (New Haven, CT: Yale University Press, 1989).

41. Lawrence O'Brien, in Robert L. Hardesty, ed., *The Johnson Years: The Difference He Made* (Austin, TX: Lyndon B. Johnson School of Public Affairs, 1993), p. 76. See also comments by Nicholas Katzenbach, p. 81.

42. See James L. Sundquist, *Politics and Policy: The Eisenhower, Kennedy, and Johnson Years* (Washington, DC: Brookings Institution, 1968).

43. Randall B. Woods, *LBJ: Architect of American Ambition* (New York: Free Press, 2006), p. 668.

44. Lawrence R. Jacobs, *The Health of Nations: Public Opinion and the Making of American and British Health Policy* (Ithaca, NY: Cornell University Press, 1993).

45. Mark A. Peterson, *Legislating Together* (Cambridge, MA: Harvard University Press, 1990), pp. 69–70.

46. Ronald Brownstein, *The Second Civil War* (New York: Penguin Press, 2007), p. 97.

47. Woods, *LBJ*, pp. 470, 582, 586.

48. Ibid., p. 560.

49. Lyndon B. Johnson, *The Vantage Point: Perspectives on the Presidency, 1963–1969* (New York: Popular Library, 1971), p. 323. See also Eric F. Goldman, *The Tragedy of Lyndon Johnson* (New York: Dell, 1974), pp. 306–7, Nicholas Katzenbach in Hardesty, ed., *The Johnson Years*, p. 81.

50. See Bill Moyers in Hardesty, ed., *The Johnson Years*, pp. 65–66.

51. Quoted in Harry McPherson, *A Political Education* (Boston: Little, Brown, 1972), p. 268.

52. See Paul C. Light, *The President's Agenda: Domestic Policy Choice from Kennedy to Carter* (Baltimore, MD: Johns Hopkins University Press, 1982), pp. 58–59, on the utility of this approach. Also see Lee White in Hardesty, ed., *The Johnson Years*, p. 84.

53. Quoted in Valenti, *A Very Human President*, p. 144. See also Kearns, *Lyndon Johnson and the American Dream*, pp. 216–17; Goldman, *The Tragedy of Lyndon Johnson*, pp. 306–7; McPherson, *A Political Education*, pp. 268, 428.

54. Quoted in McPherson, *A Political Education*, pp. 267–68.

55. Carl Albert, interview by Dorothy Pierce McSweeny, July 9, 1969, interview 3, transcript, pp. 7, 11, Lyndon Baines Johnson Library, Austin, TX; Carl Albert, interview by Dorothy Pierce McSweeny, August 13, 1969, interview 4, transcript, pp. 22, 25, Lyndon Baines Johnson Library; Carl Albert, interview by Dorothy Pierce McSweeny, April 28, 1969, interview 1, transcript, pp. 22–23, Lyndon Baines Johnson Library; Carl Albert, interview by Dorothy Pierce McSweeny, June 10, 1969, interview 2, transcript, p. 14, Lyndon Baines Johnson Library.

56. Russell Renka, "Comparing Presidents Kennedy and Johnson as Legislative Leaders." Paper presented at the annual meeting of the Southern Political Science Association, Savannah, GA, November 1984, p. 18, table 4. See Light, *The President's Agenda*, p. 57, on the size of Johnson's legislative program.

57. O'Brien in Hardesty, *The Johnson Years*, pp. 76–77. See also Nicholas Katzenbach, p. 81; Barefoot Sanders, p. 83; and Lee White, p. 84.

58. Peterson, *Legislating Together*, p. 68.

59. Woods, *LBJ*, pp. 440–41, 562, 747. See also John Brademas in Hardesty, *The Johnson Years*, p. 79.

60. O'Brien in Hardesty, *The Johnson Years*, p. 75.

61. See Edwards, *At the Margins*, pp. 204–5; Joseph A. Califano, Jr., *The Triumph and Tragedy of Lyndon Johnson* (New York: Simon & Schuster, 1991), pp. 119–20.

62. Nevertheless, Johnson was always ready to exploit an opportunity. For example, he saw an opportunity to exploit the assassination of Martin Luther King, Jr., for a fair housing bill and the assassination of Robert Kennedy for a gun control measure. See Califano, *The Triumph and Tragedy of Lyndon Johnson*, pp. 276, 292.

63. Woods, *LBJ*, p. 805.

64. Jacobs, "The Promotional Presidency and the New Institutional Toryism."

65. Henry Hall Wilson, interview by Joe B. Frantz, April 11, 1973, transcript, pp. 6–7, Lyndon Baines Johnson Library, Austin, TX.

66. Mike Manatos, interview by Joe B. Frantz, August 25, 1969, transcript, pp. 13–14, Lyndon Baines Johnson Library, Austin, TX.

67. John McCormack, interview by T. Harrison Baker, September 23, 1968, transcript, pp. 20, 39–40, Lyndon Baines Johnson Library; Albert, interview by McSweeny, interview 3, p. 4, Lyndon Baines Johnson Library; Goldman, *The Tragedy of Lyndon Johnson*, p. 68; Charles Halleck, interview by Stephen Hess, March 22, 1965, transcript, p. 27, John F. Kennedy Library, Boston; Lawrence F. O'Brien, *No Final Victories* (New York: Ballantine, 1974), pp. 106, 145–49, 188–89; Richard Bolling, *Power in the House* (New York: Capricorn, 1974), pp. 218, 229; Joseph A. Califano, Jr., *A Presidential Nation* (New York: Norton, 1975), p. 155; Manatos, interview by Frantz, pp. 14, 29–30, 57–58 (see also p. 32); James L. Sundquist, *Politics and Policy* (Washington, DC: Brookings Institution, 1968), pp. 476–82; Joseph Cooper and Gary Bombardier, "Presidential Leadership and Party Success," *Journal of Politics* 30 (November 1968): 1012–27; Aage R. Clausen, *How Congressmen Decide* (New York: St. Martin's, 1973), p. 146. See also Rowland Evans and Robert Novak, *Lyndon B. Johnson: The Exercise of Power* (New York: New American Library, 1966), p. 364.

68. Arthur M. Schlesinger, Jr., *Robert Kennedy and His Times* (New York: Ballantine, 1978), p. 742.

69. Quoted in William Greider, "The Education of David Stockman," *Atlantic*, December 1981, p. 52.

70. Renka, "Comparing Presidents Kennedy and Johnson as Legislative Leaders," p. 26. See also Albert, interview by McSweeny, interview 3, p. 3.

71. Michael R. Beschloss, *Taking Charge: The Johnson White House Tapes, 1963–1964* (New York: Simon & Schuster, 1997); Michael R. Beschloss, *Reaching for Glory: Lyndon Johnson's Secret White House Tapes, 1964–1965* (New York: Simon & Schuster, 2001).

72. George C. Edwards III, *Presidential Influence in Congress* (San Francisco: W. H. Freeman, 1980), pp. 197–99.

73. Jon R. Bond and Richard Fleisher, *The President in the Legislative Arena* (Chicago: University of Chicago Press, 1990), pp. 215–18.

74. See, for example, Halleck, interview by Hess, p. 28; Hale Boggs, interview by Charles T. Morrissey, May 10, 1964, transcript, p. 26, John F. Kennedy Library, Boston.

75. For useful discussions of the dispersion of power, see Thomas E. Cavanagh, "The Dispersion of Authority in the House of Representatives," *Political Science Quarterly* 97 (Winter 1982–83): 623–37; Eric L. Davis, "Legislative Reform and the Decline of Presidential Influence on Capitol Hill," *British Journal of Political Science* 9 (October 1979): 465–79; and Barbara Sinclair, *The Transformation of the U.S. Senate* (Baltimore, MD: Johns Hopkins University Press, 1989).

76. Quoted in "Single-Issue Politics," *Newsweek*, November 16, 1978, p. 58.

77. See, for example, Steven H. Haeberle, "The Institutionalization of the Subcommittee in the United States House of Representatives," *Journal of Politics* 40 (November 1978): 1054–65.

78. Quoted in Barbara Sinclair, *Majority Leadership in the U.S. House* (Baltimore, MD: Johns Hopkins University Press, 1983), pp. 19–20.

79. See, for example, Norman J. Ornstein, "The Open Congress Meets the President," in Anthony King, ed., *Both Ends of the Avenue: The Presidency, the Executive Branch, and Congress in the 1980s* (Washington, DC: American Enterprise Institute, 1983), pp. 197–99; Norman J. Ornstein, Robert L. Peabody, and David W. Rohde, "The Contemporary Senate: Into the 1980s," in Larry C. Dodd and Bruce I. Oppenheimer, eds., *Congress Reconsidered*, 2nd ed. (Washington, DC: CQ Press, 1981), pp. 16–19; Michael Foley, *The New Senate: Liberal Influence on a Conservative Institution, 1959–1972* (New Haven, CT, and London: Yale University Press, 1980), chap. 4.

80. See in James L. Sundquist, *The Decline and Resurgence of Congress* (Washington, DC: Brookings Institution, 1981), chap. 13; "In the Senate of the '80s, Team Spirit Has Given Way to the Rule of Individuals," *Congressional Quarterly Weekly Report*, September 4, 1982, p. 2175.

81. Quoted in Light, *The President's Agenda*, p. 211. See also Edwards, *Presidential Influence in Congress*, pp. 194–95.

82. Shirley Elder, "The Cabinet's Ambassadors to Capitol Hill," *National Journal*, July 29, 1978, p. 1196.

83. Quoted in Light, *The President's Agenda*, p. 209.

84. Quoted in Steven R. Weisman, "No. 1, the President Is Very Result Oriented," *New York Times*, November 12, 1983, p. 10.

85. Quoted in Elder, "The Cabinet's Ambassadors to Capitol Hill," p. 1196. See also William J. Lanouette, "Who's Setting Foreign Policy: Carter or Congress?" *National Journal*, July 15, 1978, p. 1119; "Organized Labor Found 1978 a Frustrating Year, Had Few Victories in Congress," *Congressional Quarterly Weekly Report*, December 30, 1978, p. 3539.

86. Quoted in "House, Senate Chiefs Attempt to Lead a Changed Congress," *Congressional Quarterly Weekly Report*, September 23, 1980, p. 2696. See also Light, *The President's Agenda*, p. 212; Roger H. Davidson, "The Presidency and Congress," in Michael Nelson, ed., *The Presidency and the Political System* (Washington, DC: CQ Press, 1984), p. 376.

87. Quoted in Light, *The President's Agenda*, p. 210. See also p. 209.

88. Quoted in "Shadowboxing," *Newsweek*, June 6, 1977, p. 18.

89. Barbara Sinclair, "Coping with Uncertainty: Building Coalitions in the House and the Senate," in Thomas E. Mann and Norman J. Ornstein, eds., *The New Congress* (Washington, DC: American Enterprise Institute, 1981), pp. 178–222.

90. Jody Powell, *The Other Side of the Story* (New York: William Morrow, 1984), p. 186. See also pp. 182–92.

91. George C. Edwards III, "Interview with President Jimmy Carter," *Presidential Studies Quarterly* 38 (March 2008): pp. 5–6, 2.

92. Quoted in Mark Peterson, "Congressional Responses to Presidential Proposals: Impact, Effort, and Politics." Paper presented at the Annual Meeting of the Midwest Political Science Association, Chicago, April 1986, p. 21.

93. Peterson, "Congressional Responses to Presidential Proposals," p. 32.

94. Some of this section is based on material in Edwards, *At the Margins*.

95. "Numerous Factors Favoring Good Relationship Between Reagan and New Congress," *Congressional Quarterly Weekly Report*, January 24, 1981, p. 172.

96. David A. Stockman, *The Triumph of Politics* (New York: Harper & Row, 1986), pp. 79–80; see also p. 120.

97. Paul Craig Roberts, *The Supply Side Revolution* (Cambridge, MA: Harvard University Press, 1984), p. 88.

98. See William Greider, "The Education of David Stockman," *Atlantic*, December 1981, pp. 38, 40, 43, 45, 54; Lawrence J. Korb, "Spending Without Strategy," *International Security* 12 (Summer 1987): 169.

99. James A. Baker III, *"Work Hard, Study . . . and Keep Out of Politics!"* (New York: G. P. Putnam's Sons, 2006), pp. 132–33, 136–37, 148, 171; Lou Cannon, *President Reagan: The Role of a Lifetime* (New York: Simon & Schuster, 1991), pp. 163, 344.

100. Quoted in Bernard Weinraub, "Back in the Legislative Strategist's Saddle Again," *New York Times*, May 28, 1985, p. A10.

101. Interview with Richard Cheney, November 19, 1982, Princeton.

102. "White House Lobbyists Find Congress Is Less Supportive," *Congressional Quarterly Weekly Report*, June 16, 1984, p. 1429.

103. Richard E. Neustadt, "Presidency and Legislation: Planning the President's Program," in Aaron Wildavsky, ed., *The Presidency* (Boston: Little, Brown, 1969), 596.

104. See O'Brien, *No Final Victories*, p. 111; Valenti, *A Very Human President*, p. 178; Jack Bell, *The Johnson Treatment* (New York: Dell, 1965), p. 37; Goldman, *The Tragedy of Lyndon Johnson*, p. 71; "Turning Screws: Winning Votes in Congress," *Congressional Quarterly Weekly Report*, April 24, 1976, p. 954.

105. Wilson, interview by Frantz, p. 9. See also Harold Barefoot Sanders, interview by Joe B. Frantz, March 24, 1969, tape 2, transcript, pp. 5, 8, Lyndon Baines Johnson Library, Austin, TX.

106. See, for example, Kearns, *Lyndon Johnson and the American Dream*, p. 235; William Chapman, "LBJ's Way: Tears, Not Arm-Twists," *Washington Post*, October 17, 1965, sec. E, p. 1; Dom Bonafede, "Ford's Lobbyists Expect Democrats to Revise Tactics," *National Journal*, June 21, 1975, p. 926; Merlo J. Pusey, *Eisenhower the President* (New York: Macmillan, 1956), p. 212; Stephen Horn, *Unused Power: The Work of the Senate Committee on Appropriations* (Washington, DC: Brookings Institution, 1970), p. 195; Peterson, "Congressional Responses to Presidential Proposals," p. 18.

107. Albert, interview by McSweeny, interview 4, p. 23; Kearns, *Lyndon Johnson*, pp. 234–36; Stephen J. Wayne, *The Legislative Presidency* (New York: Harper & Row, 1978), p. 151; Bonafede, "Ford's Lobbyists," p. 926; Johnson, *The Vantage Point*, p. 459; Wilson, interview by Frantz, pp. 11–13.

108. Wilson, interview by Frantz, transcript, pp. 8–9.

109. Quoted in Peterson, "Congressional Responses to Presidential Proposals," p. 20. See also M. Stephen Weatherford and Lorraine M. McDonnell, "Ronald Reagan as Legislative Advocate: Passing the Reagan Revolution Budgets in 1981 and 1982," *Congress and the Presidency* 32 (Spring 2005): 15–16.

110. See Weatherford and McDonnell, "Ronald Reagan as Legislative Advocate," pp. 1–29.

111. Quoted in "White House Lobbyists Find Congress Less Supportive," *Congressional Quarterly Weekly Report*, June 16, 1984, p. 1433.

112. Wayne, *The Legislative Presidency*, p. 151; John W. Kingdon, *Congressmen's Voting Decisions* (New York: Harper & Row, 1973), pp. 184, 187; Malcolm E. Jewell, *Senatorial Politics and Foreign Policy* (Lexington: University of Kentucky Press, 1962), pp. 160–61; McPherson, *A Political Education*, p. 192; Abraham Holtzman, *Legislative Liaison: Executive Leadership in Congress* (Chicago: Rand McNally, 1970), p. 247.

113. Quoted in Peterson, "Congressional Response to Presidential Proposals," p. 20.

114. Quoted in "Reagan's First Defeat," *Newsweek*, September 20, 1982, p. 26. See also Wilson, interview by Frantz, p. 11.

115. "Turning Screws," pp. 947, 949, 954. See also Sinclair, *Majority Leadership in the U.S. House*, p. 156.

116. Quoted in Gary W. Reichard, *The Reaffirmation of Republicanism* (Knoxville: University of Tennessee Press, 1975), p. 173.

117. Jonathan Fuerbringer, "Pressures and Rewards Face House Members on MX Vote," *New York Times*, March 26, 1985, sec. A, p. 1.

118. Quoted in Greider, "The Education of David Stockman," p. 51.

119. See Mark Peterson, "Congressional Response to Presidential Proposals," p. 20.

120. Stockman, *The Triumph of Politics*, pp. 217–18.

121. Weatherford and McDonnell, "Ronald Reagan as Legislative Advocate," pp. 7–8. See also Barbara Kellerman, *The Political Presidency* (New York: Oxford University Press, 1984), p. 243, for some different numbers.

122. Weatherford and McDonnell report that on the final vote on the tax bill on July 29, 1981, 90 percent of the Democrats the White House had identified as solid supporters or leaning toward the presi-

dent voted for the bill. Half of those the White House identified as uncommitted or leaning against the bill voted for it in the end. "Ronald Reagan as Legislative Advocate," pp. 24, fn. 17.

123. Quoted in Hedrick Smith, "Coping with Congress," *The New York Times Magazine*, August 9, 1981, p. 16.

124. See, for example, Weatherford and McDonnell, "Ronald Reagan as Legislative Advocate," pp. 8, 16–17; Ornstein, "The Open Congress Meets the President," in King, *Both Ends of the Avenue*, p. 206 and sources cited therein; Anthony King, "A Mile and a Half Is a Long Way," in King, *Both Ends of the Avenue*, pp. 264–65; "White House Lobbying Apparatus . . . Produces Impressive Tax Vote Victory," *Congressional Quarterly Weekly Report*, August 1, 1981, p. 1372. On the success of appeals of other presidents, see McPherson, *A Political Education*, p. 192; Neil MacNeil, *Forge of Democracy* (New York: David McKay, 1963), p. 265; Horn, *Unused Power*, p. 195; Everett M. Dirksen, interview by Joe B. Frantz, July 30, 1969, tape 2, transcript, p. 7, Lyndon Baines Johnson Library, Austin, TX.

125. See, for example, Edwards, *Presidential Influence in Congress*, p. 128 and sources cited therein; "Winning One for the Gipper," *Newsweek*, August 30, 1982, p. 25; James A. Miller, *Running in Place* (New York: Simon & Schuster, 1981), pp. 45–46; Stephen E. Ambrose, *Eisenhower the President* (New York: Simon & Schuster, 1984), p. 116.

126. "How Two GOP Freshmen in the House . . . Rate the White House Lobbying Effort," *Congressional Quarterly Weekly Report*, June 16, 1984, p. 1431.

127. Albert, interview by McSweeny, interview 2, pp. 11–12.

128. Manatos interview by Frantz, p. 18.

129. Quoted in Paul C. Light, *The President's Agenda: Domestic Policy Choice from Kennedy to Carter (with Notes on Reagan)* (Baltimore, MD: Johns Hopkins University Press, 1983), p. xiii.

130. "House Reverses Self, Passes Major Tax Overhaul," *Congressional Quarterly Weekly Report*, December 21, 1985, pp. 2705–11; Elizabeth Drew, "A Reporter in Washington," *New Yorker*, January 6, 1986, pp. 80–81.

131. See, for example, Fred I. Greenstein, *The Hidden-Hand Presidency: Eisenhower as Leader* (New York: Basic Books, 1982); and John P. Burke, "Political Context and Presidential Influence: A Case Study," *Presidential Studies Quarterly* 15 (Spring 1985): 301–19.

132. Gerald Ford termed Nixon's relations with Congress "terrible." Gerald R. Ford, *A Time to Heal* (New York: Harper & Row, 1979), p. 156.

133. Edwards, *At the Margins*, chaps. 9–10; George C. Edwards III, *Governing by Campaigning: The Politics of the Bush Presidency*, 2nd ed. (New York: Longman, 2007), chaps. 5–8.

134. Quoted in Lou Cannon and Carl M. Cannon, *Reagan's Disciple* (New York: Public Affairs, 2008).

135. Jon R. Bond and Richard Fleisher, *The President in the Legislative Arena* (Chicago: University of Chicago Press, 1980), chap. 8; Richard Fleisher, Jon R. Bond, and B. Dan Wood, "Which Presidents Are Uncommonly Successful in Congress?" in Bert Rockman and Richard W. Waterman, eds., *Presidential Leadership: The Vortex of Presidential Power* (New York: Oxford University Press, 2007).

136. Joseph Cooper and David W. Brady, "Institutional Context and Leadership Style: The House from Cannon to Rayburn," *American Political Science Review* 75 (June 1981): 411–25. See also David W. Rohde and Kenneth A. Shepsle, "Leaders and Followers in the House of Representatives: Reflections on Woodrow Wilson's Congressional Government," *Congress and the Presidency* 14 (Autumn 1987): 111–13; and Barbara Sinclair, "Party Leadership and Policy Change," in Gerald C. Wright, Jr., Leroy N. Rieselbach, and Lawrence C. Dodd, eds., *Congress and Policy Change* (New York: Agathon, 1986).

137. For Carter's description of this process, see Edwards, "Interview with President Jimmy Carter," pp. 7–8, 12.

138. Calvin Mouw and Michael MacKuen, "The Strategic Configuration, Personal Influence, and Presidential Power in Congress," *Western Political Quarterly* 45 (September 1992): 598.

CHAPTER 5: Leading Congress: Less Favorable Contexts

1. Richard E. Neustadt, *Presidential Power and the Modern Presidents* (New York: Free Press, 1990), p. 234.

2. See George C. Edwards III, *At the Margins: Presidential Leadership of Congress* (New Haven, CT: Yale University Press, 1989).

3. Edwards, *At the Margins: Presidential Leadership of Congress*, chap. 8; David Peterson, Lawrence J. Grossback, James A. Stimson,

and Amy Gangl, "Congressional Response to Mandate Elections," *American Journal of Political Science* 47 (June 2003): 411–26.

4. For more on the conditions that encourage perceptions of a mandate, see Edwards, *At the Margins: Presidential Leadership of Congress*, chap. 8; and Lawrence J. Grossback, David A. M. Peterson, and James A. Stimson, "Comparing Competing Theories on the Causes of Mandate Perceptions," *American Journal of Political Science* 49 (April 2005): 406–19.

5. Michael Duffy and Dan Goodgame, *Marching in Place: The Status Quo Presidency of George Bush* (New York: Simon & Schuster, 1992), pp. 19, 37.

6. George Will, "Bush Promised Little; We Got What He Promised," *Bryan–College Station Eagle*, January 21, 1990, p. 8A.

7. Quoted in Duffy and Goodgame, *Marching in Place*, p. 82.

8. Arthur M. Schlesinger, Jr., *The Politics of Upheaval* (New York: Houghton Mifflin, 1960), p. 654, chap. 35. See also Arthur M. Schlesinger, Jr., *The Coming of the New Deal* (Boston: Houghton Mifflin, 1958), p. 585; James MacGregor Burns, *Roosevelt: The Lion and the Fox* (New York: Harcourt, Brace and World, 1956), pp. 143–45, 155–56, 171, 238, 334, 476.

9. See Kerry Mullins and Aaron Wildavsky, "The Procedural Presidency of George Bush," *Political Science Quarterly* 107 (Spring 1992): 31–62.

10. George Will, "535 Political Rookies Surely Can't Be Any Worse Than Present Bunch," *Bryan–College Station Eagle*, October 14, 1990, p. A8.

11. George C. Edwards III, *On Deaf Ears: The Limits of the Bully Pulpit* (New Haven, CT: Yale University Press, 2003).

12. See, for example, Richard A. Viguerie and Steven Allen, "To Bush: The Right Has Other Choices," *New York Times*, June 14, 1990, p. A15.

13. See Edwards, *On Deaf Ears: The Limits of the Bully Pulpit*, chap. 7.

14. George C. Edwards III, William Mitchell, and Reed Welch, "Explaining Presidential Approval: The Significance of Issue Salience," *American Journal of Political Science* 39 (February 1995): 108–34.

15. See George C. Edwards III, *Governing by Campaigning: The Politics of the Bush Presidency*, 2nd ed. (New York: Longman, 2007), chap. 1.

16. Gallup poll, January 15–16, 2001.

17. Quoted in Bob Woodward, *Plan of Attack* (New York: Simon & Schuster, 2004), 28.

18. Dana Milbank, "Bush Goes With the Bold Stroke: Outsize Proposals Key to Strategy—but Not Without Risk," *Washington Post*, January 9, 2003, p. A1.

19. Alexis Simendinger, "The Report Card They Asked For," *National Journal*, July 21, 2001, 2335.

20. Of course, engaging in a highly partisan fight over taxes early in the administration while simultaneously seeking bipartisan support on other issues may have had counterproductive consequences for future coalition building.

21. The Project For Excellence in Journalism, *The First 100 Days: How Bush Versus Clinton Fared In the Press*, 2001.

22. Joseph J. Schatz, "With a Deft and Light Touch, Bush Finds Ways to Win," *Congressional Quarterly Weekly Report*, December 11, 2004, p. 2900.

23. Richard E. Cohen, "Where's the Beef?" *National Journal*, September 20, 2003, 2866–70; Elisabeth Bumiller, "Sharply Split House Passes Broad Medicare Overhaul; Forceful Lobbying by Bush," *New York Times*, November 23, 2003, p. 21; Schatz, "With a Deft and Light Touch, Bush Finds Ways to Win," 2903; Marilyn Werber Serafini, "A Prescription for Defeat," *National Journal*, August 30, 2003, pp. 2612–13.

24. Bob Woodward, *State of Denial* (New York: Simon & Schuster, 2006), p. 15.

25. Serafini, "A Prescription for Defeat," pp. 2612–13. The president did work with George Miller of California, the ranking member of the House Committee on Education and the Workforce on the No Child Left Behind legislation.

26. Gallup poll, News Release, January 5, 2001.

27. Gary C. Jacobson, "The Bush Presidency and the American Electorate," *Presidential Studies Quarterly* 33 (December 2003): 701–29.

28. See, for example, Jeffrey M. Jones, "Bush Ratings Show Historical Levels of Polarization," *Gallup News Service*, June 4, 2004.

29. This point is nicely illustrated in Gary C. Jacobson, *A Divider, Not a Uniter: George W. Bush and the American Public*, 2nd ed. (New York: Longman, 2007), chap. 1.

30. Jones, "Bush Ratings Show Historical Levels of Polarization."

31. Jeffrey M. Jones, "How Americans Voted," *Gallup News Service*, November 5, 2004.

32. Jacobson, *A Divider, Not a Uniter*, p. 190.

33. Thomas E. Mann and Norman J. Ornstein, *The Broken Branch* (New York: Oxford University Press, 2006), pp. 146, 151–79, 213–17.

34. Ronald Brownstein, *The Second Civil War* (New York: Penguin Press, 2007), pp. 240–48, 252, 287.

35. Robert Novak, "Bush's Problem with Congress," *Washington Post*, June 6, 2005, p. A19.

36. See, for example, Sheryl Gay Stolberg, "Instead of Dialogue, Bush Gives Senators Bottom Line," *New York Times*, October 18, 2003, p. A6.

37. For a full discussion of this point, see Edwards, *Governing by Campaigning*, chap. 4.

38. R. W. Apple, Jr., "After the Attacks: Assessment: President Seems to Gain Legitimacy," *New York Times*, September 16, 2001, p. A1.

39. Gallup poll, February 28–March 3, 1991.

40. Quoted in Dana Milbank, "Bush Popularity Isn't Aiding GOP Domestic Agenda," *Washington Post*, June 16, 2002, p. A4.

41. Richard E. Cohen and Alexis Simendinger, "Like Father, Like Son?" *National Journal*, March 29, 2003, pp. 991, 993.

42. William Schneider, "The Bush Mandate," *National Journal*, November 9, 2002, p. 3358; Adam Nagourney and Janet Elder, "Positive Ratings for the G.O.P., If Not Its Policy," *New York Times*, November 26, 2002, pp. A1, A22.

43. William Schneider, "A Popularity Contest," *National Journal*, November 16, 2002, p. 3346.

44. Charlie Cook, "Off to the Races: So Much for the GOP Sweep," December 10, 2002, Washington, DC.

45. Bob Benenson, "GOP Won Midterm by Winning Series of Small Battles," *Congressional Quarterly Weekly Report*, November 9, 2002, p. 2890. See also Jim VandeHei and Dan Balz, "In GOP Win, a Lesson in Money, Muscle, Planning," *Washington Post*, November 10, 2002, pp. A1, A6, A7.

46. Gary C. Jacobson, "Terror, Terrain, and Turnout: Explaining the 2002 Midterm Election," *Political Science Quarterly* 118 (Spring 2003): 1–22.

47. Charlie Cook, "A Landslide? That Talk Is Mostly Just Hot Air," *National Journal*, November 9, 2002, pp. 3346–47.

48. Richard E. Cohen, "New Lines, Republican Gains," *National Journal*, November 9, 2002, p. 3285; Gregory L. Giroux, "Redistricting Helped GOP," *Congressional Quarterly Weekly Report*, November 9, 2002, pp. 2934–35.

49. Cook, "A Landslide? That Talk Is Mostly Just Hot Air," pp. 3346–47.

50. Peter H. Stone and Shawn Zeller, "Business and Conservative Groups Won Big," *National Journal*, November 9, 2002, p. 3355.

51. Jacobson, *A Divider, Not a Uniter*.

52. See Edwards, *Governing by Campaigning*, chaps. 7–8.

53. Brownstein, *The Second Civil War*, pp. 229–30, 249–52, 287–96.

54. See Edwards, *Governing by Campaigning*, chap. 3.

CHAPTER 6: Reassessing Leadership

1. Richard E. Neustadt, *Presidential Power and the Modern Presidents* (New York: Free Press, 1990), p. 265.

2. George C. Edwards III and Andrew Barrett, "Presidential Agenda Setting in Congress," in Jon R. Bond and Richard Fleisher, eds., *Polarized Politics: Congress and the President in a Partisan* (Washington, DC: Congressional Quarterly, 2000).

3. George C. Edwards III and B. Dan Wood, "Who Influences Whom? The President, Congress, and the Media," *American Political Science Review* 93 (June 1999): 327–44.

4. Stephen Skowronek, *The Politics Presidents Make* (Cambridge, MA: Harvard University Press, 1993).

5. Stephen Skowronek, "Leadership by Definition: First Term Reflections on George W. Bush's Political Stance," *Perspectives on Politics* 3 (December 2005): 818, 826.

6. Skowronek, "Leadership by Definition," pp. 818, 821, 826–27.

7. Jeffrey K. Tulis, *The Rhetorical Presidency* (Princeton, NJ: Princeton University Press, 1987), pp. 179–80.

8. David Zarefsky, *President Johnson's War of Poverty* (University: University of Alabama Press, 1986).

9. See, for example, Charles M. Cameron, *Veto Bargaining: Presidents and the Politics of Negative Power* (New York: Cambridge University Press, 2000); Kenneth R. Mayer, *With the Stroke of a Pen, Executive Orders and Presidential Power* (Princeton, NJ: Princeton

University Press, 2001); Phillip J. *Cooper, By Order of the President: The Use and Abuse of Executive Direct Action* (Lawrence: University Press of Kansas, 2002); William G. Howell, *Power without Persuasion* (Princeton, NJ: Princeton University Press, 2003); Adam L. Warber, *Executive Orders and the Modern Presidency: Legislating from the Oval Office* (Boulder, CO: Lynne Rienner, 2006).

10. Michael Nelson, "The President and the Court: Reinterpreting the Court-packing Episode of 1937," *Political Science Quarterly* 103 (Summer 1988): 277–78.

11. William E. Leuchtenburg, *The Supreme Court Reborn: The Constitutional Revolution in the Age of Roosevelt* (New York: Oxford University Press, 1995), pp. 134, 137–47.

12. Ibid., p. 156.

13. William E. Leuchtenburg, *Franklin D. Roosevelt and the New Deal, 1932–1940* (New York: Harper & Row, 1963), p. 234; Robert Maddox, "Roosevelt vs. The Court," *American History Illustrated* 4 (November 1969): 10–11; Arthur A. Ekirch, Jr., *Ideologies and Utopias: The Impact of the New Deal on American Thought* (Chicago: Quadrangle Books, 1969), p. 197; James MacGregor Burns, *Roosevelt: The Lion and the Fox* (New York: Harcourt, Brace and World, 1956), pp. 307, 315. FDR's diminished authority resulted in part from other developments such as the harsh recession of 1937–1938, anxiety over relief spending, and resentment at sit-down strikes. See Leuchtenburg, *The Supreme Court Reborn*, p. 156; Leuchtenburg, *Franklin D. Roosevelt and the New Deal, 1932–1940*, p. 250.

14. George Tindall, *The Emergence of the New South, 1913–1945* (Baton Rouge: Louisiana State University Press, 1967), p. 623.

15. James T. Patterson, *Congressional Conservatism and the New Deal* (Lexington: University of Kentucky Press, 1967), p. 95; Leuchtenburg, *The Supreme Court Reborn*, pp. 157–58; Leuchtenburg, *Franklin D. Roosevelt and the New Deal, 1932–1940*, p. 252.

16. Leuchtenburg, *The Supreme Court Reborn*, pp. 158–60; Leuchtenburg, *Franklin D. Roosevelt and the New Deal, 1932–1940*, pp. 238–39.

17. Leuchtenburg, *The Supreme Court Reborn*, pp. 157–58; Leuchtenburg, *Franklin D. Roosevelt and the New Deal, 1932–1940*, pp. 250–51, chap. 11.

18. Leuchtenburg, *Franklin D. Roosevelt and the New Deal, 1932–1940*, pp. 272–74.

19. Leuchtenburg, *The Supreme Court Reborn*, pp. 160–61.

20. Robert Dallek, *Franklin D. Roosevelt and American Foreign Policy, 1932–1945* (New York: Oxford University Press, 1979), pp. 136–37, 140.

21. George C. Edwards III, *On Deaf Ears: The Limits of the Bully Pulpit* (New Haven, CT: Yale University Press), pp. 35–37.

22. Lawrence R. Jacobs and Robert Y. Shapiro, *Politicians Don't Pander* (Chicago: University of Chicago Press, 2000), pp. 76, 81–83, 105, 115–16, 136, 149, 152.

23. Ibid., pp. 115, 149.

24. Elizabeth Drew, *Showdown: The Struggle between the Gingrich Congress and the Clinton White House* (New York: Simon & Schuster, 1996), p. 66.

25. Jacobs and Shapiro, *Politicians Don't Pander*, p. 115.

26. Quoted in Jim VandeHei and Mike Allen, "Bush Rejects Delay, Prepares Escalated Social Security Push," *Washington Post*, March 3, 2005, p. A4.

27. Mike Allen and Jim VandeHei, "Social Security Push to Tap the GOP Faithful: Campaign's Tactics Will Drive Appeal," *Washington Post*, January 14, 2005, p. A6.

28. Thomas B. Edsall, "Conservatives Join Forces for Bush Plans; Social Security, Tort Limits Spur Alliance," *Washington Post*, February 13, 2005, p. A4.

29. Allen and VandeHei, "Social Security Push to Tap the GOP Faithful."

30. www.strengtheningsocialsecurity.gov/60stops/accomplishments _042705.pdf.

31. See George C. Edwards III, *Governing by Campaigning: The Politics of the Bush Presidency*, 2nd ed. (New York: Longman, 2007), chap. 7.

32. Pew Research Center for the People & the Press poll, February 16–21, 2005.

33. Pew Research Center for the People & the Press poll, March 8–12, 2006.

34. Bill Clinton, *My Life* (London: Hutchinson, 2004), p. 514.

35. Seth A. Rosenthal, Todd L. Pittinsky, Diane M. Purvin, and Matthew Montoya, *National Leadership Index 2007: A National Study of Confidence in Leadership* (Center for Public Leadership, John F. Kennedy School of Government, Harvard University, Cambridge,

MA), p. 2. Interviews of the national sample were conducted on September 4–17, 2007.

36. See, for example, Ronald Brownstein, *The Second Civil War: How Extreme Partisanship Has Paralyzed Washington and Polarized America* (New York: Penguin Press, 2007).

37. Quoted in Robert Draper, *Dead Certain: The Presidency of George W. Bush* (New York: Free Press, 2007), p. 230.

Index